T0330224

Transactional Culture in Colonial Dakar, 1902–44

Rochester Studies in African History and the Diaspora

Toyin Falola, Series Editor

The Jacob and Frances Sanger Mossiker Chair in the Humanities
and University Distinguished Teaching Professor
University of Texas at Austin

Additional Titles of Interest

A complete list of titles in the Rochester Studies in African History and the Diaspora
series may be found on our website, www.urpress.com

Transactional Culture in Colonial Dakar, 1902–44

Rachel M. Petrocelli

UNIVERSITY OF ROCHESTER PRESS

First published 2024

University of Rochester Press
668 Mt. Hope Avenue, Rochester, NY 14620, USA
www.urpress.com
and Boydell & Brewer Limited
PO Box 9, Woodbridge, Suffolk IP12 3DF, UK
www.boydellandbrewer.com

ISBN-13: 978-1-64825-077-4
ISSN: 1092-5228

Library of Congress Cataloging-in-Publication Data

Names: Petrocelli, Rachel M., author.
Title: Transactional culture in colonial Dakar, 1902–44 / Rachel M. Petrocelli.
Other titles: Rochester studies in African history and the diaspora ; 101 1092-5228
Description: Rochester : University of Rochester Press, 2024. | Series: Rochester
    studies in African history and the diaspora, 1092-5228 ; 101 | Includes
    bibliographical references and index.
Identifiers: LCCN 2023054287 (print) | LCCN 2023054288 (ebook) | ISBN
    9781648250774 (hardback) | ISBN 9781805433200 (epub) | ISBN
    9781805433217 (pdf)
Subjects: LCSH: City and town life—Senegal—Dakar—History—20th century.
    | Dakar (Senegal)—Economic conditions—20th century. | Dakar (Senegal)—
    Social life and customs. | Dakar (Senegal)—History—20th century. | France—
    Colonies—Africa—Administration—History—20th century.
Classification: LCC HC1045.Z7 D3465 2024 (print) | LCC HC1045.Z7 (ebook)
    | DDC 330.966303—dc23
LC record available at https://lccn.loc.gov/2023054287
LC ebook record available at https://lccn.loc.gov/2023054288

A catalogue record for this title is available from the British Library.

To Zach,
who gets it all.

Contents

Illustrations

Acknowledgments

This is a book about living in Dakar during a time when the city was growing up. I wrote it after having spent a great deal of time in Dakar over the years, during which I also became closely acquainted with the fascinating stories in the collection of justice records I studied. Part of my goal was to share my understanding of what those stories might convey, but the other part of it was to acknowledge a city whose people and spaces have inspired me in their great resilience and accomplishments. Writing the book and bringing it to completion took time and support from many others.

Considering the time it takes to write a historical monograph, and the endless conversations about it that are unavoidable in the households of people who write them, the most important acknowledgment is of my husband, Zach West. He listened to me go on and on about this case or that case. He handled our children while I pushed through a chapter revision. He supported this book from start to finish, knowing it would bring no monetary reward and/or new title. He saw this book as a must-do for me personally, and so he made it a priority for our family. To our two children, Emmanuelle and Joshua, who later will not remember the days when I devoted so much time to writing this book, I say: I will. I thank them for letting me race through the bedtime song, and for giving me those ten extra minutes I needed alone in my office in the morning.

It took me forever to get to this book because for years I was enjoying living in Dakar more than I wanted to start writing about it. That made all the difference because the work means more to me than it might have had I not made Dakar such an integral part of my life for a decade. During those years, certain people became unwavering supporters of any and all things I was interested in, and ultimately, they shaped how I experienced Senegal and the nature of my work.

I thank first and foremost Moussa Diouf for his constant friendship and guidance. He opened countless doors and stood in my corner. His wife, Mariama Diao, sustained open hospitality toward me year after year, and I cannot thank her enough. I offer equal appreciation to Babacar Diaham, who ensured I experienced nearly every aspect of Dakar and Senegal's regions, and to his wife, Fatou Ndao, for her warm support. At the most profound level, I thank Oumoul Sow for a friendship that grew deeper than either of us could have imaged. What started as daily walks through Dakar that we passed off as Wolof lessons evolved into lazy, hours-long Sunday brunches of beignets and omelets on the cushions and rugs of her living room and then regular visits to the USA to extend the tradition to my home. Oumoul became an older sister who also could answer all questions Wolof and Senegal, and she still is today. It speaks to our friendship that my next acknowledgment is of her daughter Aissatou Barry, who was seven when we met and has grown to be as my niece over twenty years. Many times while revising this book, moments of concentration I needed were made possible by Aicha during her stays with us. The many hours we have spent laughing over meals we make and eat together have been reinvigorating.

At Stanford, before I began dissertation research, I met Babacar Fall, who became an important friend and colleague in Dakar. His efforts to integrate me into conferences and professional activities were and continue to be incredibly important. It was through my collaboration with him that I began to publish my work. He has been a committed supporter and he has always been sincere and generous in his friendship. As I frequented the National Archives of Senegal, I became close with its staff, many of whom went above and beyond in the assistance they provided. Director Fatoumata Cissé Diarra and, before her, Babacar Ndiaye, treated me like family and made the research process inviting. The smoothness of daily work never would have happened as it did over the many years I came into and out of the archives without the assistance of Mossane Diouf and Mamadou Ndiaye. I am so appreciative for the extra files, the basement access, the searching help, and for their friendly approach and warm correspondence. Finally, I was fortunate enough to have lived for a time in Senegal with Kelly Duke-Bryant, whose level of professionalism as a historian is matched by her openness and good cheer, all of which made the earlier phases of research so enjoyable.

Emily Burrill and Rachel Jean-Baptiste took a special interest in this book—and in me—as I completed it. They each went through its first full drafting with a fine-toothed comb, offering a depth of feedback I never could have expected. It allowed me to use my time in the most efficient way possible when revising, a process in which they each accompanied me. Emily turned chapters around within days, and Rachel pushed hard for changes or additions I was at times reluctant to consider. They offered every type of advice. The many calls that diverged from the book into tangents on all sorts of things, from teaching to raising children, sustained me during the revision and editing process. There is a solidarity we share, and I cannot thank them enough for the support and friendship both Emily and Rachel have provided.

Cara Anzilotti has been a mentor whose role I cannot acknowledge enough. She read my research, encouraged me to pursue my goals, gave me the honest advice everyone needs, and became an indispensable and devoted friend. Cara's interest in my success and professional fulfillment has carried me through at so many key moments. Richard Roberts was my graduate advisor. I thank him for his ongoing advice and encouragement. He is a model for teaching historians like me, and his legendary status as a mentor to many people within the world of African history exists for good reason. I also acknowledge James Ferguson and Sean Hanretta for their work with me during my graduate candidacy. Several important ideas emerged from those reading and discussion sessions, and their guidance was formative.

Scott Howell read chapters of this book and offered ideas from the perspective of someone not entrenched in the world of African history. I am appreciative of his time and the interest he took in my work. Narges Rabii-Rakin also offered support for my efforts to produce scholarship, making certain my schedule afforded me the time and space, and standing firmly next to me in my professional goals. Lindsay Wildt provided valuable assistance with research in Dakar on the Cape Verdeans, and Dean Hughes's organization and classification of case records were extremely helpful to my work on this project. My sincere thanks go to Michelle Beckett for her attentive editing of the manuscript and to Erin Greb for her fine custom cartography. During the initial days of writing as a graduate candidate, Natalia Mehlman Petrzela and Brenda Frink offered feedback on my early work on this topic. Finally, Gabriel Petrocelli read all of my chapters for style and errors (as a result, he is the only Petrocelli besides me who basically knows all kinds of niche things about Dakar's history).

There are a lot of people, some now in my past, who supported me as I worked on this project, lived in Dakar, and navigated the winding road that leads one through graduate school, into professorhood, and just generally to being an adult with many stories to tell. Those people have been part of the story, and I thank them for the roles they played.

My work was supported by various grants over time. Several Foreign Language Area Studies fellowships helped me develop my Wolof skills. I thank Paap Sow for expert instruction in this regard. A Fulbright-Hays Doctoral Dissertation Research Fellowship supported intensive research, and a Mellon/ACLS Dissertation Completion Fellowship supported write-up of the thesis on which this book is based. A Summer Stipend from the National Endowment for the Humanities supported manuscript revision.

My mother hosted many friends from Senegal in her home and understood the road I was on. She had a knowingness. My grandmother pushed me hard in the loving, deeply supportive way only she could. My father is the ultimate professional role model. I appreciate how much he sees my efforts. I know he's pleased now that I didn't opt to study the history of New Jersey.

Introduction

Transactional Culture and Transience in African Urban History

In 1922, the Tribunal de Première Instance, Dakar's principal civil court, received a complaint from Diame Diop. It alleged that Makha Diouf had borrowed a bracelet from the complainant with the purpose of temporarily pawning it to be able to purchase an animal for his butcher's shop. Once Diouf had sold the product at his butcher's shop he would be able to reclaim the bracelet and return it to its owner. Still awaiting the return of the bracelet, Diop sought its restitution and brought the matter to the court.[1] This ordinary case was just one among thousands brought over the course of the first several decades of the twentieth century in Dakar, capital of former French West Africa (FWA) and today the capital of Senegal. People in colonial Dakar approached the court to broach the obstacles and stalemates they encountered as they managed their resources and the networks of transactions in which those resources were embedded. As they did so, they carried with them ideas and assumptions about what was acceptable and what was not in the expanding social and economic landscape of Dakar. In this way, a case such as *Diop v. Diouf* was about more than simple reclamation of property or breach of faith. It was also about needs, practices, and expectations in a French West African colonial urban setting.

This book is about those needs, practices, and expectations. The lens it adopts is one that focuses on Dakarois' strategies for living in and negotiating the city with each other and within a world of racism espoused by a colonial state that was self-contradictory and unable to achieve the degree of control it sought. By peering into corners of life that ostensibly were mundane but in actuality were central to an urban existence while minding the overarching umbrella of state rhetoric and imperatives, this book explores the contours of life in Dakar over the formative period of its development as a major regional city. It is not a history of a city. New neighborhoods and

---

1   Diop v. Diouf, November 29, 1922, Archives Nationales du Sénégal (ANS), 5M/208(184).

lines drawn, streets named and spaces reshaped, political debates and mechanisms of rule installed, port and the military installments—these aspects of Dakar have been examined and explained elsewhere, providing an excellent sense of how Dakar featured in the stories of French colonialism in West Africa.[2] Here, the focus is on bringing into clearer view Dakar is as a lived experience. The city was the field on which encounters took place between colonial imperatives and people as well as within the population itself. This book concerns itself with the city Dakar became over four decades by focusing on what that meant for those who called it home in some way. To get at this, the chapters that follow examine the two most central aspects of urban life in colonial African cities: economic survival and success, and the workings of belonging within those priorities. Both of these were shaped by the French colonial state and its own ideas of what its capital city was supposed to be and how those in it should act. In Dakar, pursuits of many types involved negotiation and positioning, objectives and frustrations, and aspirations and unintended outcomes. As lives were lived, a way of life in the city was made.

Layered dimensions were and are inherent to African cities as they have been to all cities. But the colonial context created a denser set of layers, a greater distance between top and bottom, and the intent for opacity to exist on one plane with knowability at the other. Dakar was a colonial urban entity and economy aimed on the official level at the exclusion and exploitation of Africans. A city created by France for its own objectives, Dakar was meant to control—policy, commerce, labor, rights, taxes, laws, and people—to the benefit of administration of the massive territorial holdings grouped as the French West Africa Federation. But the colonial capital was not only the world city dwellers occupied. The function of Dakar was multidimensional, and for those who forged belonging in the city, it took on other roles and forms of meaning. It was a place for people's own pursuits, which inevitably took place in the context the colonial state had created, but were their own pursuits nonetheless. The ways in which Dakarois lived and operated were imbued with flexibility, ingenuity, and situational awareness that allowed needs to be met, obstacles to be overcome, and communities to congeal and thrive.

---

2   Works on Dakar range in topic, with a substantial number centered on its physical nature, including the processes and politics of the planning of the city. An early, authoritative work is Seck, *Dakar*. See also Bigon, *French Colonial Dakar*. Additional works on Dakar's physical development include the following: Shaw, *Irony and Illusion*; Harris, *Constructing Dakar*. The city features heavily in other historical narratives and analyses as well. See Echenberg, *Black Death, White Medicine*; Jones, *The Métis of Senegal*; Barbary, "Dakar et la Sénégambie"; Melly, "Inside-Out Houses"; and Gamble, "Navigating the Fourth Republic."

Ways of life in Dakar were not divorced from its identity as a colonial capital. The fact that Dakar was the capital of FWA was the prime source of all administrative anxieties and ideas about controlling space and people in the city. A preoccupation with African bodies inhabiting urban space—with African practices unfolding before French eyes with proximity to symbols of colonial power and with a projection of cultural whiteness—was evident in the discussions and policies of French colonial officials and bureaucrats. City dwellers' everyday practices and expectations developed as shaped by that powerful context. Ultimately, attitudes and efforts among administrators became part of the greater set of forces operating in Dakar, moving into interplay with other priorities and perceptions, which were neither their own nor under their control. Those were the needs and desires of city dwellers themselves, as well as the mechanisms they developed to see to and cultivate them. That interplay threads throughout this book, revealing the limits and unintended consequences of power and the iterations and effects of colonial state racism in quotidian terms.

Central to the urban world this book reconstructs is what I term the *local transactional culture*, comprising the set of accepted practices and assumptions that permeate the many interactions within a broad spectrum of exchanges in a specific location. There were norms city dwellers implicitly understood as they carried out their economic and material lives, and these were rooted both in the specific parameters of what was possible and preferable in the colonial capital city of Dakar as well as in what urban residents sought and were determined to create. The transaction has been essential to urban life. AbouMaliq Simone has pointed to it as a means of identifying "varied interests" as well as "functional compromises" in African cities, where negotiation is a constant.[3] Localizing a city's transactional culture is a way of giving coherence to various engagements typically understood within their own spheres of activity—credit, housing, employment, and so forth—by interpreting them in the particular urban context in which participants acted. In this way, a rental agreement and an employment contract in 1930s Dakar could have been driven by similar dynamics despite their obvious initial differences because they were carried out within the framework of the city's local transactional culture.

This device is also useful in understanding the colonial capital of FWA, because cities did not invent transactions but rather were sites of changing norms developing around them. The economic world of colonialism in African cities was one of control—efforts to establish it, carry it out, subvert

---

3   Simone, "Introduction," 4. Simone discusses the general public as a place of bargaining, negotiation, and renegotiation among actors from all corners of urban life, inclusive of institutional sectors, and asserts that the transaction stands at the crux of these, particularly in a diverse setting in which economic activities are complex and urban development is ongoing.

it, and reshape it. Transactions were wrapped up in that changing landscape. Commerce was deeply rooted in the broader region, and very much so in Senegal. Scholars of West Africa have pointed to the role of trade in generating mobility as well as in creating new communities.[4] Colonialism brought about a labor-oriented economic world. Although labor often took place outside cities with the onset of cash crop regimes, urban areas were most visible and concentrated in their role in labor mandates. Struggles over work were inherent to urban regimes, as Frederick Cooper's pioneering work on Mombasa showed.[5] Luise White's seminal work on Nairobi revealed that cities also provided economic opportunities that reproduced the male labor system, all while creating urban permanence for men and women alike.[6] Charles Van Onselen has explored the extension of control from sites of work to the arteries connecting them in his study of exploitative systems of rail transport that commoditized the workers moved amid Southern Africa's segregated landscape.[7]

In colonial Dakar, the local transactional culture was largely shaped by two forces: transience and identity-based notions initiated by the colonial state. At times implicit and at other moments overt, both contributed to the possibilities available to people as they pursued the activities of daily life. Transience and identity thread throughout the aspects of urban life explored in this book, revealing their centrality to the steady building of systems of interaction, which were normalized over time in the city. Together, they allow for a sort of inside-outside understanding of life in Dakar. That is, transience was so common among those who lived in Dakar that it became

---

4   West Africa's place in the Atlantic slave trade was significant in this respect and has been the subject of a great number of works, many of which elucidate economic change in Senegal both during and after the trade, when commodities arose as the object of commercial exchange. Selected contributions have included the following: Barry, *Senegambia and the Atlantic Slave Trade*; Green, *Rise of the Trans-Atlantic Slave Trade in Western Africa*; Cappelli and Baten, "European Trade, Colonialism, and Human Capital Accumulation"; Jones, "Women, Family and Daily Life in Senegal's Nineteenth-Century Atlantic Towns"; Swindell and Jeng, *Migrants, Credit and Climate*. In addition, the expansion of Islam in West Africa, including the region's ties to North Africa through Islamic networks, have provided fertile ground for explorations of community, movement, and economic strategies. For notable examples, see Cohen, *Custom and Politics in Urban Africa*; Lovejoy, *Caravans of Kola*; Curtin, *Economic Change in Precolonial Africa*; Hanson, *Migration, Jihad, and Muslim Authority in West Africa*; Lydon, *On Trans-Saharan Trails*.

5   Cooper, *Struggle for the City*.

6   White, *Comforts of Home*.

7   Van Onselen, *Night Trains*.

part of its fabric, and yet the very nature of transience is that those who experienced or utilized it might have resisted considering themselves as part of the city. Similarly, identity categories were in large part constructed by the colonial framework and state policy itself, but the existence of them produced dynamics, groupings, and boundary settings that were very much internal to urban society and the ways it operated. These two themes run throughout the chapters in this book, allowing a deep dive into people's everyday considerations without sacrificing an understanding of the broader urban world in which they lived.

The French officials who ran Dakar saw themselves as presiding over a special project, a colonial capital meant not only to serve an administrative purpose but to convey France's imperial hegemony in West Africa to the region and larger world. Dakar was not to be a city of blurred lines, mixed heritage, or shared power. Those features of its late mercantile and early colonial regime had shaped the earlier Senegalese communes, dynamics Hilary Jones recreates in her work on society in the colony from the late eighteenth to early twentieth centuries.[8] As much as they could in a nonsettler colony, they pursued policies that aimed to create a dual city in which a "European" core was separate from and served by a peripheral African population that the state tried to limit. This was the premise of a long series of race-based theories, policies, and aspirations administrators pursued in their creation and management of the city. It relied on the categorization of people, an area to which French bureaucrats were increasingly attentive as colonial rule congealed and settled in West Africa. Racial politics imbued colonial urban management at every level, as many works treating cities across the continent explore.[9] In colonial Senegal, this was an ever-present fact of the urban experience, as Jones's work reveals, as does Myron Echenberg's study of public health policies in Dakar.[10] Gwendolyn Wright's study of architecture explicitly addresses the built space as part of colonial urban racial politics and the quest to control urban spaces.[11] That desire to control cities also revealed itself in the systems of urban surveillance the French colonial state established in Africa, as Kathleen Keller has discussed.[12]

Most people in Dakar, however, did not fall clearly within the categories to which the state ascribed, complicating the very categories themselves and undermining the reasons for which they existed. Dakarois did the things

---

8   Jones, *Métis of Senegal.*
9   See, for instance, Freund, "Contrasts in Urban Segregation"; Goerg, *Pouvoir Colonial, Municipalités et Espaces Urbains.*
10   Echenberg, *Black Death*; Jones, *Métis of Senegal.*
11   Wright, *Politics of Design in French Colonial Urbanism.*
12   Keller, *Colonial Suspects.*

they needed to do and understood themselves in the ways they found most appropriate. The local transactional culture was a principal venue for this, and thus it chiseled away at official expectations and frustrated the city's managers. At the state level, an internal struggle simmered between the real and the ideal, pushing administrators to devise and revise mechanisms of control in Dakar over the course of decades. The resulting parameters of life in the colonial capital informed city dwellers' actions, which they shaped in an adaptive way that was geared toward resilience.

The exercise of categorization in which the colonial state engaged pertained not only to race but also to place. Officials were deeply uncomfortable with the fluidity of movement among Africans precisely because it was widespread and determined by the priorities of those who did the moving. This book takes that fluidity of movement from the perspective of the city, identifying transience as one of the central features of Dakar's transactional culture. It provides another category beyond mobility and migration, showing that transience operated as a state of being and a condition that met the needs of people and was possible for them because of the sort of city Dakar was. As the chapters that follow delve into the interactions of people within the urban world of transactions, they shed light on the transient condition as an important aspect of the colonial city. This book does not follow people as they moved through time and space as studies of migration and mobility have done.

A long-standing interest in movement among Africanists has laid a foundation for exploring and understanding transience by providing deeper insights into networks, options, initiatives, and connections.[13] James Ferguson's pivotal work on the Zambian Copperbelt presented a fluid conception of migration, freeing it from the modernization theories that underlay most prior work on African cities.[14] He revealed the deep flaws

---

13 From the late 1930s into the 1960s, the study of cities in Africa was the nearly exclusive domain of social anthropologists based primarily in southern and southern-central Africa. Scholars of the period examined the dynamics of kinship, migration, and adaptation to cities. That last issue was one of particular interest as both colonial administrators and social scientists considered cities to represent a wholly new physical, economic, and especially social paradigm for Africans. See Wilson, *Essay on the Economics of Detribalization*; Mitchell, *Kalela Dance*; Epstein, *Politics*; Mayer, *Townsmen or Tribesmen*; Van Velsen, "Labor Migration as a Positive Factor in the Continuity of Tonga Tribal Society"; Gluckman, "Tribalism in Modern British Central Africa."

14 Ferguson, *Expectations of Modernity*. As Ferguson has explained, foundational as they were, mid-century scholars were wrapped up in a theoretical construct that took modernization as its premise. They principally investigated mechanisms of adaptation, seeing a stark divide between African ways of life and

in teleological assumptions that migration eventually would give way to permanent urban residence. Instead, Ferguson was able to show the city to be part of mobility patterns and options rather than the end result. As this study moves the focus to transience as a form of city dwelling, it draws on Ferguson's argument on the broader worlds people inhabited. The work of Jorge Duany provides additional depth to this effect by pointing to mobile livelihoods, positing the notion of multiple poles of activity rather than one prime center.[15] The agency of individuals in crafting their own geographies is one of the central features of arguments regarding movement, even when that agency operates within the framework of imposed conditions, as was the case under colonialism. François Manchuelle explored such dynamics among Soninke migrants, whose labor-related movements involved multiple locations and were driven by the quest for an improved economic outlook in the early twentieth century in West Africa.[16] Other scholars have been attentive to age, gender, and religion as factors in decisions to move, migrate, and create new communities.[17] Within the Africanist tradition, works have integrated these perspectives to provide greater nuance in our understanding of the forces at play in people's lives and their priorities in broaching both movement and urban lives, allowing the scholarship to transcend prior concerns with adaptation and modernization that had woven throughout the work of prominent social anthropologists.[18] Implicit in this scholarship was the idea that new behaviors in cities were modern behaviors, and the city demanded new ways of thinking about self and community that were distinct from those entailed in rural life.

In many cases, the effects of migration are studied in rural areas, while cities are understood as the recipients of populations. Bruce Whitehouse embodies this approach in his work on Togotalans in Brazzaville, a city he identifies as a "receiving community," standing in opposition to the "sending

---

the sort of city dwelling brought about by industrialization, specifically in the white settler and mineral regions of southern and central southern Africa.

15　Duany, "Mobile Livelihoods."

16　Manchuelle, *Willing Migrants.*

17　Works are extremely numerous. For some examples overtly addressing these topics, see Ocobock, "Earning an Age"; Mudeka, "Gendered Exclusion and Contestation"; Simelane, "State, Chiefs and the Control of Female Migration in Colonial Swaziland"; Van den Bersselaar, "Imagining Home"; Rain, *Eaters of the Dry Season*; Penvenne, *Women, Migration, and the Cashew Economy in Southern Mozambique*; Premawardhana, *Faith in Flux.*

18　Prominent among mid-century sociologists who studied French-speaking zones and West Africa were Georges Balandier, Claude Meillassoux, and Kenneth Little. See Balandier, *Sociologie des Brazzavilles Noires*; Meillassoux, *Urbanization of an African Community*; Little, *West African Urbanization.*

community."[19] My approach shifts the focus from the mover and what the mover left behind in other places or what the intentions of the move were, relocating the focus to a single location in which residents were movers and movement was accommodated. To do that, this book locates people in a moment—the time of a transaction of some sort—and place, which was Dakar. Transience was an undeniable fact of life in the capital of FWA. Even those who did not experience it as actors experienced it through the mechanism of broader involvement as it was embedded in interactions and transactions across sectors and pursuits. Important here is what the ensemble of moments of contact in a transient setting meant to both individuals and the city itself. It seeks to make sense of transactions in light of not only people's own apparent priorities but also the contours the state laid down in Dakar as related to race and identity. The transient lifestyle that became prominent in Dakar was one of the means by which people confronted a specific colonial condition, protected themselves within it, and attempted to draw out maximum gain.

Unlike migration, transience represented unpredictability as well as a firm sign of the limits of French power over people and space. Transient city dwelling broke down the concept of the city as controlled, permanent, and stable. In the colonial mind, the true role of a capital city like Dakar could not be realized if people—particularly Africans—were able to enter and exit the urban space and economy as they pleased. Colonial bureaucrats who manned offices that fielded justice complaints also witnessed the role of transience in the local transactional culture, bringing them closer to the reality of things, including the inability of the state to account for its population in real terms. Parties in a legal matter disappeared easily amid an investigation. People worked for two weeks and left, known only by their first name to their employers. Contracts were broken, positions of employment were abandoned, and debts were left unsettled. Coming and going among urban society lent a particular friability to transactions of every sort. Agreements, when they existed, tended to be short-term to avoid these hazards. At the

---

19 Whitehouse, *Migrants and Strangers in an African City*, 10. The notion of the city as the receiver is also inherent to studies of what has been termed *circular migration* linking urban and rural spaces into an overarching space of movement, typically for labor purposes. For a more recent example, see Posel and Marx, "Circular Migration." When the city is the destination or receiver, rural areas may be cast not only as a place of origination but as a site of true belonging of home. See, for instance, Njwambe, Cocks, and Vetter, "Ekhayeni." For an example of the rural-centered approach, see Sunseri, *Vilimani*. Peter Geschiere and Josef Gugler point to the continued role of the rural-urban paradigm in exploring movement and African cities. See Geschiere and Gugler, "Introduction: The Urban–Rural Connection."

same time, arrangements were drawn out over time to allow them to bear fruit over the course of several sojourns in town. In their dealings with one another, people expected, exploited, and deplored the effects of transience. It was, therefore, an important force in shaping the local transactional culture, within which movement was not disdained but known as a fact of urban life and confronted as needed.

In many ways, the French colonial economy and the policies the state adopted overtly required migration and sought to be predictive of people's patterns of movement, with the objective of maintaining a labor force that would remain trapped within the work cycle.[20] But transient city dwelling was in contradiction to this. It signaled agency, even a form of stealth existence. A Dakarois who kept a room and an armoire but often locked both up to leave town, who worked at will and left often for other pursuits, who pawned items and took out credit was an uncontrolled, unpredictable economic and urban actor. Yet, the French colonial state did not require transience as a pretext for seeking to shape a capital city in which African presence was limited. Dakar was never meant to be an African city in a true sense. It had been envisioned since its inception as an iteration of a dual city defined by a small class of haves—primarily Europeans—and a large mass of have-nots serving the colonial state and economy from as great a distance as possible. By focusing on race and what was seen as a correlating lifestyle, colonial officials sought time and time again to protect central Dakar from Africanization. Devices of control and exclusion were at the heart of the physical aspects of that project, as works on the city have shown. But state efforts to peripheralize Africans existed at nonphysical levels as well, particularly in the spheres of pay and employment.

Urban life emerged within the context of such colonial imperatives. People devised flexible and creative resource allocation to make life possible and pursuits worthwhile, even within the confines and limits of racist colonial policies. Van Onselen's work on the Witwatersrand remains foundational in reminding us of the ingenuity everyday people applied to their lives, even in the arguably most oppressive racist regime in Africa.[21] For every act of exploitation and domination, there was impact that was more complex and profound than colonial policy architects ever could have imagined. Colonial administrators created financial institutions meant to exclude Africans in the capital city of its largest territorial holding. But in doing so, the state birthed a sort of urban poverty as they built up Dakar. And within

---

20 This is a topic many historians have tackled. See Babacar Fall's work for an authoritative and grounded study of forced labor in the French colonial context. Fall, *Le travail forcé*.

21 Van Onselen, *Studies in the Social and Economic History of the Witwatersrand*.

that local transactional culture of limited resources, Dakarois expanded their own options through creative means, operating within what Jane Guyer has called "their own institutional frameworks," most of which existed informally.[22] Very often in Dakar, parties involved in transactions had social ties of some sort. Economic activity often mobilized social networks and drawing upon ethnic boundaries, whether real or perceived. As Viviana Zelizer has discussed, social structures impact the ways people conceive of and use their monetary resources based on locally embedded understandings of the relationship between monetary value and social norms.[23] Thus, the socioeconomic way of life in Dakar was one that not only provided the sense that one could locate spaces in which to belong and be successful but also created a depth of resources—cast in new forms that were born of city life—on which Dakarois could rely. Dakar was a fragile economic landscape for most, but its fragility was understood.

Over the course of some forty years, from the moment when Dakar was made capital of FWA to the waning days of the Second World War, after which colonialism across Africa took a dramatic turn toward reform and what was termed "development," a transactional culture imbued with transience and delicately balanced on colonial policies emerged and transformed in Dakar. Its beginnings reflected the modest size and scope of the city, as well as the relative laxity of official attention to local habits and ways. By the 1920s, when what is typically termed "high colonialism" set in, it began to congeal as the city's identity settled and policies aimed at control became more real. The city also incorporated immigrants of foreign origin, revealing the adaptability of the transactional culture to changes in its urban setting. Indeed, this was not simply an African transactional culture; it was a local one. The Depression brought new pressures to Dakar as it did elsewhere, and the transactional culture of the 1930s revealed the stresses placed not only on economic life but on the social ties and networks that were its foundations. By the 1940s, a colonial capital in the clutches of a grand-scale war saw its transactional culture adjust once again, integrating illicit activities that became available and even necessary to an urban population living through new experiences and exposures.

This book is the history of life in a growing, changing city viewed through the lens of urban dwellers' needs, practices, and expectations as they operated amid the race-based rhetoric and actions of the colonial state. It identifies both significant themes that permeated the urban economic experience and major elements of Dakar's adolescence, relating them to one another in a way that shows how useful a consideration of transactions can be. By

---

22   Guyer, *Money Matters.*
23   Zelizer, *Social Meaning of Money.*

entering the world of transactions, this book moves through what were arguably the most ordinary aspects of people's lives, aspects that typically remain hidden from view. In what might be considered mundane moments, Dakarois confronted their most urgent concerns—those that addressed that very moment. We are thus able to witness change at a level that is at once intimately personal and socially significant.

As an intervention in urban social history, the approach this book takes also permits us to transcend narrow urban communities and fields of activities. Many works on cities focus on ordinary people but zero in on specific populations: women, workers, autochthons, children, migrants. The richness in those specific routes of inquiry is clear in the contributions such works have made. Yet, there is the need to understand the city from multiple angles, locating what connected people in their urban experiences. This book replaces the subsegment of urban society with its cross-section. The means by which this book represents the different constituents of colonial Dakar is through an analytic field—a local transactional culture imbued with transience—that cut through and bound together many diverse members of the urban society. Here, the transaction, arguably the building block of any urban entity, is central to each aspect of urban life explored throughout the chapters to follow.

Working with Testimony in Justice Records and Oral Form

Identifying the needs, practices, and expectations of an urban population, especially one living under colonial rule, can be challenging because they are not only hidden but implicit. The questions of quotidian life, which compose any local transactional culture, emerge only in evidence generated by the population: newspapers, oral histories, novels, letters, and court cases. Just as they did in the field of urban history, historians exploring law and courts in colonial Africa were able to build on and diverge from an existing social science scholarship. A. L. Epstein, Max Gluckman, and Lloyd Fallers were among those social anthropologists who turned to courts and legal practices as windows into the inner workings of society.[24] A generation later, historians were developing their own methodological approaches to law and court records, and the field of African colonial legal history opened up with the publication of Martin Chanock's work on Malawi and Zambia, followed

---

24   Epstein, *Juridical Techniques and the Judicial Process*; Gluckman, *Custom and Conflict in Africa*; Fallers, *Law without Precedent*.

a few years later by that of Richard Roberts and Kristen Mann, whose edited collection signaled a new generation of work on law and court records.[25]

This book pairs the use of oral testimonies and colonial state documents with a large collection of records from Dakar's Tribunal de Première Instance, the civil court that served anyone who had French status, including *originaires*, colonized people who possessed certain rights such as access to French courts which used metropolitan law. A majority of cases brought to the court involved transactions: grievances concerning loans, terms of employment, purchases and credit, rental agreements, and all manner of breach of faith reached the Tribunal by way of letters and in-person complaints. French officers charged with administering justice often summoned the plaintiffs and defendants to testify before forwarding the cases to the next stage for judgment. The particular archive of the Tribunal employed here is a collection labeled *sans suite*, which means there was no legal follow up, typically because of an irregularity or obstacle. Litigants disappeared from Dakar, dropped their cases, did not appear when summoned, presented what was considered weak evidence, or were simply in the wrong court. Since the judicial outcome is unknown, focus on judgment recedes and analysis of the records can take place in a qualitative way. The aim here is not to assess how people accessed the courts, as has been done in other studies,[26] but rather to locate the intricacies of urban life that are visible in the case data. The content of complaints, the profiles of the litigants, and the combination of patterns and details that reside in the Tribunal dossier are all rich sources of local history. For the purposes of this book, the *sans suite* classification is of interest as it reinforces the theoretical premise that the transactional culture of Dakar was imbued with transience. A number of cases discussed in the chapters that follow would have moved further down the justice pipeline but did not because litigants could not be located.

Mine is the first substantial work done with this important archive. In the 1990s, Roberts, among the most prominent historians of law and courts in West Africa, explored the possibilities of the Tribunal records.[27] His article examined the docket entries from a methodological perspective, yielding important considerations about the legal process as a productive one that crafted and shaped the voices that historians access. This gave rise to

---

25 Chanock, *Law, Custom and Social Order*; Mann and Roberts, *Law in Colonial Africa*.

26 Chanock, *Law, Custom, and Social Order*; Christelow, *Muslim Law Courts and the French Colonial State in Algeria*; Mann and Roberts, *Law in Colonial Africa*; Shadle, "Changing Traditions to Meet Currently Altering Conditions."

27 Roberts, "Text and Testimony in the Tribunal De Première Instance, Dakar."

more works that employ justice records to access social history.[28] My intensive work with the records of the Tribunal shifts our focus to the content of it, drawing out the broad strokes that emerge as one canvasses many court records. This is not a statistical approach as has been pursued in other works.[29] Although I identify the themes and trends that thread throughout the records to best understand the primary practices and issues that pervaded Dakar's transactional culture, I do not seek conclusions drawn from aggregate data. Instead, I pay equal attention to single cases that present great historical insights and to patterns that emerge from cases in context. In this way, I draw in part on the work on Mann, whose book on colonial Lagos examined individual cases in depth, stressing the "human face" they contain.[30] Indeed, my use of Tribunal records sees the actor and his or her understandings and expectations as paramount. I do not concern myself with the factual integrity of complaints people lodged against one another in Dakar.[31] Instead, I concentrate on what those assertions say about the notions Dakarois possessed about the matters at hand and the world in which their claims were made.

Since conflict is necessary for such justice records to exist in the first place, the information mined from the Tribunal archives is the product of situations that reached an impasse. Scholars long have identified the representational potential in disputes.[32] Conflicts in courts were important moments that provide insight into the broader field of relationships and activities in which dilemmas emerged.[33] People in colonial Dakar did not require major crises to access the courts. Many of the cases in the Tribunal records were resolved by the time an official treated the case. One administrator in Dakar noted in his comments on the court's activities the "public's tendency . . . to come to the police for even the most minor incidents of daily life."[34] Dispute, inherent to such archival sources, does not make them anomalies. By seeking out details of transactions that reveal social relationships, local norms, and urban constraints, we take the dispute as an opportunity to access information that otherwise might not have surfaced in archival records. The court

---

28   Of particular note here is Burrill, *States of Marriage.*

29   Roberts, *Litigants and Households.*

30   Mann, *Slavery and the Birth of an African City.*

31   Shadle, *"Girl Cases."*

32   Bohannan, *Justice and Judgment among the Tiv*; Epstein, *Administration of Justice and the Urban African*; Epstein, *Juridical Techniques and the Judicial Process*; Gluckman, *Custom and Conflict in Africa*; Fallers, *Law without Precedent*; Moore, *Social Facts and Fabrications.*

33   Fallers, *Law without Precedent*; Roberts, *Litigants and Households.*

34   Dakar et Dépendances, Annual Ensemble of Reports—Police and Safety, 1932, ANS 2G32/22.

records also allow us to place the priorities of city dwellers in conversation with those of the colonial state.

Alongside civil court records, this book makes use of colonial state documents and oral testimonies. Covering the four decades of what I term Dakar's adolescence, the state documentation employed here provides insights into the concerns and objectives of colonial officials as they managed and sought to control a growing city from the mid-1910s through the mid-1940s. Principal among these archives are reports in which administrators reflected on and strategized ways to shape the urban population to suit the colonial state and economy. They provide the important context for an analysis of Dakar's transactional culture. In the 1910s, as the number of inhabitants began its genuine increase, documentation reveals state fixation on *refoulement*, or pushing back, of Africans from the central areas of town envisioned to represent European grandeur in West Africa. In the 1920s, dialogues about immigrants and the changing economic landscape of the city emerged. By the 1930s, presiding over a large capital moving through economic crisis and important political change in France, colonial officials expressed concern over who belonged in Dakar and what the roles and needs of such city dwellers were. Finally, the nature and concerns of state documentation experienced major shifts in the 1940s with the onset of the Second World War, which brought first Vichy rule and then an American presence to FWA.

Oral testimonies serve to enrich the insights that emerge from both the Tribunal records and state documentation. These testimonies were not collected under the rigid circumstances of a researcher on the quest for respondents to a set of predetermined questions. Rather, the oral histories presented here were collected slowly from 2007 to 2012, a span of time during which I pursued regular long stays in Dakar for the purposes of research, field instruction, and leisure. This permitted me to acquire the social contacts crucial to oral research. My archival research informed the oral testimonies I collected. Because the records held in both the Tribunal archives and the colonial state archives reveal a high degree of diversity and fluidity among the urban population at all phases of its development, my own oral research sought out informants of various backgrounds, both genders, and different fields of economic activity. Lebu, Cape Verdean, Lebanese, Wolof, Toucouleur, and other Senegalese with origins outside of the Cap-Vert peninsula shared their personal narratives and impressions about the city that is the subject of this book.

The question of diversity in the collection of oral history arose as an important topic in the earlier phases of this research. Initially, my requests for informants who might provide insights on the history of individual lives in Dakar yielded what became predictable references to only a handful of people—men who would be considered Lebu notables and "valid" holders of the city's history. The collective logic held among Dakarois that led me to local Lebu notables in the earliest phases of this research was based on the common local assumption that Lebu history was the history of Dakar. The central place of the notion of autochthony in both Lebu self-perceptions and public life have contributed to those ideas. As compelling as encounters with Lebu notables were, the testimonies I collected in the years to follow from ordinary people who would not have called themselves Dakarois when asked were far more revelatory. Informants of various backgrounds had long histories in the city. Their testimonies, however self-consciously presented as linked to other themes, such as a place of origin or a field of work, revealed a social urban history highly relevant to the transactional culture explored here. It was indeed this notion that one is not truly from Dakar despite lives led and generations raised in the city that is noteworthy. My line of questioning thus quickly changed from any emphasis on Dakar itself to a focus on life and family histories.

Participants were questioned in their homes and often in the presence of other family members and friends who became informants if they chose to become involved in our conversations. No forms or predetermined lists of questions were presented. While I originally sought to record our meetings, I quickly understood that the dialogue was much more organic without a recording device. Meetings at times involved meals or drink, and I returned to some homes several times as the informants became more comfortable with sharing the details of their lives with me. More often than not, informants offered the names of other potential participants, and thus some of the oral testimonies examined here are linked to each other through social and kinship networks. Although early in my work I sought the assistance of an interpreter for testimony collected in Wolof, I soon had no need for one as my proficiency in that language rapidly developed. In addition, many interviews were given in French, a language in which I long have been fluent. This did not preclude the presence of other parties, however. Friends and contacts in Dakar who recommended potential participants often accompanied me to the first interview, lending me the social legitimacy required of someone requesting to peer deep into the life of another. The interview dynamic, therefore, was at times that of a group, with occasional contributions from those who facilitated the interviews, producing discussion among several people even as the interview focused on the personal history of one individual.

Summary

Transactional Culture proceeds through seven chapters to explore various corners of Dakar's transactional culture and the dynamics of transience and identity that were central to them. Chapter One explores the foundations of transience in colonial Dakar, illustrating the complex nature of the question of permanence that infused both official thought and local practices. While the webs of movement in which African cities historically have been entrenched are often seen as being couched in local urban-rural networks, such a premise overlooks the very nature of most colonial cities in Africa as transient entities from their inception. We learn that, in Dakar, from an early stage, both the French presence and autochthonous community contributed to locally accepted ideas about residence. At the same time, the colonial administration created an urban regime that privileged autochthony and established Europeans, who were inherently transient in Dakar, as ideal city dwellers, seeking to establish the vast majority of Africans, many of whom rejected one foothold in favor of several, as an undesirable urban population.

Chapter Two examines the race-based philosophy of *refoulement*, the French term for "pushing back" that administrators used to express their goals as they pertained to Dakar's African population and the flow of people into the capital. The concept emerged in official rhetoric on the city in the mid-1910s. Despite their objective to create a version of French urban modernity in Dakar free of the trappings of African life, state policies and actions based on *refoulement* had far-reaching outcomes with unintended consequences. New modes of residence flourished under state policies that sought to separate African and European city dwellers in a deliberate manner. The creation of the Medina, a neighborhood made for African habitation, was the most obvious concrete result of such state imperatives. Understood as an African "village" that did not require the same regulatory oversight as Dakar-ville, Medina was free to expand, accommodating people in ways that were highly flexible. Far from producing any pushing back, it yielded an easy entry into—and exit out of—Dakar.

Chapter Three delves into the local transactional culture as the embodiment of that transience. It explores court cases that invoked residence to trace the ways Dakarois managed the challenges of a city that sought to establish barriers to African permanence. The Tribunal cases on disputes surrounding rental agreements, roommate relationships, and other housing matters show that from the 1910s to the 1930s, people in Dakar established a number of strategies to make flexible residence possible. For some, these solutions involved expanding the concept of residence to include living entirely at one's place of work. These court cases also reveal that transience created inherently friable residential situations filled with risk. With arrangements easily broken, housing transactions became short-term or easily changeable affairs.

Chapter Four traces the economic theories and policies that the French colonial state, confronted with a diverse and growing urban society, espoused and enacted to control city dwellers in the 1930s. It shows that the racist theories that imbued the colonizer's immigration and urban planning policies also shaped its approach to wages. Committed to the idea of African fiscal irresponsibility, Dakar's administrators sought to keep the Africans at the bare minimum of economic resources. A major premise on which they relied was that most Africans in the capital were not truly urban residents. Because the local transactional culture was responsive and flexible, Dakarois devised practices that stretched resources the colonizer deliberately kept as limited as possible. This chapter explores the practices that made up the local transactional culture of "just enough," in particular pawning possessions and taking out credit. These practices, hallmarks of informality, became well established by the 1930s and 1940s.

Chapters Five and Six introduce into an exploration of Dakar's trajectory the important cosmopolitanism that existed in the city and point to the ways in which diversity shaped both colonial rhetoric and the economic landscape of the capital. Chapter Five brings to the fore the Cape Verdean community of colonial Dakar. It considers the ways immigrants from the Portuguese colony of Cape Verde carved out economic spaces in Dakar and examines the deployment of identity that was intrinsic to that process. In establishing areas of economic specialty, they mobilized boundaries in the context of the fluidity inherent to the categories that French administrators, in their constant quest to read the urban population in terms of distinct categories, attempted to apply to them. In colonial Dakar, as the example of Cape Verde reveals, identity and economic niches were related, and city dwellers were active participants in this dynamic, even influencing the ways the state understood them.

Chapter Six continues an investigation of the role of diversity in the colonial capital, shifting to an examination of Dakar's Lebanese community. Although Lebanese immigrants in Africa were considered an intermediary class, a view forwarded during the colonial era by French business interests, justice records reveal the integration of Lebanese Dakarois into the local transactional culture at many levels. The needs and norms of economic life meant that the colonial city was accommodating of diversity both in the spaces it allowed newcomers and innovators to fill and in the weakness of the colonial state's ability to prevent success among those it had not included in its plans. Like Cape Verdeans in Dakar, Lebanese were able to establish themselves in certain areas of economic activity in ways that closely associated such activities to their identity.

Chapter Seven moves that informality into the realm of the illicit, identifying the Second World War as a catalyst for both illegal transactions and state surveillance of them. These two elements are related. The war brought a new scarcity of resources in Dakar, which reported to the Vichy regime in France. The clutch of wartime shortages affected everyone, from vendors to the state itself. Already adapted to a system of limited resources, Dakarois became resourceful in their strategies to survive and thrive. Illicit trade in ration tickets, controlled commodities and foodstuffs, and small military wares sprouted up during the war. By the 1940s, transience was very much part of Dakar, which allowed people to devise the movement of such items in and out of the city. The thriving illicitness within Dakar's transactional culture was brought on by the war but also was more frequently documented because of heightened state attention to anything seemingly illegal. In the later years of the war, as the balance of power shifted in Europe, the Vichy regime gave way, and Americans landed in Dakar. Their presence brought a new set of linkages to Dakar as soldiers and goods from the United States circulated the city, quickly appearing in both state documentation and Tribunal records.

Note on Orthography

This book employs French and Wolof terms as well as names drawn from many cultures and languages. For place names, I have retained French-derived spellings as conventionally accepted and employed in English. For instance, French Soudan retains the "o" in the second word. For the names of litigants, I refer to the archival documentation. French administrators who recorded grievances that primarily were given in oral form often struggled with Wolof and other local languages and thus were inconsistent in their spelling. Transliteration from local languages to French spelling at the time was at the choice of the translator. Since these were entered as official record, I retain the spelling as it was provided in the Tribunal de Première Instance archives, even if such spellings contradict today's locally accepted orthography. The same practice applies to any names provided in writing in other colonial state archives. The spellings of oral informants' names are based on either explicit instruction from the participant or my own understanding of how a name is spelled today in contemporary Senegal, where Wolof is the vernacular but French is the official language of business and government.

Chapter One

Illusory Roots

Europeans, Autochthony, and Visions of a Capital City

Rooting Transience through Residence without Settlerism

Dakar was not a deeply rooted Atlantic city born of the earlier commercial era but a new city erected during and following the moment of colonial conquest, representing the new relationship between France and West Africa. France did not consider its major cities in Africa to be sites of indirect rule or places in which native authority as conceived by the state would hold sway. Rather, they were sites of France's power, embodied in signs of French civilization and ideals, which were not masked but overtly conveyed. French administrators saw the presence of their own as a boon and marker of modern urban life in their cities in sub-Saharan Africa, which they understood to be inherently nonurban and unmodern.

This chapter explores the complex relationship with residence that existed at the level of the colonial state, pointing to the importance of its ideas regarding two populations—one that it termed European and another that it recognized as autochthonous—in helping it project attitudes toward everyone else. It reveals that white residence dictated French priorities in Dakar, even in the absence of a settler dynamic, while also showing that the existence of a community of autochthons provided a language of rightful urban belonging to only a limited group of Africans. Dakar was not built atop a tabula rasa. The society that inhabited the Cap-Vert peninsula shaped the evolution of urban forms and dynamics, as occurred throughout colonial Africa. John Parker's work on Accra showed that many of the important debates that emerged with urban growth occurred not only between the state and Africans but within African communities, especially autochthonous ones.[1] Working in Yoruba towns, Margaret Peil proposed a model for the interactions between autochthons and newcomers, positing the ways in which each adapts to the other by way of turning to different livelihoods.[2] These are important perspectives that intervene in the tendency to perceive dynamics involving autochthons as ethnically defined or principally tied to land ownership concerns.[3] For Dakar, autochthony influenced both transactional culture and the model of transient residence as well as the racial contours of French assertions regarding city dwelling.

Even with an overwhelmingly African majority in Dakar, a nonsettler city, the presence of the French was important to the state's vision. This served a number of purposes, one of the most principal of which was setting up an ostensible model of Western, white modernity that functioned to facilitate racist policies and exploitation of Africans in the capital. France supported a small, elite European population in Dakar that was meant to thrive and represent a concreteness of the civilizing mission. Yet the state fully acknowledged such a population as impermanent; the French residing in the city had neither local roots nor serious local attachments other than assignments within the bureaucracy commitment to commercial ventures.

Unlike Saint-Louis du Sénégal, which long had been the site of France's negotiated interplay with local societies and of the emergence of a strong, visible *métis* class,[4] Dakar was a capital city largely inhabited by Africans but built on a form of white hegemony and residence without settlerism. It was the power center not of a nearby region but of a vast territory France moved to conquer after having remained on the Senegambian littoral for over two centuries.[5] Despite the presence of nearby Gorée, which possessed a *métis* culture and history akin to that of Saint-Louis, Dakar was not, for France, an extension of the island. Military installations were the key first steps in France's establishment of Dakar, and land acquisitions achieved through negotiations with or seizures from the Cap-Vert's Lebu population followed. Lebu political concerns were oriented toward the maintenance of independence not only vis-à-vis France but also expansionist Wolof powers

---

1   Parker, *Making the Town.*

2   Peil, *Cities and Suburbs.*

3   Gobbers, "Territorial Découpage and Issues of 'Autochthony' in Former Katanga Province, the Democratic Republic of Congo"; Prestholdt, "Politics of the Soil"; Colin, Kouamé, and Soro, "Outside the Autochthon-Migrant Configuration."

4   The most comprehensive overview of the history of mixed communities in Senegal is provided by Jones, *Metis of Senegal.*

5   Liora Bigon also points to the difference between Dakar and the older communes in her *French Colonial Dakar*, 5–6.

in the regions to which the peninsula was attached.[6] Those priorities existed amid intensified French political and military activity in western Senegal that sought to consolidate control and facilitate a railway between the older city and the new one, which possessed a superior port and physical space for larger colonial installations.[7] The new era Dakar represented had at its core the importance of the primacy of France in West Africa as a greater region as opposed to the negotiated, ambiguous spaces of its occupancy of the littoral in the past. For a city to convey power in a new, different way from the three older communes, its physical and social makeup needed to reflect the twentieth-century colonial order. The demotion of France's *métis*-dominated principal city to capital of Senegal, and the establishment of Dakar—understood by French officials as a project of their own undertaking—as the capital of FWA entailed a shift to greater transience as, unlike the power brokers of Saint-Louis, those who ruled and ran Dakar were rarely permanent. By and large, French men and women did not settle in Dakar.[8] The arrived, stayed, and left.

As Dakar began to grow in earnest in the early twentieth century, colonial administrators attentively monitored the presence of whites in Dakar, delineating "Europeans" and "natives" in censuses and other documentation. Yet, the population of Europeans was neither monolithic nor stable. The term *European* was synonymous with *white*, and in its construction of whiteness, the state found itself often in the traps that racial categorization necessarily entailed, as this book's exploration of Dakar's Cape Verdeans reveals. In establishing a line between the city's "European" and "native" populations, administrators saw the latter as easily identifiable and definable, thereby allowing most others to be grouped into the former category. French colonial officials saw population very much in terms of black and white, often looking to perceived race rather than nationality or place or origin when delineating categories in population censuses. In this way, Algerians and Moroccans residing in Dakar were not considered African by the local administration, and under circumstances of basic census taking in the earlier decades of the twentieth century would have possibly found themselves counted among the capital's European population. As time went on, more population designations were added, in large part as a response to the

---

6   Barry, *Senegambia and the Atlantic Slave Trade*, 179. The ability of the Lebu to maintain independence throughout the nineteenth century was noted by French observers. See, for example, Laurent, *De Dakar à Zinder*, 6.

7   Barry, *Senegambia*, 215, 225; Robinson, "French Africans," 27.

8   Bignon notes the French experience in Algeria as having informed France's experience with tension when white settlement became entrenched, but sees the topical climate as the primary reason for the absence of analogous white settlement in Dakar. *French Colonial Dakar*, 7, 28–29.

growing Lebanese and Syrian population in Dakar from the 1920s onward. The notion of a cohesive European population in the capital was also offset by the presence of other European expatriates in Dakar. As a coastal capital within the immediate vicinity of non-French colonies that were in some ways less prime in terms of economic activity and urban growth, Dakar attracted opportunists of British and Portuguese backgrounds. British parties surfaced in the Tribunal de Première instance, for instance. Thus, although colonial administrators implied that the term *European* referred to their own compatriots, their concern was above all with race. It was the fact that the French were white that set them apart from the local population in the eyes of officials, not the fact that they were of French nationality.

As Dakar was the capital of the vast French colony in West Africa, a majority of whites in Dakar were French, and the state had an interest in their presence in the city under frameworks that were as equally racist as they were nationalistic. The presence of French people in Dakar, the administration understood, needed to serve a purpose and not be the result of personal venture or opportunism that would take individuals and groups outside the boundaries of state service or control. While it was the state's objective to make Dakar a sort of Paris of West Africa and stabilize a French core there, FWA was not a settler colony. White residence was driven by opportunities that had temporal parameters: colonial service, commerce, diplomatic posts, and similar sectors in which French and sometimes other European agents were needed for specific periods of time. Frequent moves were intrinsic to the French colonial system to which many in Dakar were attached. FWA's highest official and Dakar's most visible European authority—the governor-general—changed frequently: of the fifteen governors-general and acting governors-general who filled the position between 1910 and 1944, eleven occupied it for three or fewer consecutive years. Alongside those working for the French administration, there were other Europeans occupying diplomatic and similar positions, each typically carrying defined length of tenure. Just as functionaries filled posts for defined periods of time, French traders came to town during the seasons appropriate to the crops or products they purchased and sold. For Europeans, Dakar was not considered a place to stay. Capitaine Laurent's 1911 account of his time in West Africa described what he saw as a sad, poorly constructed new capital city, telling his readers that the details in his sketch of the city would serve "the unfortunate who will stay in Dakar," and pointing out that he would be moving on from the city.[9] Raymond Betts emphasized this point, stating that the "military, administrative and commercial elements were in a rather constant state of

---

9   Laurent, *De Dakar à Zinder*, 6.

motion."[10] He noted that observers remarked that one "does not remain at Dakar; one passes through it."[11]

Quarterly reports in which the state kept track of the city's numbers clearly reveal the transience the French adopted in their patterns of residence in Dakar. "The European population has remained as large as during the previous trimester, the time of the year when it generally reaches its maximum density," the first quarterly report of 1917 observed.[12] Dakar's fluctuation in population numbers was a plain description of the ebbs and flows that were a normal part of the city. Indeed, administrators expected patterns of movement among French inhabitants. It was no surprise to colonial officials that by the second quarter of that same year, many Europeans had left for France either to avoid the pending rainy season, for health reasons, or to participate in the war going on in Europe. By July, the hottest time of year and the moment of the onset of the rains, the "exodus" was at its zenith.[13] The transience of the capital's French residence was not without observable consequence. Administrators noted that the low period for European residence in Dakar resulted in fewer available police agents, a fact that concerned officials since the city needed adequate law enforcement because of the regular arrival of newcomers into town.[14] Mid-autumn saw the return of the French community, though it was not necessarily composed of the same individuals who had left. New opportunists were not unusual, with the intent to find work with the large colonial *maisons de commerce* in Dakar.[15] French functionaries cycled in and out of official posts in the capital as well. Just as urban labor opportunities during the dry season brought Africans to reside seasonally in town, the flow of Europeans to Dakar followed the trend of incentives and obligations.

The colonial state encouraged the view held among the French that Dakar was not a place to stay in the very nature of many of its operations in the capital. Public works and construction, domains in which the state required people with expertise, were among the major reasons the administration contracted European men to relocate to Dakar. The periods prior

10   Betts, "Dakar," 199.

11   Betts, "Dakar," 199.

12   Senegal, Territories of Direct Administration, General Report, 1st Trimester, for Dakar, Gorée, Rufisque, and Suburbs of Dakar, 1917, ANS 2GG17/26.

13   Senegal, Territories of Direct Administration, General Report, 3rd Trimester, for Dakar, Gorée, Rufisque, and Suburbs of Dakar, 1917, ANS 2G17/26.

14   Senegal, Territories of Direct Administration, General Report, 2nd Trimester, for Dakar, Gorée, Rufisque, and Suburbs of Dakar, 1917, ANS 2G17/26.

15   Senegal, Territories of Direct Administration, General Report, 4th Trimester, for Dakar, Gorée, Rufisque, and Suburbs of Dakar, 1917, ANS 2G17/26. Dakar, 1917, ANS 2G17/26.

to and following the Depression saw the expansion of building and public works projects in Dakar that both demanded French builders and workers and created opportunities for Europeans filling in the secondary sectors that served the white population.[16] Such projects were temporary in nature and did not encourage a high rate of long-term resettlement in the capital. Each new project required a potentially new set of French experts, especially since the administration's policies were to keep only whites in positions of authority while providing only basic training to Africans. This yielded a system by which projects always necessitated recruitment of whites. Instead of seeking to foster a generation of Africans who could compose a stable corps of city dwellers equipped to manage and undertake Dakar's ongoing public works and construction projects over the interwar period, the state's racist policies meant to keep Africans at the lowest levels of labor resulted in a system of French expertise acquired on an as-needed basis. This was a fact clearly laid out in official reports. A 1937 public safety report, for instance, noted that projects being undertaken in Dakar would soon bring additional Europeans to town.[17]

Dakar was not simply an administrative city. It also housed various military installations, and from the 1910s into the 1940s, the city became an important base. French soldiers, in particular those at the officer ranks, were always present in Dakar but, naturally, were never permanent. Although France had long employed African soldiers by the time the twentieth century dawned, they reserved high-ranking posts commanding African forces for whites, and thus a corps of French officers was a constant contingent of the capital's European population. Military assignments were transitory, and the coming and going of French servicemen was a fact of Dakar's social landscape. During times of war, this was even more the case, and the capital's four decades of major growth in the high colonial era saw two world wars in which France was deeply embroiled. Those wars carried their own patterns of residence in Dakar, causing the white population to balloon at times when France leveraged its West African capital as a base. Wartime also entailed difficulties in and restrictions on movement. This was particularly true during World War II, the period of time that saw the least transience and greatest stability among the white population. FWA's allegiance to the Vichy regime from mid-1940 through 1942 and the conditions of war obliged French civil servants to sustain longer tours of duty in Dakar, which was loyal to that

---

16   See, for example, Dakar et Dépendances, General Annual Report, 1930, ANS 2G30/25; and Dakar et Dépendances, Police and Safety, Annual Report 1937, March 1, 1938, ANS 2G37/33.

17   Dakar et Dépendances, Police and Safety, Annual Report 1937, March 1, 1938, ANS 2G37/33.

regime. Wartime was not a state of normalcy, however, and the conditions of World War II in France were such that French bureaucrats and commercial agents or others working in Senegal would have had little desire or impetus to return to the metropole when war was ravaging France. The large white population in Dakar during that period was also the result of the heavy presence of servicemen—French and then American—who were posted in Dakar at various points over the course of the war.[18]

While Dakar had a larger French population than most points in FWA,[19] its model was white residence without settlerism. There was a stable, long-term white society that was primarily engaged in the colonial commerce associated with ground nuts and the port, but even many of those residents

---

18 The wartime European population of Dakar rose visibly: the administration counted 17,480 on January 1, 1943, and then 19,276 in December 1943. See Dakar et Dépendances, Annual Economic Report, 1943, ANS 2G143/52. See also O'Brien, *White Society in Black Africa*, 65, 275.

19 While white communities were scattered throughout the towns and trading posts of FWA and of Senegal itself, Dakar held a high proportion of Europeans, and this percentage increased as time passed, and more activities became concentrated in the capital and main port of FWA. According to Rita Cruise O'Brien's analysis, from the city's establishment as capital of FWA until the 1930s, Dakar's European population represented roughly 40 to 45 percent of the population of Senegal as a whole; in the 1930s, that percentage began shifting visibly toward Dakar, with the capital housing nearly 60 percent of Senegal's Europeans. See O'Brien, *White Society in Black Africa* for these numbers. Her analysis of the postcolonial period shows the continuation of that trend toward white flow to town: by the early postindependence period, 27,500 of the 29,000 French of Senegal resided in Dakar. O'Brien, *White Society*, 17. However, it should be noted that on the whole, O'Brien's statistics are generally lower than those found in a range of archival sources. Census taking was an infrequent and inexact science in the colonial era, and even while counting Europeans was easier than counting Africans, the numbers vary from one archival source to another. Different services (immigration, administrative and political affairs, police, and safety) took estimates of the population of Dakar at various times for their individual reports. A local count done under the municipal authority of the mayor of Dakar at the end of 1934, for example, counts the total European population (French and other European, but not including Lebanese) at 8,220. See Circumscription of Dakar and Dependencies, City of Dakar, Population—Table Summarizing the Foreign Population of White Race in the Circumscription of Dakar, December 31, 1934, and Circumscription of Dakar and Dependencies, City of Dakar, Population—Table Summarizing the European Population, December 31, 1934, ANS 1Q322(77). O'Brien's population statistics are much lower for the first half of the 1930s. The European population of Dakar was counted at 19,276 in December 1943.

were impermanent in the long run. The French in Dakar and the major cities of Senegal were of working age and lived expatriate rather than permanent settler lives, maintaining strong ties to France throughout their tenure.[20] Living in Dakar was part of a life of movement for many. William Ponty, who served as governor-general from 1908 until his death in 1915 and has been considered a key figure in architecting the French republican aspects of colonial rule, had moved throughout the region as part of his colonial military career, spending eighteen years in various parts of the region before his promotion to the federation's top administrator, seated in Dakar.[21] Early twentieth-century photographer Edmond Fortier chose Dakar as his place of residence; his images became the face of colonial Dakar to the rest of the world through their use in the production of postcards, which today are seen as iconic visual colonial representations of the city. He arrived in Dakar in his forties, having already moved within Europe, even acquiring German citizenship at one point.[22] His life in Dakar was in many ways defined by mobility as his craft took his to regions throughout French West Africa. As Rita Cruise O'Brien points out in her study of French society in Senegal, decades later, even among the most settled white residents "regular leave and plans for eventual retirement to France always helped to sustain their roots with their families and regions of origin."[23] Transience—whether in the short or long term—among Dakar's European population became accepted and expected over the first half of the twentieth century.

Although nonsettled white residence had highly variable modes, the role of the French population as dominant transients in Dakar represented an unspoken but obvious contradiction for the state. The colonial administration sought to craft a capital city according to European needs and norms while discouraging instability and stemming what it saw as unnecessary movement to and from town among Africans. While it is not the argument here that Africans imitated French habits of temporary or cyclical residence, it is the claim that the white population and the French state contributed to a culture of transient residence in which Africans were by no means unique actors when they accessed Dakar in the same ways. By establishing a hegemonic elite in Dakar that was neither local nor locally invested, the colonial administration normalized a model by which one could establish residence in Dakar while not only rejecting it as a place of permanence but also adopting it into broader geographies of belonging and activity. Administrators attributed what they perceived as the city's ills on the liberal movement and

---

20   O'Brien, *White Society in Black Africa*, 17.

21   Foster, "Rethinking 'Republican Paternalism.'"

22   Moreau, "Edmond Fortier."

23   O'Brien, *White Society*, 17.

Figure 1.1. Postcard image of the Port of Dakar, c. 1910s. Edmond
Fortier postcard collection. Courtesy of edmondfortier.org.

informal residential arrangements of Africans, but the French population was
often in a greater state of flux, accepting life in Dakar as temporary. It was
not a city in which one was meant to settle for good. Indeed, the observer
quoted by Betts in his portrait of colonial Dakar proclaimed in 1929 that
"for the greater part of the inhabitants" of the colonial capital, coming and
going was "life."[24] In Dakar, transience was intimately tied to residence.
There were few means by which to differentiate between inhabitants on the
basis of greater or lesser states of permanence.

France shaped a city that required and sought to maintain white residents
for specific reasons and for identifiable lengths of time. Both the state and
the French population understood Dakar was a short-lived experience for
most whites. There was a deep contradiction in the roles Europeans played
in helping to define colonial Dakar. The state's emphasis on whites as essential and modern effaced the reality of their transience, which, when linked
to Africanness, was the anathema of urban development for the colonial
administrators. The European core was the laboratory of orderly urban
development for such officials, despite the fact that they knew its inhabitants would rarely become permanent in it. In the colonial capital's local set
of norms, transience was a foundational element, and the French in Dakar
were bound up in it as intimately as the society as a whole. Colonial administrators never sought to stabilize the white community of Dakar in the way

24   Betts, "Dakar," 199.

they very pointedly attempted to control the city's nonwhite population. For them, Africans were not natural city dwellers; rather, whiteness ascribed a set of rights to live in a modern city and act as if the city were home—even if it was not.

Dakar's Autochthons in the Construction of the Urban Resident

As a nonsettler city with a majority-African population, Dakar was a place in which Senegalese and other West Africans resided regularly and increasingly over time. Similar to the French who found themselves in the capital, not all African Dakarois were there to stay; in fact, for many, the city was a place alongside others in which the activities of life were carried out. With the exception of the autochthonous Lebu population, whose settlements on the Cap-Vert peninsula had been disrupted but not destroyed by French conquest, most people were not from Dakar. The Lebu possessed land rights as well as political rights derived from their status as *originaires*, setting them apart from other Africans in Dakar, both in real terms and in the mind of colonial officials. The existence of an autochthonous community established a premise upon which administrators could judge Africans more broadly, encouraging and solidifying the notion that those without obvious rights had to demonstrate utility to warrant residence in Dakar. Utility was defined not in personal terms to the individual but rather in terms of what the state deemed useful to itself. Across the continent, policies were put in place to either discourage or outright exclude nonwhites from establishing themselves in cities, particularly those with no precolonial roots. Nowhere was this more obvious than in southern Africa, where pass laws, which effectively criminalized urban unemployment, were the epitome of this.[25] Although Dakar did not legislate to this extent and made sure to point out in its own reports that it was not overseeing a segregatory regime akin to those in British colonies in Africa, the French colonial state certainly was preoccupied with African movement and enacted policies to limit when, how, and why subjects of FWA could move around.[26]

---

25   There is a large literature on the repressive South African regime in which the pass law system developed. For an overview, see Beinart, *Twentieth-Century South Africa*. See also Van Onselen, *Studies in the Social and Economic History of the Witwatersrand*; Evans, *Bureaucracy and Race*; Crais, *Politics of Evil*; Hindson, *Pass Controls and the Urban African Proletariat in South Africa*.

26   These controls were built into France's *indigénat*, the "native code" devised to create a regime of forced labor, submission, and restricted movement

In its management of Dakar, the French administration turned not only to its identifiable white urban community but also to the autochthonous population in managing policy and expectations for residence and rights in the city. It adopted the notion of autochthony both as a means of seeking segregation it could claim was not based on race and as a continuation of France's nineteenth-century establishment of special rights for certain city dwellers. Peter Geschiere points out that the use of the term *autochthony* in the French colonial administration was an invention of the moment around the turn of the twentieth century, when the creation of ethnic categories meant to render the large population of FWA legible to those who sought to control it emerged as a specialization of the colonial state.[27] Invoking one population as possessing inherent rights allowed for the casting of all others as outsiders, a framework that served not only the categorization in which the colonial state engaged but also the efforts at *refoulement* to which it was committed in a city such as Dakar. However, there was a tension in this model since, as Geschiere explains, French colonial administrators such as Maurice Delafosse demonstrated preference in their ethnographic work for migrant groups, interpreting movement as evidence of industriousness and energy, which was to be harnessed to the benefit of the state.[28] The idea of autochthony provided stable ground for foundations, though, and in the quest for urban development, such groups needed to be identified and differentiated from others.[29]

French officials paired the ethnically informed concept of autochthony with the historical consideration of first contact, conferring rights as a result of the latter but interpreting them as somehow inherent to the former. The colonial state granted autochthons legal and electoral rights based on what it saw as an inherited right to residence in the *communes de plein exercise* based on the fact that they already were there when France established those

---

throughout the areas outside the four communes. Mann, "What Was the Indigénat?"; Gueye, *Le Code de l'indigénat*; Doho, *Le Code de l'Indigénat*; Slobodkin, "State of Violence"; Bogosian, "Forced Labor, Resistance and Memory": Fall, *Le travail force en Afrique Occidentale française*; Rossi, "From Unfree Work to Working for Free."

27 Geschiere, *Perils of Belonging*, 4.

28 Geschiere, *Perils of Belonging*, 14–15. See also Amselle and Sibeud, *Maurice Delafosse Entre Orientalisme et Ethnographie*.

29 Pointing to the emergence of ethnic categorization most substantially under Governor-General William Ponty's *polique des races*, Gescihere asserts that a local ethic was adopted by the colonial state, which wished to implant itself locally and thus required autothchonous populations to validate in doing so. This was as philosophical as it was physical. See Geschiere, *Perils of Belonging*, 15.

communes. There was a pairing of physicality and subjectivity in this policy. The French colonial state selected locations of interest and made them sites of power. People already established in that place at the time of that selection were its original inhabitants, even if a region had previously undergone contests for power or resettlement trends over time. For the French colonial administration, the crucial point was not to accurately assign rights but to conveniently do so. France, a foreign entity, acted as both interpreter of existing rights and architect of new ones, ultimately deciding what to "preserve" and what to invent outright since this served its purposes and placed it at the center of control.[30] In a newer city such as Dakar, the designation of certain inhabitants as original city dwellers with rights established those communities as valid and permanent members of an urban society and marked them off from everyone else.

Initiated in the mid-1800s, the principle of *originaire* status was based on the idea that inhabitants of France's key towns in Senegal, under the Third Republic, should exercise rights permitted under French metropolitan law and be able to elect local officials. At the time, towns such as Saint-Louis and Gorée were the centers of economic activity and social life in colonial Senegal, with a prominent mixed population that carried out its own set of politics.[31] Prior to the shift from assimilation to association, the creation of this status was the way French authorities sought to bring inhabitants of their key Senegalese cities more fully into the fold of French influence. The notion that urban dwellers were in particular the proper candidates for French status was congruent with France's identification of cities as sites of performative civilization.[32] As the cities of FWA grew and as the state consolidated its hold over the extended colony that reached inland across the Niger River and into the Sahara, the debate as to what rights *originaires* truly held and how to acquire or maintain them heated up. French authorities

---

30 There is a large literature on this broader trend in colonial Africa, primarily framed as the "invention of tradition," named for Ranger's article on the theory. See Ranger, "Invention of Tradition in Colonial Africa"; Chanock, *Law, Custom and Social Order.*

31 Jones's *Métis of Senegal* provides a comprehensive overview; Johnson's *Emergence of Black Politics* is an earlier exploration of these political dynamics.

32 This has been explored across works on colonial cities of the industrial age. Ousseynou Faye has made this point in his work on Dakar, as has Bignon in examining the nature of place names in Dakar's evolution. Ambe Njoh points to the process of urban planning as an exercise of control. Wright's work has shown this point in detail through the analysis of architectural planning and genesis. Faye, *Dakar et ses cultures*; Bigon, *French Colonial Dakar*; Njoh, "Urban Planning as a Tool of Power and Social Control in Colonial Africa"; Wright, *Politics of Design in French Colonial Urbanism.*

shifted their philosophy about the relationship between France and Africans, favoring a system by which France sought not to integrate Africans as pseudo-citizens but to "protect" them as subjects. The creation of a multilayered legal system, with metropolitan, native customary, and Muslim codes, opened space for new attempts by the state to channel Africans, even *originaires*, into the latter categories. *Originaires* vigorously defended their rights to access French law, and the election of Blaise Diagne and the onset of the First World War helped confirm those rights. Military conscription, which was pursued heavily in FWA, opened space for Diagne to link military service with the other elements of *originaire* status to yield fuller French citizenship for the residents of the four *communes*.[33] The confirmation of *originaires'* rights also served to solidify the very different status of subjects, or non-*originaires*. These changes meant something important for urban residence: by the end of the First World War, there was a clear contingent of the urban population that had seen its rights reasserted.

In Dakar, that group of city dwellers was predominantly the autochthonous Lebu community. By the twentieth century, France's knowledge of the Cap-Vert's Lebu societies was based on a century of anecdotes, observation, and experience in its conquest efforts in the adjoining regions. An 1814 work that sought to describe the indigenous communities of Senegal pointed to the distinctive ability of Lebu societies to "defend their rights," referring to the independence Lebu leaders had maintained vis-à-vis African power brokers in the Wolof regions.[34] By the time Dakar was made the *chef-lieu* of FWA, colonial authorities recognized an existing political organization among the Lebu and folded it into the city's local administration of African residents. The state gave official roles to local Lebu authorities, making them the "traditional" counterparts to officials serving in the French system. Councils of Lebu notables elected key figures to preside over the Lebu communities of the Cap-Vert peninsula. Their functions included political and religious capacities. The French administration identified certain of those positions as Lebu interlocutors with the colonial state. That interaction became important over time as the growth of Dakar gave rise to questions regarding property rights and the Lebu stake in municipal management. The Lebu mobilized their *originaire* status and autochthonous identity on critical issues to assert their natural rights as both the traditional inhabitants of Dakar and as the citizens of the French capital.

---

33 For accounts of these processes, see Roberts, *Litigants and Households*; Roberts, "Text and Testimony"; and Johnson, *Emergence of Black Politics*. In his book, Roberts probes the earlier legal debates, while in his article he addresses the debates of the 1910s. Johnson outlines the politics of Diagne in the citizenship struggle.

34 Villaneuve, *L'Afrique*, 58.

France preserved what it saw as the existing rights of the autochthonous Lebu by recognizing them as the majority *originaire* community of Dakar, the last Senegalese colonial city to be made a *commune de plein exercise*. The Lebu had the legal and electoral rights commensurate with *originaire* status. French colonial policy created segregation among Africans, and this impacted the administration's understanding of whose residence in a city such as Dakar was appropriate and whose was not. Despite France's use of underhanded, racist tools to displace Lebu communities to the areas of Dakar beyond the Plateau, they were positioned as undeniable Dakarois. As Ousseynoue Faye points out, the Lebu were the most visible of the majority—that is, the African population—and were particularly implicated in the generation of urban culture in Dakar.[35] Other Africans became migrants by default, he asserts, fulfilling the state's desire to transform the majority of the population into a "sociological minority."[36] The existence of the Lebu community and the autochthonous status associated with it provided the colonial state with a vocabulary by which to exclude other Africans whose tenure in town was interpreted to be ultimately fleeting and undesirable. Thus, non-Lebu Africans in Dakar needed to demonstrate either utility, or perceived stability, if they lacked autochthony and an inherent set of privileges—whether self-ascribed or bestowed—to justify urban residence. At the same time, this framework allowed officials to cast their policies as unrelated to race, since neither Lebu nor other African residents of Dakar were white. Rather, the administration could maintain, these were issues of rights and autochthony, despite the fact that administrators were very clear in their correspondence and reports that they abhorred the idea of developing and presiding over an African city in Africa.

This inherently contradictory stance emerged around the same time as the creation of the Medina, the moment when the colonial administration became more acutely attentive to the composition and habits of Dakar's population. Population growth spurred by the designation of Dakar as the capital of FWA, expansion of trade through the enlarging port of Dakar, and the First World War brought about an urgency in the state's impulse to control the city. Reports on Dakar's demographics demonstrated careful attention on the part of administrators to a distinction drawn between autochthons, who were accepted as residents, and other Africans, who were essentially cast as foreigners. In a 1915 report explaining Dakar's growing and increasingly diverse population, the lieutenant-governor told the governor-general that the capital possessed 25,000 inhabitants, including people in various jobs ranging from dockworker to domestic, as well as "residents." He pointed

35   Faye, *Dakar*, 17.
36   Faye, *Dakar*, 17.

out that autochthons represented between 8,000 and 10,000 of the total population; everyone else had come "from all points in French West Africa, some by accident, . . . others to escape their native land, and others lastly to look for work or giving in to the attraction of the big city."[37] Thereafter, it was common in reports on the city's population, economic life, and standard of living for officials to count the Lebu as a separate group from other Africans. The rest of the African urban population in Dakar, however, was rarely broken down according to ethnic background or place or origin in such reports; their shared status as nonautochthons defined them to the state.[38] An insider-outsider distinction for Africans was formed within the existing race-based framework that operated to the same effect.

There was a reality to autochthony, of course, despite the colonial state's framing of it as a form of exclusivity that served the purposes of the state in urban management. The Cap-Vert peninsula was the site of a robust Lebu social and political system prior to the move France made from its nearby offshore stronghold on Gorée to the mainland. Precolonial Lebu history, and the diplomacy that ensued between the community and the French arrivals, became engrained in local collective memory, which holds that the Lebu constituted a unique community with status as the owners of Dakar's heritage, history, and lands.[39] This common understanding about Dakarois is rooted in the fact that autochthony established *originaire* status and entailed, in addition to voting and juridical rights, certain land tenure assurances, creating a double affirmation—political and physical—of the Lebu as state-sanctioned residents. The Lebu community protected and defended its *originaire* status and rights in the political arena.[40] This was particularly true

---

37 Confidential letter from the lieutenant-governor to the governor-general, July 18, 1915, ANS 11D1/1284.

38 See, for example, ANS 11D1/1284, 3G2/9(120), 4G/107(105).

39 Lebu oral histories are the first to assert the primacy of their community in Dakar, but on the whole, collective memory among Lebu and non-Lebu alike point to the separate and unique nature of the Lebu population. When asked to interview long-standing Dakarois, I was nearly always referred to Lebu families, even though a great number of the oldest families in the city are not of Lebu origin. So strong is the understanding of Lebu autochthony as distinct from other urban identities that it was only after many explanations of my objective of speaking with all city dwellers, not simply the original residents, that contacts in Dakar introduced me to a fuller range of informants of varied backgrounds. There is thus no specific interview to cite here; this is rather an observation made over months of field research in Dakar.

40 The early portion of the period this chapter treats was a time of great discussion about *originaire* rights and status, articulated more fully in the promulgation of the Diagne laws of 1915 and 1916 concerning French military service.

in matters of property. Land was an ongoing and contentious issue because even autochthony did not protect the Lebu from state appropriation of their urban lands. Despite the erosion of those rights with increased confiscations by the state, Lebu continued to constitute the majority of African property owners in colonial Dakar.[41] They were not the only landowners in the city. Many Lebu sold to the French and, eventually, the Lebanese and other Africans, and most leased land to other city stakeholders as a financial strategy. Still, their dominance in property holding remained part of the Lebu identity in Dakar. While there were many avenues to creating success in the city—employment, trade and commerce, creation of social networks, education—property transactions were particularly important for Lebu city dwellers.

In addition to claims to land, autochthony carried preexisting activities—notably, local fishing and horticulture. Those occupations had constituted the precolonial subsistence economy of the Cap-Vert peninsula, and the Lebu population was able to continue them into the colonial era. The French administration wanted such activities to flourish as they created a local supply of food for Dakar. Lebu fishers in particular were able to gear their catch toward the local market that served a largely African consumer base. The link between Lebu societies and the fishing occupation was strong and long-standing by the twentieth century, having been noted as the primary way of life for coastal people of the Cap-Vert and Petite Côte for two centuries. Georges Balandier and Paul Mercier's 1948 study, *Particularisme et Évolution*, made clear the enduring relationship between a historic livelihood and the autochthons of the region.[42] During the years of Dakar's growth, small-scale farming among Lebu communities in town was also

---

With the enlargement of Dakar into the Circumscription in 1924, Lebu of the suburbs became active in establishing their *originaire* status, activity noted in the 1925 Summary of Reports from the FWA Group of Colonies, 1925, ANS 2G25/10, and in the 1926 Annual Report for the Circumscription of Dakar, ANS 2G26/9. The general question of the *originaires* of Dakar has been explored in a number of works. Of particular note is Johnson, *Emergence of Black Politics*.

41 Land questions run throughout the archives on Dakar and are located in several collections. See, for instance, the ANS series L prior to 1920 as well as the Dakar Regional Archives series C—this chapter has specifically examined ANS L28, L30, L35, and L59, and ANS Service Régional des Archives de Dakar series C/211 and C/228.

42 Balandier and Mercier, *Particularisme et Évolution*.

encouraged, and colonial officials kept track of what was locally procurable in the Dakar region.[43]

The distinction between African communities who inhabited the Cap-Vert peninsula prior to France's arrival and those who came to it after that fact was drawn not only by the French but also by local Lebu stakeholders. Lebu terminology for other Africans who came to reside in Dakar bears witness to their own self-conceptions as autochthons or "primo-residents," as Faye explains, drawing on the work of Pape Sakho.[44] Immigrants from other regions who arrived in the earliest waves prior to World War I were referred to as *doxandeem*, drawing on the Wolof word for walk, *dox*.[45] Africans who settled and became Dakarois by virtue of establishing their families there did not assimilate into the local community, in this terminology, but rather continued to be designated as outsiders. The term *doomi doxandeeem* became used to refer to the descendants of non-Lebu who settled in Dakar—*doom* is the Wolof word for offspring.[46] Although the historical depth of such terms is not established, their usage provides insight into the role of Lebu self-perceptions and status under French colonial rule in creating a premise for exclusion of other Africans as rightful, appropriate, or natural residents of Dakar. The Lebu ultimately shifted to minority status as Dakar's population expanded by the 1930s and 1940s, but an implicit understanding remained of non-Lebu African residents as belonging elsewhere.

Colonial authorities did not require an autochthonous African community in Dakar to come to policies that excluded nonwhites from full, equal urban life. Officials already understood urban residence as an inherently modern and non-African practice, and the parameters for an African presence in town were crafted around their own objectives. But the existence of the Lebu, their history with France, and their locally based economic activities—such as landowning and fishing, which were seen as markers of stability—fed the colonial mindset about movement, belonging, and city dwelling. Other Africans were engaged in far more ephemeral jobs either because of the nature of the work or because of their own preferences to move from place to place. Those other occupations—trade, manual labor, domestic service, employment in commercial houses and the administration,

---

43 See annual reports entitled "Rapports d'ensemble" for the years 1914, 1917, 1925, and 1944 for examples of comments to this effect: ANS 2G14/40, ANS 2G17/26, ANS 2G25/10, and ANS 2G44/19.

44 Faye, *Dakar*, 37.

45 Faye, *Dakar*, 37.

46 Faye, *Dakar*, 38.

port work—became largely filled by non-Lebu.[47] While city dwellers in those positions could demonstrate utility, that utility was only valid so long as the work was in progress. Many of the employment opportunities in Dakar entailed a necessary element of mobility and encouraged transience, destabilizing the worker's identity as a resident. With the Lebu engaged in other activities, other Africans took such jobs, and the differences between *originaire* and others added to its legal aspect an economic dimension.[48]

The figuring of Lebu Dakarois in opposition to other Africans who came to inhabit Dakar by no means entailed an accompanying assumption of proximity between the Lebu and the white community that the French colonial administration intended to dominate the city. The contrary was embedded in French policy. Lebu ownership status was original and factual in nature but was rendered marginal and symbolic in practice by the colonization of the Cap-Vert and establishment of Dakar. The second half of the 1800s saw various means of land appropriation, as well as speculation driven by purchases by inhabitants of nearby Gorée and others.[49] The creation of Dakar according to the European core model the French administration pursued required the movement of Lebu communities out of what would become the Plateau into peripheral spaces that would be understood as native villages as opposed to neighborhoods of the city itself.[50] The positioning of Lebu as different from other Africans in Dakar informed an overall native policy in Dakar that operated fully outside the sphere of what was considered the modern, French city and its identity.

The function of the binary delineated among Africans was to facilitate policies that discouraged non-Lebu from settling in town and to cast the systems of movement in which non-Lebu Africans operated as inherently

---

47 This is in no way meant to suggest the Lebu did not undergo change; in fact, the contrary is obvious in the transformation of Lebu political institutions under colonialism and in the orientation of fishing, horticulture, and land owning. These latter activities became a major source of income for many Lebu families.

48 Interview with Oumar Ba, September 2007, Dakar, Senegal. Wesley's discussion of Lebu politics in Dakar suggests the same dynamics; see Wesley, *Emergence of Black Politics*. Colonial documents confirm this by signaling out Lebu activities as different and separate from others—a good example is the report on "The Standard of Living of Natives in the Circumscription of Dakar," February 4, 1939, and "Response of the Governor-General to the Report of Inspector of Colonies Bargues," ANS 4G/107(105).

49 Faye, *Dakar*, 40–41.

50 The division of Dakar into a European core and African periphery is widely discussed in works addressing the city and the French colonial administration in Senegal. See Faye, *Dakar*, 46–50; Bigon, *French Colonial Dakar*, 79, 90.

inimical to stable urban development. Central to French understandings of Dakar was an internal contradiction that conveyed the simultaneous message of belonging and exclusion regarding the Lebu. Yet this layered othering pursued in French colonial thought, which positioned Africans in opposition to whites and then positioned Africans in opposition to one another, was neither novel nor exclusive to France. It was a foundational device of colonial control honed during conquest and elaborated in theories of rule across the continent. At larger-scale levels, it drove the politics of division in colonies such as Nigeria and Rwanda, and in the Senegambian region it had informed the campaign against El Hajj Umar Tal.[51] In Dakar, it took shape in the marshaling of autochthony as a device of urban control.

Foundations of Transience and Residence

Dakar was a city of expectations layered atop one another. All who came to the capital possessed them, as did those who saw new communities rise around their own. But colonial Dakar was not a landscape of equal participants, and the colonial state and its adjacent stakeholders—white residents—were hegemonic in crafting the ways those in Dakar understood and expected the urban world to operate. Colonial administrators were committed to what they perceived as a modern project that would become a model city in tropical Africa, led by a small but important corps of white

---

51   Hall, *A History of Race in Muslim West Africa*; Pondopoulo, "The Construction of Fulani Otherness in Faidherbe's Writings"; Arowosegbe, "Hausa-Fulani Pastoralists and Resource Conflicts in Yorubaland"; Carney, "Beyond Tribalism"; Mamdani, "The Racialization of the Hutu/Tutsi Difference Under Colonialism"; Law, "Hamitic Hypothesis"; Maiangwa, "Conflicting Indigeneity." Islam's role in engendering colonial portrayals of alienness has been discussed across the literature on Islam in Africa. Initial conquests in the nineteenth century that intruded upon Islamic states and their expansion drove the attitudes colonial authorities adopted vis-à-vis Muslim African leaders. See Harrison, *France and Islam in West Africa*; Soares, *Islam and the Prayer Economy*, 53–59. David Robinson points out that the shift in French policy to *Islam noir* was a concept that permitted a rapprochement under the umbrella of colonial control and efforts at Muslim leaders to maintain spiritual and local authority. Paul Lovejoy points out that Islamic states acted as a bulwark against European hegemony well before colonial conquest. In other work, Lovejoy points out that slave status, not dominant status, was associated with alien identity in pre-colonial-Saharan Africa. Europeans cast Africans who held larger African populations in slavery as alien. Robinson, *Paths of Accommodation*; Lovejoy, "Islam, Slavery, and Political Transformation in West Africa," 280; Lovejoy, *Transformations in Slavery*, 1–6, 20.

residents whose lives in Dakar would closely resemble the urban lives of the inhabitants of a major metropolitan city in France. But the capital of FWA was an African city, one that few French residents sought to make their permanent home. The model they established was residence without settlerism, and in that they became the dominant transients, carving out lives in Dakar as necessary and for highly variable amounts of time. This was the role the city played for thousands of Africans across the region, but ultimately many more Africans established more regular residence habits in Dakar than French inhabitants did. The colonial state found in its European core population a group of people whose behavior did not encourage the sort of stability administrators wished to see entrenched in the new capital.

Whatever the nature of the white community of Dakar, officials maintained the premise of a European city and employed it in the exclusionary process upon which urban expansion and policies were constructed. By defining segments of urban society in opposition to one another, the state envisioned a socio-spatial hierarchy in which closeness to France was mirrored by proximity to the city center and the rights and privileges life within it afforded. Administrators mobilized the existence of autochthonous residents in this process, and Lebu Dakarois acted in their own interests against both exclusion by the French and erasure by the incoming waves of new arrivals from regions of Senegal, Mali, Guinea, and beyond.

Dakar needed newcomers, visitors, sojourners, and migrants. They filled the growing and diverse roles that emerged as a colonial capital developed into a major city. Dakar's non-European, non-autochthonous population drove the new directions society took. These new residents came from nearby regions and those further afield in West Africa, as well as from places of origin such as the Cape Verde Islands and Lebanon. Their reasons for being in Dakar were equally diverse, as were their understandings of how and when to live there. But in sum and over time, they dramatically expanded the city's population and spatial expanse from the 1910s to the 1940s, and with that growth came a unique culture of how to live in the city.

As Dakar grew, French officials crafted both a rhetoric and a set of policies regarding urban residence that they conceived as the natural order of things, and racism was inherent to the logic they applied. Prioritizing whiteness, they fashioned an elaborate apparatus of ideas meant to congeal identities and categorize people in order to render the city easier to understand and manage. Critical in that was drawing up an understanding of what it meant to be a true resident of Dakar, even if that required overlooking the transient nature of French inhabitants or singling out the autochthonous community as intrinsically unique. With the Lebu and French as residents, a category of everyone else was brought into being. Those others come from all over to live in Dakar, entered against a background of an existing French colonial lexicon of city dwelling that sought to exclude in a way framed as rational and even rightful.[52] The mobile lifestyles in which many African Dakarois engaged only bolstered the administration's idea that they were not residents. However, as the next chapter will show, such mobility was, contrary to state discourse, neither unique to the African community nor destructive to Dakar. By the close of the interwar period, transient residence became a more common model than that of autochthonous, established residence in the capital.

---

52   Nancy Rose Hunt uses the term "colonial lexicon" in her examination of the medicalization of childbirth practices and discourses under colonialism in the Belgian Congo. Hunt, *A Colonial Lexicon*.

Chapter Two

The Rhetoric of *Refoulement* in Colonial Dakar

Refoulement in the French Colonial Conception of the City

The two decades from 1914 to 1934 saw increasingly heightened concern in the colonial state's perception of Africans as the principal undesirable element of the capital of France's important West African colony. Administrators adhered to a race-driven concept of urban modernity, one that was threatened by Dakar's growth even as that growth brought the city to greater prominence. State vision was for a grand capital, major Atlantic port, and modern city. This was expressed throughout the years of high colonialism—key decades for the development of Dakar—but was also accompanied by a current of concern among officials that the capital's African setting and social makeup could compromise its potential. As the men who staffed the colonial state attempted to hone their professional approach to urban management, they brought into their work a rhetoric around Africans that was embedded in the language of modernity. Within it, the majority of Africans were cast as inappropriate to city dwelling, making the generation of strategies to discourage them from coming to or remaining in town a vital aspect of running the capital. Part of the project of making Dakar what they believed was modern was dealing not only in the technical details of urban planning but also in the social attributes of the city. Yet, these ideas did not correspond to realities on the ground. Ultimately, the energy and effort devoted to making Dakar a modern European city did little to wrest the day-to-day power to shape urban life from the hands of those who lived it. The way in which this was perhaps most obvious was in the simple fact of Dakar's growth from the 1910s through the 1930s to an African-majority city, a process that stood in deep contrast to the goals and visions of the state.

In France, a reconceptualization of urban space began in the 1850s with Haussmann's transformation of Paris, but it was in the early decades of the twentieth century that its relationship to urban life, human development, and modernity was more explicitly drawn out in circles of urban planners, architects, and sociologists. As colonial administration of FWA congealed, the concept of professionalized rule took shape in Dakar, informed not only by colonial imperatives but by global trends. The official mind was particularly set toward social control, seeing the urban space as one in which the potential to create ordered Europeanness could be hindered by uncontrolled African presence. Urban management as a device of social control was consistent with the era across world regions. The year 1911 saw the birth of the Société Française d'Urbanistes, a professional organization that influenced viewpoints on urban development and management in the French colonies and other southern cities such as those of Latin America.[1] Just as Dakar's administrators attempted to reconfigure their city, projects were being undertaken in places such as Rio de Janeiro to modernize along a model that took Haussmann as inspiration, and officials in FWA were participants in the movement.[2] In the French colonies of Africa and Asia during the first several decades of the twentieth century, urban architectural projects were infused with objectives of Western modernity even as they struggled with the specific indigenous contexts in which they were set.[3] Architecture alone did not constitute the concern with urban life at that time. In places like Mexico City and Shanghai, struggles with informal settlements and activities in cities had already emerged by the 1920s and 1930s.[4] It was also during these years that modern cosmopolitan life dominated discourse in the United States. The influential Chicago school of sociologists came to prominence in the 1920s, bringing ideas about the role of cities in influencing social behavior. Specialists saw spaces and society as intertwined, and they sought to control both. Efforts to shape Dakar were thus part of a global trend, but at the same time the discourse about modern urban needs was particularly shaped by—and for—the racism of the colonial state in France's largest colony.

---

1   Guillot, "La Société Française des Urbanistes et l'Institut d'Urbanisme."
2   Underwood, "Alfred Agache, French Sociology, and Modern Urbanism in France and Brazil." For an overview of the general trend, see Hall, *Cities of Tomorrow*. Freund also gives a broad overview of colonial aspirations of cosmopolitan modernity in African cities in *The African City*. In Dakar, new structures were seen as an opportunity to cast colonial power as modern, expressing it through buildings in which Africans would go about daily tasks, such as markets. Bigon and Sinou, "Quest for Colonial Style in French West Africa."
3   Wright, *Politics of French Colonial Urbanism*.
4   Ochoa, "Coercion, Reform, and the Welfare State"; Lu, "Creating Urban Outcasts."

Modernity as linked to urban spaces was a central concept, operating at several levels in the colonial context. Generally, cities around the world were understood to be a result of the new age but also a vehicle for advancing it. It was essential that cities be exemplary, controlled environments of progress. The concept of what modern meant was contextual, and for French colonial administrators, it was deeply entrenched in the association with whiteness. Even as officials who understood themselves to be part of a global trend devised theories and plans to shape Dakar into a modern capital city, they undergirded their work with the premise that such cities were inherently designed and occupied by Europeans, their proxy term for whites.[5] Africans were understood at best to be naturally unsuited to modern urban life and at worst to be deleterious to a city's ability to thrive. In this way, the urban modernity movement among Dakar's managers occurred in two layers of paternalistic thought, one that saw well-conceived cities as able to shape human behavior, and the other that saw whites as able to control the lives of blacks.

Like all urban spaces, Dakar was neither a single space, nor was it a blank slate by the time state officials began to take a more concerted hand in shaping the next stage in its development. Having been established in 1857 atop dynamic preexisting Lebu settlements, and linked into networks that reached in all directions via land and sea, Dakar was a growing city that already had its own specific characteristics and tendencies. Communities both nearby and further afield already possessed ideas about and relationships with Dakar, affecting its function and form. Any physical agenda for the capital was to confront its social and economic realities. Official goals for urban development and curation constantly faced the challenges posed by the circumstances of the colonial situation itself. The act of founding a city on the premise that its majority population and the spaces they inhabited would be hidden from view resulted to a great extent in that outcome, but without the subservience that was assumed to follow. Laid out from the start in a way that meant to ensure distance between the colonizer and the colonized, its corners were opaque and its alleys obscure. The city's expanding population inhabited it at will and for the purposes people deemed necessary, and their exchanges and interactions, while proscribed by the limits of colonialism, were pursued within that framework. The 1910s represented the last decade in which administrators believed they could separate those they understood to be white and black in Dakar in any real way. By the 1920s and 1930s, officials shifted their race-based and ideologically driven question for a specific

---

5   David Nelson has emphasized this vision held by the French colonial state regarding Dakar in his overview of its development. Nelson, "Defining the Urban."

type of modernization to the concept of stemming new arrivals to town and sending back those considered unnecessary.

From the moment Dakar was designated as the capital of FWA, it took on a new complex identity that was meant to express the grand imperial capital, significant southern Atlantic port, center of West African trade and administration, and colonial urban jewel. For the French state, these multiple identities not only worked together in the achievement of modernity but were natural outgrowths of Dakar's physical characteristics, situation on the map, and placement among what was perceived to be a docile population. Because colonial officials held that Africans were barriers in the modernization of Dakar, it believed it could effectively minimize African residence in the city. Officials were acutely aware of the fact that the colonial regime over which they presided was not meant to be an overtly segregatory one. The foundational concept of modernity thus married the paternalism imbued in the urban social endeavor to the racist premise built into colonialism. To achieve a "modern" city, undesirable elements needed to be removed. This strategy was embodied in the term *refoulement*, or pushing back, that became central to communications among administrators on managing Dakar's population.

This idea corresponded with the deeply entrenched notion of the French mission to shepherd the colonized in his evolution from traditionalist African to modernized Frenchman. That ideological premise for colonial rule had occupied a major space in French colonial theory for many decades and held sway into the 1930s, even if it was no longer always verbalized in as overtly assimilationist language as in prior years (though the term *évolué* still surfaced frequently in colonial communications). Over the course of the 1920s and 1930s, philosophies about managing urban space and those who inhabited it upheld this racist foundation but evolved with changing circumstances. Rather than discussing assimilation of their colonial subjects, administrators emphasized rehabilitation and curation of the spaces people inhabited and used. Human occupants of Dakar were in many ways discussed in the same manner as roads and buildings, electricity, and sewers: the underlying premise was that members of the urban population were physical elements of the city that could be crafted, moved, eliminated. Managing people's access to that space—both from within and without—was among the central strategies administrators attempted to define and implement from 1914 through the mid-1930s in order to wrest control over growing Dakar. The logic consistently espoused policies of de facto segregation, which was a path France never took on in a full regulatory manner even as it worked to create a modern West African metropolis based on notions of European superiority.[6]

---

6   For this notion of functional, as opposed to legal, segregation in French West
     African cities, see Freund, "Contrasts in Urban Segregation."

Reducing Dakar to its forms and spaces, with the population as secondary to those, was deeply out of touch with the realities of how a city worked. City dwellers understood the capital as a place of opportunity. For people who lived in and made the city, Dakar was not a physical representation of ideas but rather a dynamic confluence of complex interactions. It was a place that, despite the close proximity of the administration, could be molded and manipulated according to individual imperatives. The boundary between urban and rural was not clearly defined. Dakarois were not all permanent, nor were most autochthonous to the city, and the range of pursuits in town represented the full scope of what was possible, as opposed to what French administrators might have considered appropriately urban. Official endeavors crafted around the effort to produce a non-African city in Africa saw endless barriers as, ultimately, Dakarois lived urban lives within a framework very largely of their own making. Although French state policies based on *refoulement* set down parameters within which city dwellers operated, the resulting urban spaces and transactional culture were those that Dakarois forged themselves.

Health, Space, and "Pushing Back"

The underlying principle behind *refoulement*—that Africans should not live in close proximity to Europeans—was not new in the 1920s and, in fact, was a long-standing pillar of France's approach to Dakar. The major efforts of the interwar years to modernize Dakar built on the steps taken by the state a decade prior when plague broke out in 1914. That health crisis served as a means by which colonial authorities could proceed more overtly in their plans to limit and control African residence in Dakar. By that time, little more than ten years into its status as capital of FWA, the city was growing but not yet large by any international standards. The commune of Dakar consisted of what is today only its downtown core. A growing city still emerging in economic potential, it had only just begun to surpass the older city of Saint-Louis, capital of the colony of Senegal, in population. The administration counted 25,630 inhabitants in Dakar in 1914, roughly 10 percent of whom were French.[7] The outbreak of plague brought on notable fluctuations as people fled the city, and as rates of death took its toll. Entry into the capital was also temporarily restricted to avoid spreading infections. In 1916, just after the epidemic subsided, the city's population had dipped to 19,808, of which 1,732 were noted as French. This slight decline was temporary, and the city not only soon recovered its population but experienced more serious

---

7   *Annuaire du Gouvernement Général de l'Afrique Occidentale Française, 1913–14* (Paris: La Rose, 1914).

growth as the decade came to a close. In 1914, however, Dakar was not victim to real population pressure, and even physically it was still quite small. The villages of Hann, Yoff, Ngor, Ouakam, and Cambérène—all Lebu settlements, as parts of central Dakar had originally been before French settlement there—functioned as part of Dakar's orbit but were not yet integrated into the city's physical limits. The early French city occupied only the southern subpeninsula of the greater Cap-Vert in prewar times.

Prior to the plague and the full onset of war in Europe, space and urban residency were not primary concerns for the administration. Official reports from the first few years of the 1910s and up to mid-1914 in fact focused on Dakar's burgeoning urban society, the productivity of the local population, and its potential for prosperity. The efforts to create larger, modern port facilities were perhaps the most important developments of the period, and a great part of the governments-general's budget for Dakar was dedicated to that project. The physical city was at the center of officials' concerns, and they expressed satisfaction at the many projects underway in the mid-1910s. "We should be proud of the implementation of this component of the public works program—done in the interest of the general public—that should significantly contribute into improving the health conditions, the beautification, and the prosperity of the city," an earlier 1914 report expressed.[8] It conveyed the administration's general sense of ease with activities among the local population as well, pointing to the engagement of urban residents in the city's local farming and to the entry of Dakar's younger residents into the local labor pool. The administration indeed viewed the local production of fruits and vegetables within Dakar's city limits to be an essential aspect of supplying the capital with such produce, and the use of urban land for such gardens was encouraged.[9] Hired labor was also in demand, with numerous job sites springing up in Dakar. The presence of young men in town was viewed as a promising response to such demand rather than a cumbersome surplus about which the state should be concerned. In early 1914, Dakar was "hungry for labor . . . allow[ing] young people to hire out their services and thereby provide for their families."[10] Amid this portrayal of a rather stable urban social outlook on the eve of what would become the capital's most significant disease outbreak, administrators also asserted that Dakar's sanitation status was "excellent," assured by a "zealous" public health service.[11]

---

8   Senegal, Territoires d'administration directe: Rapports trimestriels des cercles, escales et communes mixtes, March 31, 1914, ANS 2G14/40.

9   Senegal, Territoires d'administration directe: Rapports trimestriels des cercles, escales et communes mixtes, March 31, 1914, ANS 2G14/40.

10 Senegal, Territoires d'administration directe: Rapports trimestriels des cercles, escales et communes mixtes, March 31, 1914, ANS 2G14/40.

11 Senegal, Territoires d'administration directe: Rapports trimestriels des cercles, escales et communes mixtes, March 31, 1914, ANS 2G14/40.

For officials, Dakar could only realize a true passage to modern cityhood if African behaviors and visible presence were displaced so that an image of whiteness and the grandeur they associated with it could be more fully projected by the city. The notion that Dakar was an urban space that needed a dramatic intervention in population management came about most concretely with the epidemic itself. The health crisis brought French administrators the opportunity to shape the city in new ways, and central to this was that it be redesigned along racial lines. The 1914 plague outbreak saw officials turn quickly to such an approach in their creation of the Medina, a "native village" just north of Dakar's city center. The Medina was officially termed a health and sanitation project.[12] Shortly after the disease appeared in Dakar, a decree creating the new entity was passed in July 1914 and efforts began immediately to move the capital's African residents to the Medina to segregate the disease, authorities emphasized, not the residents themselves. It was "neither a question of race nor of color," Senegal's lieutenant-governor wrote to the governor-general one year later, in July 1915, but "purely concern[ed] hygiene."[13] In responding to the plague outbreak, administrators pointed to what they said was a wide divide between the health habits and lifestyles of Africans and those of Europeans, one so important that when disease hit the city, the segregation of Africans and Europeans was their first line of action in slowing its spread. Officials' readiness to adopt such an approach revealed their long-standing belief that creating separate French and African zones in Dakar was desirable.[14] Indeed, the lieutenant-governor confessed to the governor-general that this had been "felt already for quite some time in Dakar," making the Medina a solution not only to the spread of disease but also the state's deeper desires.[15]

Dakar was a new kind of Senegalese city for France in colonial Africa, one founded not via early French trades and *métis* society but rather amid an African autochthonous community with a deep regional history. This brought administrators face-to-face with the realities of an African city as opposed to an early colonial *comptoir*, or colonial town functioning largely

---

12 For works on the Medina and the use of public health regulations in Dakar to control space and population, see Echenberg, *Black Death, White Medicine*; Betts, "Dakar." See also M'Bokolo, "Peste et Société Urbaine à Dakar"; Bigon, "A History of Urban Planning and Infectious Diseases."

13 Confidential letter from the lieutenant-governor to the governor-general, July 18, 1915, ANS 11D1/1284.

14 Dakar was not the only city in which French officials took this approach, which was widespread throughout colonial Africa. For an analysis of a similar approach in Porto-Novo, see Brunet-La Ruche, "Discipliner Les Villes Coloniales."

15 Confidential letter from the lieutenant-governor to the governor-general, July 18, 1915, ANS 11D1/1284.

as a trading post. They desired new mechanisms of control, however clothed in other rhetoric those might have been. In 1915, the lieutenant-governor explained such views frankly in a confidential letter.

> There is danger and to a certain extent a mutual discomfort in letting two groups with very different lifestyles live together. We therefore should let them and even force them, if need be, at least for the sake of good public health and harmonious social relationships, to live in two settings according to their own preferences: on the one side there will be the European city with all the amenities of modern health, and on the other side there will be the indigenous city with total freedom to build in either wood or straw, to beat drums all night and to pound millet at as early as four in the morning.[16]

Couched in the language of harmony and freedom, segregation was meant to keep Africans out of new, modern areas, which were labeled the "European city," while the Medina became the "native city." In 1915, the lieutenant-governor was pleased to note that already five thousand Africans were living in the recently created neighborhood of Dakar. Even though the city had reemerged from the epidemic, the administration wished to see this number grow. In pursuit of this goal, urban managers did not plan urban development in Dakar in a manner that saw the city as a unified whole. Rather than applying standards in the areas of building and public health to the entire city, colonial officials enacted them differently for the new white and black zones. In that way, the state accepted that Africans could live below the standards it had established in the new public health codes for the city center, so long as they did so outside of that area. The lieutenant-governor made clear that he saw no need for the services associated with urban health and safety to be installed in the African area of Dakar. Harmonious coexistence, then, was not one that entailed equal access or uniform urban experiences. The plague thus served to usher in a full commitment to the unequal, segregated dual city in Dakar.

Although the segregated city that was created in 1914 was delineated by a *cordon sanitaire*, or protective buffer zone, which in Dakar was an empty space of a few hundred meters dividing the city center from the Medina, that division was in many ways more conceptual than real. Dakar had been from its inception an African city, not a settler one, and it continued to develop in that respect. Of the twenty-five thousand residents in Dakar in 1914, more than twenty thousand were African. Thus, it could not displace its

---

16 Confidential letter from the lieutenant-governor to the governor-general, July 18, 1915, ANS 11D1/1284. This quote, which I ran across in the National Archives of Senegal, is an opposite illustration of the colonial mentality that conflated hygiene and segregation; it also appears in Echenberg, *Black Plague, White Medicine.*

Figure 2.1. Postcard image of an African neighborhood in Dakar, c. 1905. Edmond Fortier postcard collection. Courtesy of edmondfortier.org.

Figure 2.2. Postcard image of Dakar's Rue Vincens, c. 1905. Edmond Fortier postcard collection. Courtesy of edmondfortier.org.

Africanness to the Medina. A great number of Africans remained in central Dakar, especially landowning Lebu who were not easily persuaded to give up their property. Many were able, having profited from rental agreements, to construct buildings up to the new codes. Constructed along the street side, those structures even sometimes concealed older dwellings that remained standing behind the new facades. In addition, dwellings and lots had to be made ready in the Medina, which was not a swift procedure. While touted as safe and healthy, the Medina was flat and marshy compared to the plateau on which central Dakar was built. A 1917 report noted that the floods in the Medina during the rainy season required new drainage projects and filling of lower areas of the neighborhood.[17] Budgetary constraints also hindered the development of the Medina. A decade after the Medina's creation, the problem persisted, and lack of funds slowed not only construction in the Medina but also state efforts to destroy "unsanitary" dwellings in the other areas of town.[18]

The physical shortcomings of the state's plans were coupled with the realities of the labor regime in the colonial capital. As French state officials understood well, the African population was Dakar's workforce. In every corner of town, French enterprises and the colonial bureaucracy required African workers. People worked downtown, and many even lived at their places of work. The notion that Dakar might be shaped into distinctly African and European zones was never a possibility in such an economy dependent on African labor. Senegal's top administrator understood this well even as he lamented that this meant Africans were always in immediate contact with the capital's European residents:

> Dakar has a population of twenty-five thousand inhabitants made up of boys, dockers, unskilled labor, workers, fishermen, farmers, as well as a good number of people without a defined profession. The autochthonous population represents about eight thousand to ten thousand, and the others come from various parts of French West Africa, some of them by chance, having lived with other Europeans who left them in Dakar, others fleeing their countries, and yet others looking for jobs or falling into the allure of a large city. All this population whose existence is necessary for the commercial and maritime life of Dakar lives here among us.[19]

---

17   Senegal, Territoires d'Administration Directe: Rapports d'ensemble trimestrielles des cercles, escales et communes-mixtes: Rapport d'ensemble 3e trimestre, 1917—Dakar, Gorée, Rufisque et Banlieue de Dakar, ANS 2G17/26.

18   Afrique Occidental Française—Résumés de Rapports d'ensemble des colonies, 1925: Circonscription de Dakar, ANS 2G25/10.

19   Confidential letter from the lieutenant-governor to the governor-general, July 18, 1915, ANS 11D1/1284.

While the administrator of Dakar saw Africans as a sort of necessary encumberment, it was more accurately the case that Dakar was for Africans a necessary opportunity. The growth of the city and the concentration of activities in it made it a central site for income seeking. The efforts to discourage residence in the city center were in some ways futile and brought on new concerns for French officials. Africans pooled resources to generate adequate housing. The lieutenant-governor observed: "With the requirement to build only in masonry in the European city, [one] could live there in very expensive conditions in regard to their average salaries. The high cost of rent leads some natives to get together in groups of seven to eight to share a room in very poor conditions for their health as well as for public health."[20] Thus colonial officials became concerned about the consequent crowding, labeling it another public health threat.

The quest for a dual city based on de facto segregation in which the housing standards, infrastructure, and services of one sector were considered best left to locals while those of the other were highly regulated was a project that could lead only to the thwarting of its of objectives. While the Medina took off swiftly, its growth did not help isolate central Dakar in the way the state had hoped. The Medina expanded Dakar's urban sprawl, creating greater space for settlement of more transplants from the regions and ultimately contributing to the growth of Dakar outside the parameters of state control. It did not take long for the *cordon sanitaire* between the Medina and downtown Dakar to shrink from both sides, joining the two to create a larger city in which one neighborhood gave way to another and people of diverse origins lived and moved in greater proximity to one another. The Medina did not evolve to be a native village on the outskirts of town but rather became Dakar's largest urban neighborhood, placed centrally on the Cap-Vert peninsula and eventually engulfed by the city. Though intended to isolate the nonmodern aspects of Dakar from the central city, it ultimately became one of the most important spaces in the capital of FWA.[21]

The state thus imagined a city that was entirely misaligned with the very system it had installed.[22] France created a colonial economy and a labor sys-

---

20   Confidential letter from the lieutenant-governor to the governor-general, July 18, 1915, ANS 11D1/1284.

21   Analyses of colonial maps over time from the 1910s to the 1940s demonstrate this rapid pattern of growth, which also has been traced in various works detailing the physical expansion of Dakar. See, for instance, Seck, *Dakar*; Bigon, *French Colonial Dakar*.

22   Lynn Schler presents this argument in her analysis of colonial Douala, which reveals in inefficacy of numerous colonial efforts to shape the New Bell quarter, which became a space in which African communities could thrive. Schler, "Ambiguous Spaces."

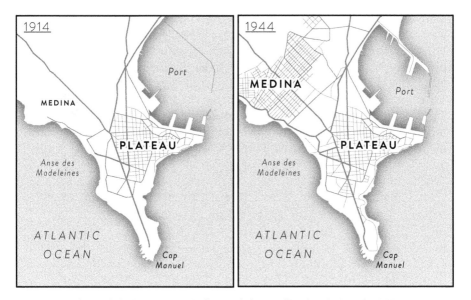

Figure 2.3. Downtown Dakar and the Medina in 1914 and 1944.

Figure 2.4. Postcard image of downtown Dakar's government
quarter, 1922. Edmond Fortier postcard collection. Courtesy of
edmondfortier.org.

tem within it, and it embarked on projects to expand its colonial capital in ways that required and invited non-European residents. State imperatives for Dakar placed Africans in a central position as city dwellers and workers, all in the context of a regime that did not seek to legally codify race-based segregation in the direct ways that were done in white settler colonies, thus leaving space for innovation and flexibility among the non-European population. The plague and its spatial outcomes had unintended consequences that led to the very sort of African attributes administrators sought to avoid developing in Dakar, further entrenching the colonial capital as an African city.

Capital-Colony: The Circonscription de Dakar et Dépendances

In the early 1920s, with the epidemic and a world war several years behind it and a new era of colonial self-confidence dawning, the administration reevaluated Dakar's status and the ways in which it would be managed. In 1924, the state created the Circonscription de Dakar et Dépendances, a new entity that was at once city and colony and the capital urban center of the region. The intent was to streamline the administration of Dakar, to free it from being doubly subjected to the government-general and the government of the colony of Senegal, and to augment its budgetary power. By 1926, shortly after Dakar had been made its own capital-colony through the establishment of the circumscription, its population was already double that of Saint-Louis. For proponents of the realization of Dakar's autonomy from Senegal, it no longer made sense that the governor of Senegal in Saint-Louis should have authority over this rapidly growing city where his superior, the governor-general, sat. In discussions about reorganizing Dakar, *autonomy* became a key term. Indeed, the port functioned semi-autonomously from the city, the French military occupied the southern section of the city, and the government-general and the commune of Dakar each had their own apparatus seated downtown.

Although the primary justification in creating the new entity was to streamline the management of Dakar by uniting different services and budgets, duplication arose.[23] Inspectors sent by the Ministry of Colonies in 1926 and 1936 to evaluate the state of the circumscription and its relationship with the colony of Senegal within which Dakar was located both found that while creation of the capital-colony was meant to enhance Dakar's ability to develop under the direct authority of the government-general, it had

---

23　Rapport sur la Circonscription de Dakar et Dépendances, Transmission par M. l'Inspecteur des Colonies, Chef de Mission, May 17, 1926, ANS 4G/87(105).

actually made the situation more inefficient and even "prodigal."[24] The inspector of colonies even asserted in his 1936 report: "The Circumscription of Dakar is far from having produced that which was expected when it was created; it should therefore disappear and its territory should be once again attached to the Colony of Senegal."[25] His complaints concerned not only fiscal wastefulness but also the insufficiency of the city's various services, the ad hoc nature of the city's bureaucracy, even the poor condition of the streets and need for more serious public works to be undertaken. He noted that so many aspects of the government-general had been transferred to Dakar that it was the preference for every civil servant to be posted there. That not only encumbered the capital with personnel but emptied other cities throughout the federation of their staff.[26]

Both the governor-general and the administrator of the circumscription defended Dakar's status as a colony and asserted that it was with the passage of time that the city would realize its destiny as a great city. In the official response to the 1926 report by the inspector of colonies, the governor-general of FWA admitted that the new circumscription was still finding its bearings and that the "imperfections" inherent in such a reorganization had not escaped colonial administrators. He emphasized, however, that the first "year coming to a close—the initial stage in the life of the large city that Dakar would become one day—was a period of evaluation and experimentation full of useful lessons for the future."[27] A decade later, the response was the same. Dakar's administrator confessed that there was still "much to do in Dakar" but rejected both the notion that the creation of the circumscription had been a mistake and the assertion that Dakar was poorly run. Those who had envisaged an "imperial city" were not wrong, he declared, adding "anyone who knew Dakar in 1920, or better still before the war, could attest not only to the efforts made but to the magnificent results obtained."[28]

---

24 Service de la Circonscription de Dakar (vues d'ensemble sur l'organisation de la Circonscription de Dakar), Rapport fait par M. Monguillot, Inspecteur des Colonies, April 25, 1936, ANS 4G/100(105).

25 Service de la Circonscription de Dakar (vues d'ensemble sur l'organisation de la Circonscription de Dakar), Rapport fait par M. Monguillot, Inspecteur des Colonies, April 25, 1936, ANS 4G/100(105).

26 Service de la Circonscription de Dakar (vues d'ensemble sur l'organisation de la Circonscription de Dakar), Rapport fait par M. Monguillot, Inspecteur des Colonies, April 25, 1936, ANS 4G/100(105).

27 Response by the governor-general to the report by the inspector of colonies, May 19, 1926, ANS 4G/87(105).

28 Response by the administrator of Dakar to the report by the inspector of colonies, May 9, 1936, ANS 4G/100(105).

The grandeur of Dakar was relative to the beholder. To those officials within it, the city was a work in progress on its way to being worthy of its title. It was also important to them to be able to showcase the city to politicians and the public in France, and even to help Dakar achieve the same status as cities in the metropole. The city commissioned studies of French cities to help them reach a better understanding of what it would take. Achieving the goals that they had set for the city—and quelling critiques such as those of the Ministry's inspectors—was, for them, a question of overcoming obstacles that stood in the way of Dakar's accession to the status of great, modern city.

Problems in People: The State's Struggle with an Urban Population, 1926–1936

In studying the question of how to realize the various goals the state had for the capital of FWA, administrators reflected much more on the impediments to grandeur than they did on strategies for context-appropriate urban development. Debates most regularly addressed that which could be added to or removed from Dakar. While additions were typically physical in nature—streets and lighting, port improvements, new markets, or even visible presence of policemen or public health agents—the proposed removals were more often human. By the 1920s, officials saw a sort of human stain as one of the most important of the multiple menaces to Dakar's modernity. Through the plague, authorities linked Africans to urban disease and sanitation, framing displacement of city dwellers as a medical urgency. As the great epidemic grew more distant, and as movement to town intensified, discussions shifted from a rhetoric surrounding public health to one focused on removing Africans from Dakar and preventing the settlement of other "undesirables" in a much more overt manner.

It did not take long after the foundation of the Circonscription de Dakar et Dépendances for people to seek to expand their own opportunities. As the inspector indeed noted, the expansion of Dakar in both status and scope brought more people into the capital's fold. While he was referring to civil servants, the same was true more broadly. Residence in Dakar for some period of time became a common goal or strategy among Africans from Senegal and the greater region. The government-general acquired more direct control over Dakar with the birth of the circumscription, but the capital itself grew and drew in more people, making it a more complex urban entity to manage and understand. Colonial administrators struggled with the fact that this growth entailed increased flow of people to the city and the diversification of their activities in town. The decade from the mid-1920s to the mid-1930s became a period of contradiction during which the administration actively vocalized its desire to make of Dakar a large, modern city worthy of its aspired status, but at the same time sought to avoid all the corollaries of urban development: migration from the interior and immigration from abroad, the emergence of entrepreneurial pursuits outside state control, the rise in the cost of living, and the decline of local subsistence activity in favor of wage earning and importation. Already in 1926, officials noted that the main issue "stirring the passions" in the suburbs of Dakar was that of juridical status.[29] Young people actively sought court statements to prove they had been born in what was now Dakar, aware that this gave them the important status of *originaire*, which included access to French courts and voting rights.[30] French legal procedures and the specific parameters around proving *originaire* status bound these efforts in red tape, but courts received numerous cases nonetheless. Administrative measures solidifying Dakar's boundaries to include the nearby suburb-villages of Ouakam, Yoff, Thiaroye, and Mbao came to fruition in 1929 and further encouraged more claims to status changes.[31] Dakar and its population of *originaires* grew as a result of the city's new physical reach.

For local officials, this was much less important than the other means by which people joined the status of city dweller: movement to town from the regions. Dakar's police commissioner's annual report in 1930 pointed to the role of the Depression in attracting more people to the capital. Coupled with Dakar's greater physical extent, the flow of new arrivals made the city harder to police, he said, and Dakar's police department had difficulty handling the entire load. In the more distant suburb-villages, security was left in the hands of the national *gendarmerie*, or military police.[32] The annual administrative report on Dakar for that year emphasized the same problem of migration to the capital: "In addition to the dismissal of employees and laborers, one of the consequences of the economic crisis has been the influx into Dakar of jobless people coming from the interior who accept the lowest salaries."[33] The 1932 report on police activity and security in Dakar conveyed greater concern. "I do not think I am exaggerating with an estimate of about 10,000, the number of people without the least means of subsistence. There is thus a permanent source of trouble not only in terms of order and

29 Circonscription de Dakar et Dépendances, Annual Report for 1926, ANS 2G26/9.

30 Circonscription de Dakar et Dépendances, Annual Report for 1926, ANS 2G26/9.

31 Commissariat Central de Police, Annual Report for 1930, ANS 2G30/59.

32 Commissariat Central de Police, Annual Report for 1930, ANS 2G30/59.

33 Dakar et Dépendances, Annual Report for 1930, ANS 2G30/25.

security, but also in terms of public health."[34] The police chief noted that night rounds and roundups were increasingly more important to Dakar's policing activity to thwart vagrancy and theft.

As authorities in 1932 observed these rising urban challenges on the local level in Dakar, representatives from throughout the French Empire gathered at the Congrès International de l'Urbanisme aux Colonies et dans les Pays de Latitude Intertropicale, held that same year. Participants were architects, urban planners, military officials, and bureaucrats who reflected on the challenges of building successful French cities in the colonies. One submission to the congress asserted that Dakar merited special attention. It noted the city's large, growing population—fifty-five thousand people, of whom six thousand were European—and its surface area of 17,500 hectares, as well as its networks of electricity, drinking water, sewers, and roads.[35] Despite this, the colonial government had committed a key mistake in developing Dakar, one that needed to be rectified:

> The principle of segregation was not observed. When that mistake was acknowledged much later, with the outbreak of severe epidemics, moving the indigenous city became more challenging as inhabitants resisted. In 1914, Governor Ponty tried to create in the Medina an indigenous center that remained unpopulated for quite a long time. Today, with a proper housing development, drinkable water, and improved housing, there are eight thousand people living there. But there are still twenty thousand black people living among the Europeans in the center city of Dakar itself.[36]

The report submitted to the congress by the colonial administration's Department of Public Works reiterated the importance of mechanisms of segregation, necessary not only because Africans "knew nothing of hygiene concerns" but also because living apart from Europeans "allowed natives to follow their customs in complete peace."[37] These arguments were not new; they had been standard policy since 1914. However, the report emphasized

---

34　Dakar et Dépendances, Ensemble of Annual Reports for 1932, ANS 2G32/22.

35　The population of Dakar was possibly greater than this by 1932. A 1934 report had Dakar's 1929 population at fifty thousand Africans; see ANS 3G2/1(1).

36　"L'Urbanisme aux Colonies et Dans les Pays Tropicaux: Communications et Rapports du Congrès International de l'Urbanisme aux Colonies et dans les Pays de Latitude Intertropicale, Réunis et Présentés par Jean Royer, Architecte et Urbaniste, Directeur Administratif de l'Ecole Spéciale d'Architecture, Secrétaire Général du Congrès," Conference proceedings (La Charité-Sur-Loire: 1932).

37　"L'Urbanisme aux Colonies et Dans les Pays Tropicaux," 1932.

the new urgency of segregation in Dakar because the city's population was growing and included a "floating population" that numbered roughly six thousand.[38]

Common to French colonial discursive practice on its urban spaces, the term *floating population* was invoked to describe any group of people the state could not properly categorize as useful, employed, controlled, or identifiable. As Phyllis Martin explained in her study of society in colonial Brazzaville, the floating population excluded workers, covering instead anyone "who might contaminate the 'stable' elements of town."[39] The concept had staying power, remaining present in a relatively straightforward manner into French language studies of African cities decades beyond the end of colonial rule.[40]

By 1934, authorities were discussing the matter of Dakar's unnecessary inhabitants with increased urgency. The "floating population" was expanding; a note from the Direction Générale des Services Économiques in May 1934 quantified it at twenty thousand, a full third of the capital's total population of sixty thousand inhabitants.[41] Most were young men who had little chances of marrying in town once settled there, hence the low birth rate among Africans in Dakar. For the colonial state, this segment of urban population represented several risks because it was not considered an identifiably useful element in town. The May note and a confidential thought piece penned by a functionary in the Department of Public safety that October of that year both argued that the "floating population" neither produced nor consumed anything in town, emptied rural villages of their young men, flooded the labor pool and brought down wages, and burdened urban African households with an unnecessary and unhealthy number of inhabitants: "Natives, ignoring the most basic health requirements, agree to live in groups of 10–12 in overcrowded rooms with enough space for 2–3 people."[42] The labor issue certainly garnered the most attention among authorities, followed closely by questions of urban health. Officials also

---

38 "L'Urbanisme aux Colonies et Dans les Pays Tropicaux," 1932.

39 Martin, *Leisure and Society in Colonial Brazzaville*, 7–8.

40 See, for instance, Coquery-Vidrovitch, "Villes Coloniales et Histoire des Africains"; Sinou, *Comptoirs et Villes Coloniales du Sénégal*.

41 Direction Générale des Services Économiques, Domaines, Note on "Développement des grandes villes en AOF," May 5, 1934, ANS 3G2/1(1).

42 Direction Générale des Services Économiques, Domaines, Note on "Développement des grandes villes en AOF," May 5, 1934, ANS 3G2/1(1); Confidential document addressed to the governor-general on the "Limitation de la population de Dakar," November 15, 1934, from the administrator of the Circumscription of Dakar, including a note from the director of political and administrative affairs dated October 19, 1934, ANS 3G2/2(2).

emphasized that the presence of people who demanded the attention of the state necessarily cost the circumscription of Dakar money.[43] FWA's director of political and administrative affairs summed the matter up rather succinctly in a July 1934 note to the director of general security, declaring that Dakar was overwhelmed with "natives whose presence is clearly useless in terms of meeting local needs and who constitute a real danger for the city."[44]

Correspondence, reports, and informal notes went over time and again the regulatory measures that could be mobilized to get people to leave town and prevent them from coming back, as well as to deter others from migrating to the city. FWA did not operate on a pass system that criminalized movement unrelated to work as had been done in South Africa. There were, however, laws in place limiting migration—Africans were generally required to obtain permission from their *chef de canton*, the French-appointed canton chief, before traveling—but these were not always rigorously enforced in town. The other major set of laws were those on vagrancy in Dakar. As in other cities in colonial Africa, people in the capital of FWA were charged with vagrancy with relative ease, providing the state with a tool by which to criminalize freedom of movement, unemployment, housing insecurity, or street vending.[45] Colonial states across Africa also implemented laws on juvenile delinquency for the same purposes. In British colonial African cities, the introduction of juvenile delinquency as a legal charge has been examined for the ways in which it was meant to be a device to control young males.[46] Indeed, Abosede George points out that in Lagos, juvenile delinquency was uniquely discussed as relevant to boys.[47] Together, vagrancy and juvenile delinquency regulations in colonial cities took special aim at the male population, seeing them as not only more mobile but more volatile and potentially threatening to the regime and its objectives.

For women, laws regulating the parameters of prostitution were more commonly mobilized by colonial states in Africa,[48] and George points out

---

43 Direction Générale des Services Économiques, Domaines, Note on "Développement des grandes villes en AOF," May 5, 1934, ANS 3G2/1(1).

44 "Note pour le Directeur de la Sûreté Générale" from the Direction des Affaires Politiques et Administratives, on "Développement des grandes villes en AOF," July 2, 1934, ANS 1H25(26).

45 White, *Comforts of Home*, 89–93.

46 Burton, "Urchins, Loafers, and the Cult of the Cowboy"; Fourchard, "Lagos and the Invention of Juvenile Delinquency in Nigeria, 1920-60"; Heap, "Their Days Are Spent in Gambling and Loafing, Pimping for Prostitutes, and Picking Pockets."

47 George, *Making Modern Girls*.

48 White, *Comforts of Home*, 176; Aderinto, *When Sex Threatened the State*; Kropiwnicki, "The Politics of Child Prostitution in South Africa";

that administrators saw marriage as removing the possibility that a girl or woman would engage in prostitution.[49] Rachel Jean-Baptiste notes that French officials in colonial Africa had varied perceptions of prostitution and its presentation of risk. Libreville officials saw sex work in Dakar as more akin to that of a European city, while viewing prostitution in the city they managed as hidden and less formal in nature, making it more difficult to pin down.[50] In general, the idea within the colonial mindset that women were easier to root in place—either by remaining in rural towns or becoming implanted in an urban household either as a member or servant—made them less prominent in discussions of the so-called floating population. In Dakar, they appeared with much less frequency in vagrancy records, and prostitution was a regulated trade that received less attention than vagrancy in official discussions of what was cast as unnecessary or excess urban population.

As authorities became more concerned with the circulation of Africans within the colony and vagrancy in the capital, they mobilized laws that had been implemented in the late 1800s, before urbanization had become an issue. In 1928 and 1931, as the question of the floating population drew increasing concern, the rules on vagrancy and bans from the city were reinforced so they could be more broadly and vigorously enforced in Dakar.[51] Vagrancy charges in Dakar carried various penalties depending on whether it was a first offense and if there were other crimes involved. The most common result of a vagrancy charge was a ban from Dakar; this could be for two years, five years, or even ten years, if a violent crime was included in the charge. A list of people convicted on vagrancy charges in Dakar in 1934 showed ninety-seven cases for which the sentences ranged from two to ten years of official ban from Dakar; most commonly in those convictions, theft charges accompanied the vagrancy charge, resulting in a ban of five years.[52]

Despite the apparent severity of such measures, the number of convictions paled in comparison to the magnitude of the problem as it was articulated by local administrators. The year 1934 was particularly active for the review of laws and regulations as the tools for what Dakar's annual report called "the purging of the city."[53] Several reports examined the effectiveness and extent of such regulatory tools, seeking to maximize their capacity to serve the new objective of ridding Dakar of "undesirables."[54] The problem was

Jean-Baptiste, *Conjugal Rights*, 209.

49   George, *Making Modern Girls*, 103.

50   Jean-Baptiste, *Conjugal Rights*, 209.

51   Justice, Interdictions de Séjour, 1930–34, ANS 5M/163.

52   Justice, Interdictions de Séjour, 1930–34, ANS 5M/163.

53   Dakar et Dépendances, Annual Report for 1934, ANS 2G34/3.

54   Dakar et Dépendances, Annual Report for 1934, ANS 2G34/3.

largely in enforcement rather than in the wording of the laws themselves, officials found. Results in Dakar were limited because the city's resources were not extensive. Complaints of an inadequate police force and immigration workers, for example, were long-standing among authorities in the capital.[55] Officials in the 1930s believed that law enforcement capacity in the capital was "behind the evolution [of the city] by several years."[56] Dakar's 1934 annual report asserted that reliance on such regulations was therefore only a "first means" of approaching the problem, adding that "police actions and the other means used are no longer enough to keep away the numerous unemployed who, out of need, become dangerous offenders."[57]

The state sought other solutions. Dakar Administrator Martine believed that it would be more efficient to turn to "a voluntary pushing back," which would be advertised among those who had been in Dakar for fewer than five years. "What I mean here," he clarified, "is giving all the natives who request it the means to go back to their homes."[58] A December 14, 1934, meeting of several key figures in Dakar's administration, including Martine, on the growing problem of urban slums in the capital, put forth that while segregation as had been achieved in the British colonies of Africa was not possible in Dakar, "it would be useful to achieve de facto segregation by means of persuasion."[59] This was to occur on two levels: first, the drawing out of people who were not needed in Dakar and who could be convinced through mechanisms such as state-sponsored transport back to the rural areas to return to their villages; and second, the continuation of measures to oblige Africans to move from the city center to more distant corners of Dakar. The creation of the Office of Affordable Housing (OAH)—a state agency that was never considered adequate in its treatment of the housing situation—occurred during this period. Discussions about the goals of the OAH explicitly linked it to the purging and segregation of Dakar, showing the ideological objective behind the OAH to be quite other than the simple provision of adequate housing for Dakarois. A conference of local administrators on the "Struggle against Urban Slums" held in Dakar in December 1934 laid out the details of the OAH's role in removing Africans from the city center to the outskirts of town through the construction of housing

55   ANS 2G/35(11).
56   Dakar et Dépendances, Police and Safety, Annual Report, ANS 2G37/33.
57   Dakar et Dépendances, Annual Report for 1934, ANS 2G34/3.
58   Dakar et Dépendances, Annual Report for 1934, ANS 2G34/3. The report used the phrase "voluntary pushing back" in its proposition to attract people back to their places of origin.
59   Direction Générale des Services Économiques, Domaines, Note on "Développement des grandes villes en AOF," May 5, 1934, ANS 3G2/1(1).

in "hard materials" not only in the Medina but also in areas farther from downtown.[60]

Refoulement, the effort to push nonwhites out of Dakar and back to their presumed place of belonging, was not simply racist but also unrealistic in light of the state's own efforts to propel Dakar to prominence. As authorities expanded the physical boundaries of Dakar and transformed its status, the city came to envelope and attract more people, especially against the backdrop of economic downturn that brought people across Africa from rural areas to towns. Persuading them to leave Dakar altogether was fruitless. Dakarois were resilient and adaptable, and most importantly they found necessity or benefit in living there. The 1930s actually saw Dakar's population increase. A July 1936 census showed an increase from 76,634 inhabitants in 1935 to 93,044 the following year: a 21 percent increase.[61] In March 1938, the annual police and safety report for Dakar estimated the capital's total population at 120,000, "if we take into account the unaccountable population that cannot be identified but that is neither the less troublesome nor the less dangerous."[62] By 1940, the colonial state's dilemma endured, with the same philosophies being tossed between administrators in an effort to stem the tide. Dakar's administrator that year articulated new plans to provide train tickets to Dakarois who were willing to return to rural areas. There were also projects for "unemployment camps" that would remove idle men from the capital and provide temporary work and housing elsewhere.[63] By the close of the decade, the dialogues of the mid-1930s, while intense, had apparently yielded very little in terms of tangible results.

The problem of people was impossible to resolve because of the way colonial authorities conceived of their West African capital: as a European city that could be isolated, protected, and linked more closely with its extra-African ties than with those it had with the place where it was actually seated. The link to maritime routes and other Atlantic cities, the economic connections to Bordeaux, the political association with Paris—these were all important but much less so than the relationship of Dakar to its own African context, both human and physical. Senegal, and FWA more broadly, was not a settler colony with settler-driven economic activities; Africans made up the vast majority of the population in town as well as in the countryside. Dakar

---

60   Direction Générale des Services Économiques, Domaines, Note on "Développement des grandes villes en AOF," May 5, 1934, ANS 3G2/1(1).

61   Demographic Reports, Census of French West Africa, July 1926, CAOM, Fonds Ministeriels GUERNUT 48.

62   Dakar et Dépendances, Police et Sûreté, Annual Report, ANS 2G37/33.

63   "Note pour le Directeur de la Sûreté Générale" from the Direction des Affaires Politiques et Administratives, on "Développement des grandes villes en AOF," July 2, 1934, ANS 1H25(26).

was a temperate, attractive location that only increased in allure when other opportunities opened up there as the city grew. Dakar Administrator Ponzio recognized this himself in his 1932 report on the circumscription: the city's "geographic position and placement in a young country" assured a "definite development."[64]

The mere existence of Dakar also changed the dynamics of the surrounding areas, a fact that officials rarely admitted. Herders found it more lucrative to sell livestock in town, men found the city to be an expedient way to earn bridewealth or augment their family's resources, the implantation of the state and its services opened up greater opportunities for jobs in the public sphere, and the transportation networks that ran throughout the colony all led to Dakar. Moreover, local agriculture was cyclical, creating periods and circumstances during which it was advantageous for people to come to the city or to return to rural areas. Dakar could not function without its majority African population. The colonial economy was exploitative and operated only insofar as it could use African labor. Dakar's managers wanted to see in the capital only the minimum number of Africans necessary to fulfill these needs, maintaining this as a goal for decades. As one essay on urbanization in FWA expressed it, "Dakar, the West African capital, crossroad of the maritime roads linking three continents, is the pride of the French who designed and built it."[65] If France had created Dakar, it had not shaped and developed it. The city's growing cosmopolitan population wielded great influence over the city's nature, instilling a great tolerance for transience within the local transactional culture that threaded through the lives of Dakarois.

---

64   Dakar et Dépendances, Ensemble of Annual Reports for 1931, April 29, 1932, ANS 2G31/32.

65   Note on "L'Urbanisme à Dakar," undated, CAOM, Fond Ministeriels, AGEFOM/377.

Chapter Three

Challenges and Solutions of the Transient City

Residence and Transience

Despite colonial ambitions for a European city stabilized through segregation that privileged whites, the realities of Dakar included a flexible, fluid model of residence. Living in town was broadly conceived. City dwellers of diverse backgrounds adopted of a range of strategies—including varying degrees of mobility—in this regard. Transience became a mode of residence, and as Dakar evolved, transience became more expansively infused into various aspects of urban life. The nature of transience makes it inherently elusive, and locating it in various aspects of city life requires a close look into the spaces city dwellers occupied. In urban settings, the most prominent of those spaces were places of residence, which in the colonial capital also entailed places of work. City dwellers formulated creative residential strategies in which movement and transience were useful. Likewise, Dakar's diverse residential landscape developed many features that catered to mobility and its consequence, transience. The commonplace nature of transience in the city instilled a fragility into housing arrangements, including those that were at places of employment.

Dakar's main civil court cases provide a window into the sorts of considerations and dynamics that often were hidden from view yet integral to urban life in Dakar. As disputes arose, matters surfaced in the Tribunal that revealed how city dwellers formulated their approaches to residence and maintaining working situations. The records show a flexibility in the practices of Dakarois as they navigated their pragmatic arrangements. While the colonial administration attempted to draw clear lines between city dwellers and everyone who belonged in other areas of the territory, Africans in Dakar pursued their own strategies with little need to define urban residence in precise terms. Many considered themselves to be from elsewhere, but this had little bearing on the fact that they lived and worked in the capital as Dakarois.

The civil court cases that Dakarois lodged from the mid-1910s through the mid-1930s reveal a number of traits in the city's transactional culture around housing. First, the arrangements made between property owners and renters were devised as needed and with no parameters at an official level regarding renting. Second, the housing market consistently suffered from shortages. The private housing sector, vibrant and creative, operated primarily on the resources of the African and other non-European communities. City dwellers became flexible in their notions of what residence entailed out of necessity in the face of limited housing supply. The expense and shortage of lodging of various kinds encouraged transient behavior—it was easier and often advantageous for people to move in and out and from one residence to another than to permanently install themselves in one place. The administration's preoccupation with hygiene and sanitation as devices of racial separation did little to increase state control over the urban population's movements and residential habits. Quite the contrary, official actions and priorities fostered the evolution of the traits evident in Dakar's residential sector: once they had implemented de facto segregation, French authorities left lodging to the locals.

Dakar's residential landscape was one of transient transactions. People chose to live together for certain reasons and on certain terms, and such arrangements were not permanent. In the urban setting, need and convenience replaced close kinship and obligation as the drivers of residential choices. Within that context, disputes were more likely to arise as Dakarois in various housing situations confronted the challenges of such situations, which ultimately were fragile and fluid in nature. The cases examined here are revelatory of these dynamics. Although cases often did not all overtly address housing as the principal matter at hand, the details in Tribunal records provide insight into the norms that emerged in Dakar around residence. In cases involving cohabitants, people broached important questions about trust, contracts, expectations, and needs. Parties often revealed how many resided at a given locale, who came and went and with what frequency, and the implicit understandings involved in such arrangements. Kinship or affinities of origin still played roles in residential choice in colonial Dakar, as did arrangements that replicated household gendered labor dynamics. Workplaces also served as sites of residence. Housing was the most essential of urban needs, and cases from Dakar's civil court demonstrate the ways in which the city was a site of specific forms of housing adapted to and integrative of the transactional culture based in transience that pervaded city life.

Passing Through and Pairing Up

Tribunal records from the late 1910s and early 1920s reveal nascent cosmopolitanism developing in Dakar, with residents from regional and international places of origin. On the eve of the 1920s, the range of cases from 1919 involved parties from northeastern Senegal, Saint-Louis, Ziguinchor, Tivaouane, Mauritania, Conakry, Great Britain, France, and villages throughout FWA. Many stayed with relatives and friends for short- and long-term engagements, while some found other solutions. Although administrators recorded place of residence in each court docket record, they were inexact in doing so. The absence of formal addresses in all but the European core of colonial Dakar coupled with the transience of Dakarois generally resulted in a norm of entering an address simply as *chez* X, indicating the name of the owner or principal occupant of a residence. A person residing with someone else might have been a renter, a guest, a temporary boarding house occupant, or a relative, but such detail was rarely included in case records as a matter of form. Rather, the details of a specific complaint often brought to light the particular relationships between occupants of a residential location. A majority of cases in downtown Dakar recorded specific addresses, although the precise type of residence was not indicated. For instance, structures that were used as individual rooms for rent or as apartments were delineated only by a street address. In such instances, the nature of the lodging arrangement emerged in the case content itself.

Even where that was not clear, the range of options available to city dwellers is evident from the case records; transience and flexibility were prominent, and the sorts of preferences city dwellers had in selecting modes of residence were clear. Many litigants stated how long they had been or intended to stay at a location. If parties were not explicit when providing personal information up front, they often revealed further information as questioning pertaining to a case proceeded. In this way, the rich transactional culture in Dakar that was developing around residence strategies comes into view.

As the 1910s came to a close—a transformative decade for Dakar that saw new developments including the creation of the Medina—greater degrees of movement and housing instability emerged in the city. Vagrancy cases became more common in the courts. These reveal not only the fact that French administrators used housing insecurity to criminalize Africans but also that stable residence was not achievable by all who sought to live in town. Officers commonly intercepted and interrogated Dakarois for possible vagrancy infractions, and by the 1920s vagrancy was regarded as a major issue that authorities attempted to quantify in statistical terms and manage with new regulations. On the ground, however, the line between vagrancy and residence was much less clear. In 1919, for instance, authorities charged

Alioune Diaye, a man in his twenties, of vagrancy. When questioned, Diaye explained that he had moved from Saint-Louis four years prior and had been stable in a job as a cook in a French household downtown. Since leaving that house, however, he remained unable to find another position and thus a place to live and called the courtyard of a coaling merchant home.[1] When place of residence came with employment, loss of a position resulted in immediate housing insecurity. Diaye's place as a working resident of Dakar is made clear in his testimony, with little to suggest he intended to leave the city for other pursuits. The colonial economic structure of Dakar, as established from the French perspective, saw work as the sole reason most Africans should be present in Dakar. In this sense, the ready availability of housing outside the context of employment was unnecessary. Access to reliable housing was ephemeral, dependent on not only procuring employment but keeping it, a task not always within the control of a worker. Employers themselves could be transient, especially within the domestic work sector. Employers set the terms of employment and considered those who worked for them to be in a position of both subservience and obligation—dynamics made clear in claims of theft and abandonment of work brought to the court against their employees. Thus, the attachment of housing to work imbued into Dakar's local transactional culture the need to produce quickly and easily obtainable residential arrangements, including those in which no money was exchanged.

In the challenging but also fluid context of colonial Dakar, living with family was a common solution. A relative's home provided immediate access to housing and drew on reliable kinship bonds that secured the arrangement. People routinely informed authorities that they lived with or were staying at the home of a family member, as was the case for Boubakar Ndiaye, who was interrogated upon a vagrancy arrest. He assured authorities he had a stable living situation at his brother's home in Dakar's Khadieul neighborhood.[2] Ndiaye explained that he was unable to find a place to live despite

---

1   Vagrancy charge against Alioune Diaye, May 9, 1919, ANS 5M/205(184).

2   Mbengue v. Ndiaye, April 26, 1919, ANS 5M/205(184). A note on the citation of sources in the ANS Series M (Justice), Sub-series 5M: This book draws heavily on this series, which contains the *procès-verbaux* explained in the introduction. The collection contains a variety of cases that can be cited in various ways, depending on the nature of the complaint, misdemeanor, crime, or other issue at hand. When the case is between two or more parties, all future citations will appear in the short form indicating the last names of plaintiff(s) and defendant(s), followed by the date and then dossier number, as in this example: Mbengue v. Ndiaye, April 26, 1919, ANS 5M/205(184). When there is no obvious plaintiff because a party was brought in for another reason, such as in the case of Alioune Diaye, a description will appear, as in the

his long tenure in Dakar. Records do not reveal whether Ndiaye's family was Dakarois to begin with. Typically, people born in Dakar or with extended family in the capital made this known in the *procès-verbaux*, as doing so was to their advantage. Ndiaye's case might have been an example of a family wave in which relatives followed each other to the city. Often, the establishment of one family member in town provided a home base to which others could then anchor themselves. Cases spanning the run of this collection suggest that pattern.[3] Kinship also permitted those receiving relatives in Dakar to draw on the income and domestic labor contribution of extended family, making it a potentially advantageous arrangement for hosts as well. Still, such arrangements were not uncommonly fleeting, as Dakarois often moved in and out of employment arrangements or encountered tensions within a living arrangement.

Other cases from the same year reveal the ways in which mobility threaded through the lives of different kinds of people in Dakar on the eve of the 1920s. Examples of passing through, rural linkages, and new arrivals were numerous in the civil court records on a variety of case matters. In some cases, the temporary nature of a person's residence in Dakar was clear, as in the example of a grievance filed by Fatogorra Traore, an artillery soldier in Dakar. He reported to the court in July 1919 that a money order for fifty francs he had sent to his wife in the village some time back had not reached her.[4] Traore was posted to Dakar as part of his military enlistment, clearly for a long enough time that he had been paid, sent money home, and was familiar enough with the local systems to have been able to access the court to file his complaint. Several other cases involved sailors residing temporarily in Dakar as their ships made berth there, which sometimes lasted up to weeks or even months.[5] In other cases, people revealed that they had come to reside in Dakar because of the opportunity to work. Sidy Diop, for instance, brought a complaint against Malla Ba, who, he said, had not paid

---

    footnote immediately preceding this one. After this footnote, no further citations in this book will provide the full title of the series and subseries. All cases from the 5M subseries in this study are from the "Justice, Affaires classées sans suite, Plaintes et procès-verbaux de police," from 1914 to 1944. Finally, when a section draws on a number of cases or indicates a common theme across cases, it will cite only the dossier rather than each individual example of such cases. Such footnotes typically contain several dossier citations.

3   It is a pattern that continues to be identifiable today. The successful settlement of one family member in the city is widely recognized as a sort of open door that can lead to the passage, if not full establishment, of other family members in that urban household.

4   Complaint lodged by Fatogorra Traore, July 7, 1919, ANS 5M/205(184).

5   See cases in dossier ANS 5M/205(184) for examples.

the wages Diop had earned during his eight months in Dakar since arriving from Podor.[6] Other records reveal the transitory effects brought on by Dakar's role as a hub. One case was submitted by the Customs Office against an Englishman, Mr. Whittington, for illegal importation of items from Germany under cover of English origin by passing them through Sierra Leone to Dakar.[7] A number of theft cases also involved parties passing through Dakar. City dwelling took diverse forms, with the city serving different purposes to the many who engaged it.

Inherent to the creation of a temporary home, regardless of duration, was the creation of a household, and this often took on gendered dimensions. Certain residential arrangements entailed provision of domestic services by women for men who required them during sojourns in Dakar related to labor.[8] Men of all backgrounds and means lived in town with the paid services of women, who provided a range of services that were both gendered and foundational to the making of household at its basic level. Domingo Dacosta, a deckhand on the ship *Gabon*, brought a complaint against a woman he said he paid to provide meals and laundry. His claim was that she had not rendered adequate service. Investigation revealed that Dacosta spent nearly two months in Dakar after hospitalization for illness and had engaged a "laundress" to care for him.[9] The woman, Diapoly Ndiaye, told authorities that Dacosta's claims of unsatisfactory service were unfounded, adding that he actually owed her money. The record leaves unclear what type of residence Dacosta occupied while engaged in the arrangement with Ndiaye. It could have been her home, a boarding house, or lodging he rented outright. Dacosta was not unique in this type of arrangement.

In colonial urban Africa, the provision of domestic tasks such as described by Dacosta was a relatively common service offered by women, including

6   Diop v. Ba, January 24, 1919, ANS 5M/205(184).
7   Customs Bureau v. Whittington, February 21, 1919, ANS 5M/205(184).
8   The role of women in recreating "home" in the urban environment for laboring men is a theme that appears in the broader literature on migrancy and urbanization in Africa. The most comprehensive treatment is Luise White's *Comforts of Home*, in which prostitution is central to the lives of working men in colonial Nairobi. One of the types of prostitution she examines, *malaya* prostitution, included domestic services such as cooking and companionship without sexual relations. It should be noted, however, that in these Dakar cases, neither the interested parties nor colonial authorities suggest that sexual services were part of the contested housing agreements. A number of the rental properties in Dakar were owned or operated by women, who also could provide laundry and meals to increase profit associated in the boarding agreement.
9   Dacosta v. Ndiaye, January 18, 1919, ANS 5M/205(184).

certain classes of prostitutes, as Luise White describes in her analysis of what was termed *malaya* prostitution in colonial Nairobi, where women's possession of a room itself offered special benefits to the men who patronized them.[10] Her exploration of the dynamics of that form of prostitution notes its role in providing safety and security to men in an urban setting in which laborers were "vulnerable to increasingly strict pass and vagrancy laws."[11] White argues for the central place of women operating within the domestic and sexual dimension of colonialism in Africa, asserting that such space "was a place where male labor power was produced and contained."[12] Colonial states were not only aware of prostitution but prone to associating it with female urban life. A July 1923 case involving a "laundress" includes notes by authorities suggesting the party was most likely a prostitute.[13] Whether or not prostitution was implicated, women who provided food, laundry, and other domestic service outside the boundaries of formal, long-term employment permitted transient residence to operate successfully in cities like Dakar. Prostitution was not the only avenue to the creation of such gendered household dynamics among men and women not bound by kinship or marriage. In her study of early postcolonial Dar es Salaam, Emily Callaci examines the avenues available to and opportunities forged by women who chose to leave rural areas for urban life.[14] She locates men as central to women's survival in the city, but points out that women adopted various strategies in this regard, "often living with male partners for whom they would provide domestic labor as a way of accessing housing and other basic necessities."[15] Calacci finds that alliances were neither exclusive nor durable but rather ephemeral and "flexible."[16]

That portrayal of gendered arrangements and relationships that were first and foremost for the purpose of creating an individual urban life is consistent with the dynamics of Dakar decades earlier. Ndiaye's dealings with Dacosta were transactional. Men's arguments in court suggested a sense of rights to women's reproductive labor of the household, while women in various arrangements insisted that their work warranted compensation as it

10   White, *Comforts of Home*, 79–102.
11   White, *Comforts of Home*, 89.
12   White, *Comforts of Home*, 90.
13   Sy v. Bokary, July 2, 1923, ANS 5M/209(184).
14   Callaci, *Street Archives*, 66.
15   Callaci, *Street Archives*, 66. While Emily Callaci reveals these dynamics of vulnerability and reliance as wrapped up in the making of urban self among women, White points to women's transactional interactions with men as a means of building wealth, ownership, and community within female spheres. White, *Comforts of Home*, 119–21.
16   Callaci, *Street Archives*, 66.

constituted paid labor.[17] In a 1923 case between Fatou Diop and Samba
Diop, testimony recorded that Fatou Diop provided cooking and laundry
services to Samba Diop while she also was employed as a cook in the central
French quarter of Dakar.[18] Both roles were positions of paid labor, even if
they took place in different contexts. Her matter with him arose once he had
left town for the countryside, making procurement of payment for services
rendered a challenge. The *Diop v. Diop* case illustrates the critical role of
transience within the transactional culture, particularly in its ability to infuse
risk into any arrangement. Payment relied on the presence of the responsible party, and men were particularly mobile in the colonial urban setting,
both due to their participation in the labor regime that stretched from city
to countryside and their prominence in colonial schemes to remove those
thought to be vagrants or members of the so-called floating population.
The household, a foundational societal building block of residence itself that
entailed deeply embedded gendered dimensions, was recreated in colonial
Dakar within the specific parameters of transient transactions.[19]

While cohabitation between men and women was at times implicit, other
matters entered into the Tribunal docket explicitly broached the topic. In
August 1923, a rental debt matter came before the court in which the renting party was a couple the landlord claimed was unmarried. The residence
had been rented for two years until the woman died, leaving the man, a sailor,
alone to pay the rent. He had assured the landlord he would do so but then
boarded a ship around the time of his partner's death, leaving Dakar.[20] It is
unclear if the man relied on his partner to pay rent, or if the woman's
death signaled the time to depart, making him reluctant to continue rental

---

17 Jane Guyer explores the notion of households as transactional in one of the
    earlier articles in the field to consider households as an object of enquiry and
    as a concept in the scholarship. See Guyer, "Households and Community in
    African Studies." Income and households are, naturally, intimately intertwined,
    and women's participation in that dynamic was not confined to the realm of
    unpaid labor. Ali Mari Tripp explores women's urban labor and contributions
    to household income in her 1989 article, noting that women who obtained
    their own sources of income were able to achieve greater independence
    within households. See Tripp, "Women and the Changing Urban Household
    Economy in Tanzania."

18 Diop v. Diop, November 24, 1923, ANS 5M/210(184). No blood relation
    existed between Samba Diop and Fatou Diop, per the record.

19 The centrality and enduring importance of households as sites that contributed
    to greater legitimacy within state and society from the precolonial through
    colonial eras are explored in the work of Emily Osborne. See Osborne, *Our
    New Husbands Are Here.*

20 Camara v. Sylla, August 11, 1923, ANS 5M/209(184).

payments. Either way, his departure as described in plaintiff testimony appears abrupt. The ability to simply leave was widespread in Dakar, and grievances regarding the disappearance of a tenant were frequently brought to court. In another case, a renter told the Tribunal she became unable to pay the rent for her lodging after the hospitalization and eventual repatriation of her lover to France. Her landlord seized her belongings to auction off while she was in the maternity ward giving birth to twins.[21] In this case, the presence of the woman's partner in Dakar was a necessary condition for the payment of rent. Because the urban setting had fewer social controls than rural areas, arrangements such as those were possible but also were inherently less stable than unions reinforced by kin groups and an entrenched sense of place. The transient nature of Dakar's population created vulnerabilities that reached into lives and livelihoods and upended living situations. The new households created in the city were imbued with distinct transactional aspects and a clear monetary value, particularly to women involved in them.[22]

The case involving Fatou Diop, the cook who brought the 1923 case against Samba Diop, shows this well. Her detailed written complaint to the Tribunal claimed that Samba Diop, in recognition of the domestic services and care she provided when he was sick, gave her the wooden dwelling he owned in Dakar. He then left for the countryside. Later, he contested her ownership of it. Fatou Diop argued that this was in discord with the good, family-like relations they had.[23] She asserted that she and Samba Diop had established a relationship whereby she cooked and laundered for him. That relationship, mirroring a husband-wife dynamic, was important to the plaintiff. However, the colonial urban context made the nature of such a "family" relationship much different. Samba Diop engaged Fatou Diop's services to facilitate ease of residence in Dakar in the absence—or unavailability—of female kin. In all this, it is important to note that Samba Diop's voice is absent from the record. Fatou Diop's letter of complaint is all that exists in the court docket.

The fact that the case received no follow-up was very likely due to the inability to locate the defendant, since he was out of Dakar. If the dwelling was indeed his, then he probably intended to return. It is possible that he could have agreed to allow Fatou Diop to occupy it during his absence, especially if she had already been residing there with him. Her assertion that he gave it to her would indicate that she believed him to be permanently gone from the city, while the second component of the case—that he contested her claims to ownership—would indicate his intention to return.

---

21   Norate v. Ndiaye, August 2, 1923, ANS 5M/209(184).
22   Callaci, *Street Archives*.
23   Diop v. Diop, November 24, 1923, ANS 5M/210(184).

What emerges from this case is the instability and flexibility of residence, influenced heavily by transient behavior. Samba Diop's mobility was evident, as was the likelihood that he considered Dakar and elsewhere both to be a form of home. Fatou Diop's side presents a less obvious but equally important aspect of residence in the city: she turned to options outside the family, finding opportunity for residential stability in work, relationships, and even in the transience of others.

Rental Relationships and Risks

Relationships between people who cohabited or between those in rental agreements entailed ingenuity and flexibility geared at making the urban environment livable. The very fluidity of the city, however, also made the residential landscape complex and often unstable. The rental property sphere was heavy with overtones of mistrust and doubt that stemmed from the understanding that arrangements could ultimately be fleeting and thus unreliable. In the early 1920s, the Tribunal saw a marked increase in rental disputes and housing challenges linked to mobile lifestyles. Ballaye Gueye's complaint to the Tribunal in 1922 against renter Ngor Ngom, a sailor, serves as a straightforward example of a common problem in the capital. Gueye said Ngom regularly paid rent but had then left Dakar, leaving an unpaid debt.[24] It was not entirely unusual for renters to leave in this fashion. In 1923, for example, Dior Diop wrote to the Tribunal to complain that her tenant Iba Seck Gallo had been absent for seven months.[25] Diop claimed Gallo was in Diourbel and had taken the key with him, locking his possessions in the lodging. Rent had accumulated and was outstanding for the months of Gallo's absence.

Dakarois' mobility was directed not only inward but also outward. Just as the interior pulled people in and out of Dakar, so did the sea. As the *Gueye v. Ngom* case above shows, the port of Dakar was a major factor in the transience that was part of Dakar's residential landscape. This was especially true by the 1920s, when significant port improvements received postwar funding thanks to Dakar's contribution to the metropolitan war effort.[26] The early 1920s also saw the development of a greater synergy between land and sea with the completion of the Thies railway line to the interior at Kayes. By the close of that decade, Dakar had become the hub of interior and exterior

---

24 Gueye v. Ngom, May 18, 1922, ANS 5M/206(184).
25 Diop v. Gallo, November. 23, 1923, ANS 5M/210(184).
26 Seck, *Dakar*, 305–35.

trade and movement.[27] A number of residential cases, such as *Gueye v. Ngom*, involved men who worked aboard ships or at the port of Dakar. They show that transport jobs brought greater transience to Dakar but, at the same time, also permitted workers to base themselves in Dakar for extended periods of time. In mid-1923, Yousoupha Basse, employed in the maritime field, appealed to the Tribunal to convince his landlord to allow him more time in the lodging he rented. He claimed he had never missed a month of rent since he had begun renting in 1920 but had now been asked to move. Finding another room in Dakar was a difficult task, he argued to authorities, and he required more time.[28] Basse's case reveals some of the expectations and risks of maritime life and the question of residence. Although Basse said he paid rent regularly, his landlord allegedly sought to terminate their rental agreement, obliging Basse to seek residence elsewhere. While many possibilities existed for the reasons for the eviction, the landlord might have perceived the eviction of Basse to be an easy matter. Basse, who was tied to the sea in his work, could have been perceived as able to be uprooted or as eventually likely to leave.

Maritime mobility also created tensions between people sharing residences. Kalibou Diagne, working aboard a ship, lodged a grievance in December 1923 against his roommate for the disappearance of items that had been stored in their shared lodging while Diagne was at sea for two months.[29] Diagne's mobility rendered his residential situation liable to ruptures. As his case against his roommate demonstrates, theft was a potential occurrence in a living situation because people left their residences with relative frequency. Dakarois lived alone, leaving lodgings empty, or they lived with others with whom they might not share kinship linkages. These new types of living situations Dakarois crafted to accommodate their movement and means involved as many new gambles as options.

The large number of theft accusations in the Tribunal records reveal that this was a risk Dakarois were willing to take—people left keys with neighbors, trunks with housemates, and residences unsecured while they were outside of Dakar. At times, they found themselves filing complaints upon their return. The marked increase in these types of cases in the 1920s reveals the growth of cohabitation and of the rental market in general. Along with that came the expansion of the movement in and out of the capital. Dakar was changing, becoming a more nebulous residential space. Most symbolic perhaps was that the Medina and downtown, envisioned by the state to be

---

27   Seck, *Dakar*, 372.
28   Basse v. Mbengue, August 19, 1923, ANS 5M/209(184).
29   Diagne v. Camara, December 11, 1923, ANS 5M/210(184).

separate and distinct, were growing and closing in on each other.[30] Dakar was becoming a large, diverse urban space.

In the expanding city, mobility brought insecurity to urban residences, as revealed in the accusations among people sharing living spaces in Dakar. In May 1922, Joseph Dia, employed at a local commercial operation, accused his roommate, Yousouf Diaye, of stealing personal possessions from the room they shared. Diaye, an apprentice typographer, confirmed that he had indeed taken these things but claimed the intent was not theft. His defense was that he took the items to store in his own trunk, locking them under key so that no one else would steal them.[31] The following month, Ismaila Keita brought a complaint against his housemate, Salifou Ndiaye, whom he had told to watch his trunk of clothes and cash while he left to sell *kolas*. Upon his return, one hundred francs were gone from the trunk. Ndiaye claimed he had not taken the cash and had actually given Keita's key to Colia Taraore for safekeeping. Keita maintained his complaint against Ndiaye since, he pointed out, Ndiaye had no right to pass the key on to anyone else. Taraore, meanwhile, was no longer in Dakar and could not be questioned.[32] In April 1924, Neby Keita filed a grievance against his roommates Mom Sylla and Maurice Bangoura, saying they shared the room where he left his trunk of personal possessions. Finding money missing from the trunk upon his return from work, he accused Sylla and Bangoura of taking it. His roommates both explained they had been out all day—Sylla at work on the docks and Bangoura on errands around town—and had no idea how Keita's money had disappeared.[33] In May 1924, Tridore Huchard lodged a complaint against Joseph Diata Dalmas, his roommate on Rue Blanchot in central Dakar. He claimed that Dalmas had taken advantage of Huchard's absence one evening to steal several items and sell them, including clothing and housewares.[34] Dalmas, when questioned, admitted his wrongdoing and

---

30 In only ten years, the Medina had grown both in population and in physical size, with a great amount of the development being undertaken by Africans. At the same time, Dakar was expanding northward with great speed. The deputy administrator of the circumscription noted: "The isolation zone between Dakar and Medina . . . has become of no purpose. [The Medina] is today nothing but an obstacle to the normal development of the city, which is pushing its inner suburbs to the north and northwest." The same official noted in his report that 131 of the 165 new buildings that had gone up in the city were built by Africans. Circumscription de Dakar et Dépendances, General Report, 1925, ANS 2G25/11.

31 Dia v. Diaye, May 11, 1922, ANS 5M/206(184).

32 Keita v. Ndiaye, June 14, 1922, ANS 5M/207(184).

33 Keita v. Sylla and Bangoura, April 29, 1924, ANS 5M/211(184).

34 Huchard v. Dalmas, May 20, 1924, ANS 5M/211(184).

eventually promised to pay Huchard back the 130 francs in value for the things he took and sold.

There are a number of important details in roommate theft cases such as these from the 1920s. The first is the cosmopolitanism that had been developing in Dakar. The names of the parties involved in the above cases represented various places throughout FWA. With that diversity, living situations forged between people who did not share common origins was common. The second is the distrust that is apparent in the cases. Residing together presented certain vulnerabilities. To mitigate the kinds of risks obvious in these examples of new kinds of living configurations, Dakarois often sought out linkages between themselves and the people with whom they lived. In *Huchard v. Dalmas*, for instance, both men were transplants from the Casamance region of southern Senegal. Both were employed in jobs in the capital, Huchard with a trading company and Dalmas with the Dakar-Saint-Louis railway. Huchard and Dalmas, though from the same region, might have found affinity in their shared geographic roots. They also may have found solidarity in their professional identities. Professional, geographic, and ethnic ties—often broadly conceived—were common devices Dakarois employed to lend stability to the fluid and often hostile urban environment.

Despite the identification of real or even fictive linkages to others, no approach to protecting one's possessions at home was fully effective. Ruptures occurred, especially in an environment in which city dwellers were not devoted to full-time life in town. In 1931, Coura Diouf told the court that a passing visitor from Kaolack named Diop had stolen a pair of earrings from her residence.[35] A complaint by Boubakar Ndiaye the same year accused an old friend, Mamadou Diogo, of stealing clothing and a wallet with money in it. Both men were from the Casamance, but while Ndiaye had a residence in Dakar, Diogo did not and needed a place to sleep after having come to Dakar from Rufisque. Despite Diogo's explanation that someone had broken into the room during the night and stole the items while both men slept, authorities charged Diogo with both theft and vagrancy.[36] Examples of such ruptures are useful in illustrating both the creativity of urban dwellers and the inherent friability of the agreements they made. This existed not only between renters and landlords and between people choosing to cohabit based on perceptions of common interests or ties.

---

35   Diouf v. Diop, August 27, 1931, ANS 5M/222(184).
36   Ndiaye v. Diogo, July 2, 1931, ANS 5M/222(184).

Figure 3.1. Image of a postcard by Edmond Fortier of houses lining a street in Dakar, c. 1902–1905.

Working to Live, Living at Work

For those who either did not have access to or opted not to seek rental residences, a viable option in interwar Dakar was to live at the place of work. Living at the workplace was especially advantageous in the low-wage environment Africans faced and within the restricted framework colonial authorities had established. Saving money, while a priority for all, was particularly crucial for those with mobile lifestyles since their objectives often included reserving a portion of their wages for needs in other places. The types of positions Europeans and the French colonial economy produced for Africans and other non-Europeans often entailed living on site. Domestic employment and work as security guards or port workers were the most common jobs that allowed people to combine residence with work. However, with such a transient European community, workers witnessed firsthand the instability inherent to transience among their employers. The residence-at-work model was thus at once a creative solution and a highly unstable arrangement. In both those aspects, African poverty, ensured by the colonial regime, drove people to reside at their workplaces.

The same forces that made residence at work the only financially viable option for some also brought about vulnerabilities for others. Colonial domestic employment assumed that the employee would reside on site and also that the provision of room and board was itself an aspect of payment. The result was difficulty in exiting such a job and remaining in Dakar. In 1922, colonial authorities received a letter from Anna Gueille, who explained that after working as a domestic worker at the Couteau home, she had now been informed that the family no longer required her services. Her letter was not a complaint but rather an appeal to the state for assistance. Her workplace had long been her place of residence, and in that context, she was paid only enough to cover food and clothing. Her relationship with the Couteau family was one of dependency, as clearly suggested through the tone and contents of her letter.[37] With her employment terminated, Gueille found herself without adequate resources to procure another housing option.[38] The difficulty of the situation did not escape the administrator who received it. His handwritten note on her letter said simply: "There's nothing I can do."[39]

Africans, Europeans, and others alike found the convenience in combining workplace and home in the colonial capital. The two most common forms of workplace residence for Africans in Dakar in the 1920s and 1930s were domestic service and employment with the state and its corollaries. Many Europeans essentially lived at work in a sense, albeit in very different circumstances. Brought to the colonial capital on a tour of duty or work contract, they often resided in lodgings provided by the administration or the private enterprises for which they worked.[40] Cases involving workplace residence became more commonly treated by the Tribunal from the 1930s onward, when Dakar's employment environment became significantly more diverse and robust. Major port improvements had been undertaken from the mid-1920s into the early 1930s, expanding its capacities.[41] The port was the most powerful element in determining Dakar's trajectory and many of its population's activities. [42] The economic crisis starting in 1929 saw the

---

37 Domestic service was an employment milieu in which dependency was common in colonial Senegal, especially for workers brought into a household at a young age, as Anna Gueille likely had been. Both the system of guardianship and the existence of pawning in colonial Senegal contributed to such dynamics. See Miers and Roberts, *End of Slavery in Africa*; Lawrance and Roberts, *Trafficking in Slavery's Wake*; Bryant, "Changing Childhood."

38 Letter to the attorney general from Anna Gueille, undated, in dossier for 1922, ANS 5M/207(184).

39 ANS 5M/207(184).

40 See the cases involving Maurice Renouard, for a clear reference to such an arrangement, in ANS 5M/254 (184).

41 Seck, *Dakar*, 334.

42 Despite the centrality of ports to colonial African cities and economies, they have not been explored in depth in historical scholarship. There is a tendency

demise of competition among regional ports in Senegal and a consolidation of export trade from the interior toward Dakar.[43] The capital took over larger portions of the important peanut trade as 1929 gave way to 1930, and by 1931 it had usurped Rufisque, the former peanut center.[44] From the mid-1920s to the mid-1930s, the population of greater Dakar more than doubled. In the early 1930s, that population increase included people who had come to Dakar as a result of economic depression hitting FWA. The conjuncture of these forces meant that finding the most financially reasonable ways to inhabit the city was an important imperative—both in terms of earnings and housing, since pressure mounted in both domains. The 1930s saw an increase in cases coming to the Tribunal involving people who combined workplace and residence.

Complaints about living at work that reached the court rarely confronted the question of residence directly but rather addressed other matters—theft and quitting without notice were the most common. In November 1930, for example, Jean Frayssenet lodged a complaint of breaking and entering. A man he referred to as his "boy," Farasamba Tabore, had intercepted the intruder in the middle of the night. Tabore, a 24-year-old from the Haute

---

to take the port system and its dockworkers as a known, common entity, understanding them as a fundamental urban component that does not require extensive discussion. Immediately noticeable is the conceptual rubric into which historians have placed ports and dockworkers: that of labor and class formation. Trade unionism remains the most common framework for analyzing the activities of port workers, and this tendency has sidelined the ability to consider the other roles such men had. Dockworkers were consumers, residents of variable tenure, farmers, renters, transients, and often not members of unions. Their workplaces and time spent in port cities included encounters with soldiers, European visitors, landlords, retailers, and a wide range of urban players. If the diversity of the experience of men who labored on docks or in port-related industries is broken down, the category of "dockworker" that has been useful to studies of class formation, unionization, and nationalism becomes more complex and can more richly contribute to the history of the port city itself. While there are a few studies of West and East African ports and dockworkers, the major historical examinations have pertained to South Africa, where the ports of Elizabeth, Cape Town, and Durban were major centers of sub-Saharan Africa's most industrialized economy. For the most explicit discussions of colonial dock work, see Cooper, *On the African Waterfront*; Luke, "Dock Workers of the Port of Freetown"; Hemson, "Dock Workers, Labour Circulation, and Class Struggles in Durban, 1940–59." Philip Curtin points to the importance of port cities in his preface to Wright and Liss, *Atlantic Port Cities*, xi–xvi.

43 Seck, *Dakar*, 393.
44 Seck, *Dakar*, 401.

Volta colony of FWA, lived in Frayssenet's house.[45] The matter at hand was the home intrusion, but the details about the residence and in what capacities were taken down for the record. "Boy" was the paternalistic term Europeans used to denote male domestic servants. It often involved living at one's place of work.[46] Offices of companies and state agencies lodged employees in similar positions as well. Maurice Tivolle, an agent with the Comptoirs Réunis de l'Ouest Africain, brought an accusation of theft of foodstuffs against an employee, Abdoulaye Diaw, in 1930. Diaw lived at the company's headquarters.[47] The same year, a complaint came from Demba Seck, a security guard at the impound section of the port. Seck lived on site and reported to police that some of his personal belongings were missing from his armoire, which had been broken. Some of the stolen items belonged to Ahmed Sy, a port laborer who also lived there.[48] Workers living at their places of employment in colonial Dakar were frequently security guards like Seck. An April 1932 case concerning money missing from a Public Works Department office included the testimony of Moctar Sow, a security guard there who also resided at the building.[49] Even though it was standard procedure to note the addresses of interviewed parties for any case, a number of records provide addresses for all except the security guard. This might suggest it was understood that the guard lived at his place of employment. Only rare cases in the Tribunal noted a guard not living on the premises for which he worked. One such instance was a home intrusion case in which the security guard, Sidy Ndiaye, lodged the grievance. Reporting a

---

45   Frayssenet v. Lopy, November 19, 1930, ANS 5M/221(184).

46   The figure of the African "houseboy" or "boy" has featured in many historical analyses and works of literature. Most well-known is perhaps Ferdinand Oyono's novel *Une Vie de Boy*, about a Cameroonian young man who becomes a houseboy in the households of a Catholic priest and a French colonial official. Charles Van Onselen argues in his social history of colonial Johannesburg that having such male house servants was part of the colonial identity, so much so that "middle-class and ruling-class families . . . considered a team of 'houseboys' to be part of their colonial birthright." See Van Onselen, *New Babylon, New Nineveh*, 36–37. The literature on domestic service has included examinations of the position of "boy," which appeared not only in Dakar but throughout the nineteenth-century colonial world, persisting throughout colonial times. See also Vizcaya, "Houseboys"; Deslaurier, "Des 'boys' aux 'travailleurs de maison' au Burundi, ou le politique domestiqué"; Pariser, "Masculinity and Organized Resistance in Domestic Service in Colonial Dar es Salaam, 1919–1961"; Bujra, *Serving Class*; Oyono, *Une Vie de Boy*.

47   Tivolle v. Diaw, July 5, 1930, ANS 5M/220(184).

48   Seck v. Sy, July 15, 1930, ANS 5M/220(184).

49   Theft complaint lodged by Gibril Wade, April 2, 1932, ANS 5M/225(184).

break-in that had occurred during the night at a European house, Ndiaye explained that although he was the guard, he did not live at Martin's house. Rather, he went to his own home to sleep.[50] He made note of that point in his testimony, which implies that Ndiaye's situation was unusual for security personnel in Dakar.

People having few residential options in Dakar might have sought out jobs in workplaces that housed their employees. A 1932 case involving a missing holding tank at a French-owned fishery in the Hann area of Dakar noted that many of the fishermen lived on the worksite grounds.[51] The same year, closer to downtown, Khary Diop brought a complaint on behalf of her daughter, Fatou, who worked in the home of Nicolas El Khouri.[52] Diop claimed El Khouri withheld wages from Fatou. El Khouri responded that Fatou had been hired to look after his children, adding that she lived at his house with them. He asserted that the root of the issue was that when he became dissatisfied with her service, he offered to let her go with one month's worth of severance pay, but Diop wanted six. An expectation of residence at domestic workplace scenarios was likely common, as a 1924 case illustrates. A dispute between a European state employee, Marie Therese Jupin, and her domestic servant, Abdoulaye Sy, about wages and theft revealed specific expectations about wages and additional benefits. Sy explained that he believed his wages of seventy-five francs per month were in addition to room and board.[53] This was important to Sy as he had arrived from northern Senegal forty-five days prior and was obliged to stay with an uncle in the Medina if he had no options through his employment. The expectation of being housed at Jupin's home was explicit in his testimony to officials. Living at work, like living with people of common backgrounds, was only one of many strategies Dakarois employed in an expensive and transient environment.

Work was not a uniform experience, of course, and for many who were not employed by the state or its corollaries, living at work meant being on the move. Certain pursuits in Dakar were inextricably linked to other places, with Dakar merely a point on a larger web of colonial economic activity. Colonial urban surveillance documents made reference to *banabanas*, traders who bought from producers and resold foodstuffs and

---

50   Theft complaint lodged by Sidy Ndiaye regarding the home of Maurice Martin, July 8, 1942, ANS 5M/261(184).

51   Theft complaint lodged by M. Le Vaillant, April 15, 1932, ANS 5M/225(184).

52   Diop v. El Khouri, June 4, 1932, ANS 5M/225(184).

53   Jupin v. Sy, June 28, 1934, ANS 5M/233(184).

products in the city.[54] *Banabana* referred to a local trade middleman, but as *banabanas* became more common in town they also became known as street peddlers. Similarly, Dakar's supply of livestock often passed through the hands of intermediaries known as *téfankés*, who, administrators reported, operated in the suburbs and sold sheep in the name of the herd's owners for sizeable commissions to buyers in the city.[55] Individual traders from other parts of Senegal and FWA were frequent sojourners in Dakar, as it was the colony's biggest market. A 1930 business dispute, for instance, implicated Moustapha El Hindaoun, a trader who had been operating in Ivory Coast and was spending December in Dakar to sell *kolas*.[56] His visit was typical of FWA's economy, in which the capital was entrenched in nearly every type of network. Conducting sales, settling accounts, developing clientele, and acquiring resources required time in the city. Fara Gueye Sar, a cheesemaker from Saint-Louis, resided at the home of Amadou Cisse, a civil servant, during a 1940 stay in Dakar that ended up involving a dispute for one of his European clients over nearly four thousand francs.[57]

Tackling Transience

By the mid-1930s, officials lamented that Dakar was overwhelmed with people and that transience was inherent to the problem. The administration had seen two decades of transient culture develop, and it demonstrated its understanding of this local urban reality maintaining the notion that it could keep Africans from driving urbanization. Africans saw their terrain of potential movement and residence more broadly than French authorities, who sought to define people according to identities that included their origins and perceived race. No matter how much they wanted to stem transience, it was woven into the very fabric of urban growth. A statement from the 1932 French conference on urbanism in the tropical colonies was particularly revelatory of this understanding among colonial officials, though it was framed in the racist, paternalistic terms that defined most French descriptions of African habits at the time:

> The native is more nomadic than the European. So many French peasants have never left their village. Berbers, on the other hand, do not hesitate to

---

54 Renseignements politiques, services de sûreté, November 27, 1943, ANS 17G/410.
55 Renseignements politiques, services de sûreté, November 27, 1943, ANS 17G/410.
56 El Hindaoun v. Rahmoune, December 16, 1930, ANS 5M/221(184).
57 Sar v. Coker, March 11, 1944, ANS 5M/268 (184).

travel 300 kilometers by foot to attend the Festival of the Lamb in Meknes. The blacks of Gabon go 500 kilometers to be hired as workers on forest worksites. As soon as a railway is built, the native takes the train without reason, out of the simple taste for being on the move. If he is attracted by the city, he will just as readily go 500 kilometers as 25 kilometers to get there.[58]

African movement, depicted with derision, was not such a simple matter. Coming and going was for the purpose of making money. Mobility was not arbitrary, and colonial officials in Dakar knew this. Colonialism had created a context in which it was unavoidable for many.

The admission that transient Dakarois were becoming a permanent feature emerged as a subcurrent beneath the discourse about stemming the *population flottante*. By the 1930s, this yielded some efforts to incorporate the members of that group so as to avoid homelessness or overcrowding of African homes. Most obvious was the Office of Economic Housing, created in 1926. It sought to address the housing shortage that perpetually plagued Dakar. The results the Office produced were never on par with the needs of the urban population, however, due to underfunding and the persisting idea within the administration that human flow to the capital could be stemmed. Very few important constructions were produced for the project before the Second World War.[59] The state also addressed short-term transients. In 1935, the administration opened the Caravansérail of the Medina, a hostel where "workers passing through Dakar, or natives who have no housing for the moment, [could] put a roof over their heads."[60] The name invoked the fortified inns that had traditionally served caravans moving across the trade routes of North Africa and the Near and Middle East, reinforcing the notion of passage.[61]

Of course, the installation of this type of institution alongside other, seemingly contrary, measures showed the ambivalence of the colonial state vis-à-vis transience. While attempting to expand housing opportunities, the state also redoubled its efforts to enforce vagrancy laws in the 1930s. The

---

58   "L'Urbanisme aux Colonies et Dans les Pays Tropicaux," 1932.

59   Coquery-Vidrovitch, "Villes Coloniales et Histoire des Africains."

60   Dakar et Dépendances, Political Report, 1935, ANS 2G35/11.

61   The term in French comes from the combination of *caravane* and *sérail*, and has several meanings, the most relevant in this case being that which refers to an inn: "*auberge, bordj, hôtellerie*," as defined by the *Grand Robert* dictionary. Additional definitions are worth noting: "En Orient, vaste cour, entourée de corps de bâtiments où les caravanes font halte," and "Lieu fréquenté par des étrangers de diverses provenances." "Caravansérail," *Grand Robert*, 2nd ed., 2001.

administration at times provided temporary lodging and at others banned people from Dakar altogether. Despite the resignation that mobility was part of city life, administrators harbored the hope that a solution could be enacted, if only the proper method could be identified. Even into the 1940s, authorities maintained that Africans could be discouraged from living in the city. Schemes to provide incentives such as train tickets back to the countryside were examples of the naïveté and racism that permeated the colonial mindset.[62] Indeed, as officials enacted small-scale initiatives, such as the Caravansérail, they expressed in everyday procedural matters the simple idea that those without adequate reason should not be in Dakar. A 1933 case between Djoulite Diop and her ex-husband, accused of abusing her after their divorce, elicited the comment from the administrator handling the matter that the woman should leave Dakar and return to Louga as soon as possible since her marriage had ended. She had "nothing to do in Dakar," the notes asserted.[63] In a case such as this, authorities made their philosophy quite clear. On the same level, the state actually encouraged transience and mobility with such rhetoric. Stable, affordable housing was not proposed or even envisaged on a scale to match the population's needs. Diop and others like her who opted to remain in town thus would need to turn to other options to fulfill their needs, and the transactional culture evolved within that context.

By the 1940s, the fragility of Dakar's residential landscape was compounded by a colonial state torn by shifting wartime allegiances, budget strains, and pressures to reform. The last major top-down urban district creation had essentially been the Medina. Around the Medina, the state oversaw the expansion of other neighborhoods, but no coherent approach to urban challenges faced by the population had been devised. The creation of an affordable housing office led only to a limited number of constructions and certainly to very few options for city dwellers who were highly mobile. There was a noticeable absence of regulations seeking to make sense of and react to what Dakarois were actually doing to reside in town. The state was not to devise a real vision for Dakar's residential landscape until 1946, when it promulgated a number of sweeping reforms throughout the colony. Only then did the administration elaborate an urban development plan for Dakar and the entire Cap-Vert peninsula that revealed, in its creation of many new

---

62 Letter-Telegram from the haut commissaire of FWA to the governor-administrator of the Circonscription de Dakar, August 24, 1940, ANS 1H25(26).

63 Diop v. Fakhry, May 22, 1933, ANS 5M/228(184).

neighborhoods to house the occupants of informal slums, that urban residence had hitherto been an entirely local matter.[64]

In 1944, such sweeping plans had not yet been articulated. Even an educated functionary like Sekou Keita, an office employee with the state railway, found himself unable to locate a stable residence. Keita wrote to authorities that for six months he and his family had been without housing. They were sleeping in different places with friends and at the homes of people who were away, and their furniture was stored on a verandah, where it was being destroyed by the elements. Previously, Keita said, they had occupied an apartment in a building owned by Aissatou Thione, who then received permission to evict her tenants and do work on the property so that she and her family could inhabit it themselves. Keita claimed that, unlike some other colleagues employed by the administration, he was unable to obtain housing through the state. His letter asked officials to help him locate a place of residence for himself and his family. Writing that life in these circumstances was painful, he added: "I am from the Soudan and do not have extensive knowledge . . . in this city where I have come not as an amateur but through administrative service."[65]

The frangible nature of the residence in the city comes through quite clearly in Keita's case. His complaint also encapsulates a number of aspects of Dakar's relationship with transience: expectations that one would be housed by one's employer, the power of property owners vis-à-vis renters, and movement from elsewhere to work in the capital of FWA. Keita very likely did not mean to settle permanently in Dakar. He was posted there on service and was one of the many transient residents looking for ways to make the city work. Innovative and flexible as Dakarois were, they were also often at the mercy of an urban environment largely unprepared to accommodate the many residents the state did not desire to be there.

Transients as Residents

Dakar developed an urban environment and society that integrated and responded to transience as a mode of existence that impacted all areas of life, infusing itself in the transactional culture. Transient residence was present in colonial Dakar in all corners of the city, and the city became at once more flexible and more fragile because of it. The colonial administration's rejection of transience was deployed through an endorsement of autochthony.

---

64   Baller, "Transforming Urban Landscapes," 59.

65   Letter from Sekou Keita to the attorney general, September 7, 1944, ANS 5M/270(184).

Yet, Dakar's growing population was fueled by places elsewhere. French company men went back to France for the rainy season, domestic servants from Guinea were employed for days or months at a time, and *téfankés* fluctuated between the city's outskirts and center. Dakar's growth and function as a city encompassed and depended on people who were not the city's full-time, autochthonous residents. At any given time, the city was full of such individuals. The administration observed this, despite its own wishes: demographic estimates taken by the most attention local functionaries—those closer to the population—were always far higher than those taken by more distant or upper-level officials because they accounted for the *population flottante*, the sojourners, the people whose activities and lodging were neither permanent nor stable. At the highest levels of the administration, authorities wanted to rule out those members of the urban society. But with time, that was increasingly difficult. The official discourse of the 1930s about *refoulement* was wrought with frustration and a sense of knowing. Dakar was a haven for those with mobile lifestyles. A single individual might return regularly or rarely, but the time they spent in town impacted both the city and that person's geography of residence. Dakar was one of the places to sleep, eat, work, spend, and trade. These were the activities of life and pursuing life in town was an act of residence, even if only for a while. The ambivalence of transience denotes not only the colonial state's conflicted relationship with movement and ephemeral city dwelling but also the understanding of residence and transience historians have when examining African urban spaces. The important idea of migration can fall short for a city such as Dakar. People such as Domingo Dacosta, Abdoulaye Sy, and even Dakar Administrator Ponzio were neither migrants nor permanent residents. Their experiences living in the capital of FWA had a start and an end, but that made them no less present or important to the economic and social fabric of the city. They represented the spectrum of transience, one of the most important elements of the urban culture of colonial Dakar.

Chapter Four

Impediments and Ingenuity in Financial Life

Transactional Relationships and State Racism[1]

In colonial Dakar, the intersection of urban African networks and colonial policies concerning African fiscal lives produced a local transactional culture in which informality was central. These dynamics were very apparent in Dakarois' everyday money management. Colonial administrations in Africa created a system in which most financial resources such as credit were available through official channels over which the state had control and were limited or inaccessible to colonized populations.[2] In Dakar, part of the mechanism of ensuring the exclusivity of the formal economy and the exploitative economic basis of colonialism was an ideological framework that cast Africans as fiscally immature, severely restricting access to funds other than the most necessary. At the height of its colonial rule in West Africa, the French state pursued the rhetoric of African fiscal responsibility to a granular level in its wage policy, marrying a paternalism that proposed a need for tutelage to shape Africans into savvy economic actors with an overt urgency to produce more and more reliable labor.

Colonial policies were fraught with unintended consequences, and as state efforts to keep permanent African settlement in town at bay ultimately encouraged expanding informal settlement, the French administration's efforts to curb African accumulation merely encouraged creative fiscal practices to flourish in colonial Dakar. In the context of racist constraints, which limited formal fiscal management and a wage regime aimed at limiting any form of real earnings, Dakarois focused on quick, adaptable, and flexible strategies of resource access. Social networks were key to such a

---

1   Certain contents of this chapter have appeared in article form in Petrocelli, "Transactions and Informality."

2   Cooper, "Urban Space, Industrial Time, and Wage Labor in Africa"; Cooper, *On the African Waterfront*; White, *Comforts of Home*.

system. People in the colonial capital forged opportunities with one another, placed in a colonial schema meant to create perpetual need among African city dwellers and retain them in the low-paid labor force. The many transactional court cases individuals brought to the Tribunal reveal that the ability of Dakarois to turn toward other city dwellers as financial resources was a key necessity in the colonial city. Particularly within the context of concerted state efforts to entrench Africans in a form of poverty prior to the end of the Second World War, maximum flexibility among city dwellers in their monetary dealings was necessary and commonplace. The French colonial state, in fact—and contrary to its own goals—helped create a vibrant informal system.

Informality is by its very nature difficult to identify and assess, particularly in the past. Invisible in many ways but obvious in others, it developed over the course of the twentieth century to dominate African economies across the continent. With equally rural and urban roots, informality takes many shapes and serves various purposes. Often taken to be a postcolonial phenomenon associated with the struggles of the eras of structural adjustment and collapsing states, informality is much more deeply entrenched. Official documentation may capture snippets of informal activity, although this typically includes only that which the state deemed illicit. Everyday informality as it existed in the lives of colonial Dakarois was pervasive and thus did little to attract a suspicious eye, eliciting instead a form of less intensive but nonetheless critical commentary from administrators who remarked in reports on the habits of local populations. However, the everyday transactions of people in Dakar were the main business of the capital's Tribunal as a civil court, and the cases lodged there provide important clues as to how informality might have emerged and operated.

This chapter delves into the records of people's complaints about one another as they appeared in Dakar's entry-level civil court, the primary venue for opening cases on matters ranging from debt to family disputes over inheritance. While this examination cannot make sweeping claims about the extent or volume of informal networks, it proposes the driving forces behind them: the French state's race-based policies on access to urban resources; and people's willingness to rely on one another as solutions to the barriers placed before them by the colonial state. Interpersonal networks were the basis of informal economy and arrangements in a racist colonial context that explicitly imposed limits on accumulation and access.

Cases revolving around a form of debt came very frequently to Dakar's Tribunal. It is clear that people not only encountered such issues on a regular basis but also saw the court as possessing the power to right a situation that had gone awry. People visited and wrote to administrators on a daily basis to seek resolutions to problems involving loans, debts, services, purchases, contracts, and all kinds of transactions that were commonplace in an urban setting. Just as frequent, though, was the abandonment of efforts to resolve such issues through official channels. The fact that so many cases ended up *sans-suite* (classified as needing to follow-up), reveals that matters were often left unresolved because either the plaintiff, defendant, or both had disappeared in the midst of an ongoing enquiry. The transient nature of life in Dakar meant that someone involved in litigation could have found exiting the city the most convenient option. But, at the same time, financial relationships in the capital were grounded in social connections, and parties might have sought multiple avenues of resolution at once, both informal and formal, with the potential for an out-of-court solution to materialize even after an initial complaint had been lodged in court. Thus, far from limiting the view of the local transactional culture, the *sans-suite* aspect of the records points to the true dynamics as they existed. Dakar was a city that offered people quick opportunities, most of which were accessible through other people.

More than simple transactions, dealings that came to the colonial justice circuit in Dakar were interactions and relationships between people. Often, they transpired between individuals or groups of people rather than formal entities or businesses. In many instances, cases involved a chain of events in which money or goods changed hands multiple times under various terms. In one another, Dakarois sought funds in the forms of currency, kind, and credit, and they provided resources based on mechanisms such as kinship bonds, neighborhood trust, cultural affinity, and patron-client dynamics, themes that have been common to monetary relations in Africa.[3] As the French colonial state refined its commitment to economic exploitation and framed it within a paternalistic language of fiscal education, such economic networks and trends expanded and solidified, coming to typify the local transactional culture in colonial Dakar.

Race and Resources: State Wage Policy in Colonial Dakar

As in many cities in Africa, access to financial resources in Dakar was through employment with the colonial state or its corollaries. Both the capital of FWA and the primary port of Senegal and French Soudan, Dakar had two

---

3   The manner in which members of urban societies created resources within contexts of restricted access, exclusion, and marginality has been explored in various key works. Jane Guyer has examined fiscal strategies and consid-erations across her work. See Jane Guyer, *Money Matters*; Guyer, *Marginal Gains*; Guyer and Stiansen, *Credit, Currencies, and Culture*. Ilda Lourenco-Lindell has examined the dynamics of needs, resources, and informality in urban Guinea-Bissau. See Lourenco-Lindell, *Walking the Tight Rope*. See also Fioratta, "A World of Cheapness."

major employment sectors: port and administration. State services employed educated Africans and laborers of various sorts. The port sector entailed handling fuel and cargo, the railway serving the port, and commercial houses. Dakar also required a range of services for visitors and sojourners. City dwellers found employment in cafés and shops serving Europeans, for instance. These sectors made up the formal employment scene of colonial Dakar, and the state attempted to monitor the availability of labor and rates of pay in many of them. Administrators' attitudes about the financial needs of the local population were based largely on their understanding of these sectors as the drivers of the capital's economy. The activities that took place underneath were either hidden from officials' view or considered by them to be signs of unsound economic behavior.

The port was the state's main economic concern. France invested in it at several intervals to assure a healthy groundnut trade as well as create a major maritime fueling station in the southern Atlantic. By 1920, forty million francs were allotted for large-scale expansion of the port, with additional sums for improvements to roads and streets that served it.[4] The economic crisis that began at the onset of the 1930s actually worked in Dakar's favor. Ships began berthing at Dakar instead of Senegal's groundnut town, Kaolack, because of higher capacity and greater commercial options.[5] As the economy recovered and groundnut production expanded, Dakar received increased traffic.[6] An entrenched role in the groundnut trade helped Dakar establish deeper connections to its hinterland from which many urban residents came in search of work. Dock work was a major draw for labor seekers, as in other African colonial ports. With a fully functioning, lucrative port sector, Dakar was positioned to thrive. To foster growth, the colonial state required cheap labor and a steady urban population that did not grow exponentially and thus increase the burden on state services. Those priorities went hand in hand with the assertions that administrators made about African fiscal responsibility.

Official priorities were to maintain cheap labor and discourage permanent settlement of Africans in town, a development they feared would tarnish the capital's outward display of European grandeur. The state joined those priorities to its paternalistic mission toward Africans in matters of modern urban life: tutelage in the areas of fiscal restraint and careful planning. Authorities held that local populations required slow training to disabuse

---

4   Seck, *Dakar*, 323–31; Sénégal. Territoires d'administration directe. Rapports trimestriels des cercles, escales et communes mixtes; Rapport du 2è trimestre 1915, Gouvernement du Sénégal, Délégation de Dakar, ANS 2G15/28.

5   Seck, *Dakar*, 399–406.

6   Betts "Dakar"; Boone, *Merchant Capital and the Roots of State Power in Senegal*.

them of wasteful, risky financial behavior.[7] That made it pointless to fix pay rates at anything other than the level of basic necessities. In communications about wages and living standards, bureaucrats consistently framed the topic in terms of need, and need was determined by race. They argued that Africans neither needed nor even desired any sort of accumulation. Earnings beyond those required to live were inappropriate for Africans, the claim held, because they had neither the same requirements as Europeans in their daily lives nor the capacity to create sound financial strategy. The phrases "very modest," "relatively comfortable," and "sufficient" were common in documentation about Dakarois and money.[8] This is crucial to understanding the evolution of local practices in everyday transactions. In a context in which the state intentionally kept earning potential low, Dakarois became flexible in their strategies to access and use financial resources.

Documents from the 1930s provide particular insight into that logic. The rise of the Popular Front in France yielded an increased interest in human welfare at home and in the colonies. A unique window thus opens to historians because the state produced a number of reports with that interest in mind.[9] The French state set up a number of missions to FWA to assess questions that ranged from food production to the condition of women, and resulting reports included a robust study of standards of living in Dakar.[10] Issued in 1939, it categorized the city's inhabitants and assessed them in terms of the state's concept of need and responsibility. Although framed in the language of its reformist era, the 1939 report echoed ideas France had held since the debut of its colonial venture in Africa about cultural superiority and the need for Africans to evolve under its guidance. The left-leaning priorities of the Popular Front merely provided a different framework within which French officials expressed its paternalism. The report reveals authorities' beliefs that Africans were unable to properly manage money and required oversight in access to it.

In laying out needs, the administration identified three primary strata of urban society: laborers, educated employees, and the autochthonous Lebu, who were landowners and fishers. The needs for each were cast differently.

---

7   For a broader treatment of the state in Africa and notions of fiscal responsibility, see Roitman, *Fiscal Disobedience*.

8   Inspector of Colonies, Report on the Standard of Living of Natives in the Circumscription of Dakar, February 4, 1939, and Response of the Governor-General to the Report of Inspector of Colonies, ANS 4G/107(105).

9   Hosington, *Casablanca Connection*; Bernard-Duquenet, *Le Sénégal et le Front Populaire*; Jackson, *The Popular Front in France*; Cooper, *Decolonization and African Society*; Chafer and Sackur, *French Colonial Empire and the Popular Front*.

10 Coquery-Vidrovitch, "The Popular Front and the Colonial Question."

In a racist construction of parameters, all were presumed to have fewer and less complex requirements than Europeans. Departing from that standard, different necessities existed within the broader category of Africans living and working in Dakar. The report asserted that an educated African head of household working for the administration could earn less than his French counterpart because he was to live in simpler surroundings and provide a basic, locally based diet to his household. A typical family was expected to have one man, one wife, and four dependents, normally indicated as children. Neither extended family and dependents, whether in the city or in rural areas, nor social obligations such as rites of passage, figured into the state's calculations of an African employee's financial burdens.[11]

For the laborer, there were fewer considerations: the objective of pay was to perpetuate work in town for a determined time. Colonial officials saw survival as the sole goal a worker's pay met, and survival was relative. As the state understood, a worker needed to earn enough to feed himself and replace the calories he had spent at work.[12] Caloric generation was specific to the context of a local African diet based on rice and fish, consumed communally with other Africans—this was expected to make caloric replacement an inexpensive task.[13] Housing was similarly framed. Laborers could "be considered, for the most part, as single men because they live[d] as such, the family (wife and children) living in the village with the ease of life in the

---

11   Inspector of Colonies, Report on the Standard of Living of Natives in the Circumscription of Dakar, February 4, 1939, and Response of the Governor-General to the Report of Inspector of Colonies, ANS 4G/107(105).

12   This philosophy pervades colonial communications of all sorts. An earlier expression of the difference in lifestyles can be found in a confidential letter from the lieutenant-governor to the governor-general regarding the Medina, July 15, 1915, ANS 11D1/1284; thirty years later, reports on rations during World War II communicated the same ideas in drawing out differences between European and African needs, ANS 2G44/19. The idea of controlling workers via food was present throughout colonial Africa. Cynthia Brantley has explored how colonial bureaucrats attempted to assess food needs among African subjects, notably for the purpose of maintaining labor. Brantley, *Feeding Families.*

13   Jeremy Rich and Megan Vaughan each has explored food and diet in African history. Rich's work on food culture in colonial Gabon explores the disconnect that existed between the colonial state and diverse Gabonese in not only production but also consumption as well as the attitude the state carried that food was a means by which to influence colonial subjects. Rich, *A Workman Is Worthy of His Meat.* Vaughan's work on Malawi showed the ways in which different levels of food self-sufficiency contributed to social stratification. Vaughan, "Food Production and Family Labour in Southern Malawi." Jane Guyer has examined the notion of cities' relationships to food production, identifying as a specific sector of economic activity. Guyer, *An African Niche Economy.* See also Twagira, *Embodied Engineering,* especially chapter 2.

bush."[14] Their earnings, therefore, did not need to support families in rural areas. Moreover, workers could be expected to live in close quarters. "The laborer will share, with one or two of his friends, a room for which rent can vary," the report asserted. Authorities argued for Africans' preference for communal living, rejecting the notion that room-sharing was a strategy resulting from low worker pay.

Other expectations existed for the autochthonous Lebu. Dakar's Lebu possessed houses with gardens and engaged in fishing, participating less in labor and civil service.[15] "The abundance of fish and the high demand . . . makes fishing among the most lucrative industries. It is estimated that a fisherman in the suburbs of Dakar can earn an average of fifty francs per day," the Ministry of Colonies reported in 1939. "But, knowing how to limit his needs, this fisherman only works one of two or three days at most and relaxes the rest of the time."[16] Such assertions clearly communicated the racist notions that buttressed the state's approach to needs and responsibility. It was common for colonial administrators in Africa to argue that Africans preferred leisure to work and did not seek accumulation, a logic known as the backward sloping labor curve thesis that held sway among European scholars into the middle of the century.[17] These attitudes toward autochthons, laborers, and educated employees were hallmarks of French colonial policy, rationalizing policies driven by inflexible and paternalistic notions about race, as well as by priorities to maintain an exploitative economy. Accumulation, even in slow increments, was impossible in such budgets. Dakarois were to earn the "vital minimum," the state held, because of the African aversion to work and inability to handle money.[18]

The commitment to the philosophy of "just enough" occurred against a backdrop of an increasingly expensive urban environment. Dakar's growth from the First World War to the Second World War witnessed dramatic rises in costs of living. In 1917, as the city's population edged above twenty

---

14 Inspector of Colonies, Report on the Standard of Living of Natives in the Circumscription of Dakar, February 4, 1939, and Response of the Governor-General to the Report of Inspector of Colonies, ANS 4G/107(105).

15 Inspector of Colonies, Report on the Standard of Living of Natives in the Circumscription of Dakar, February 4, 1939, and Response of the Governor-General to the Report of Inspector of Colonies, ANS 4G/107(105).

16 Inspector of Colonies, Report on the Standard of Living of Natives in the Circumscription of Dakar, February 4, 1939, and Response of the Governor-General to the Report of Inspector of Colonies, ANS 4G/107(105).

17 Berg, "Backward-Sloping Labour Supply Functions in Dual Economies."

18 Inspector of Colonies, Report on the Standard of Living of Natives in the Circumscription of Dakar, February 4, 1939, ANS 4G/107(105).

thousand residents,[19] administrators took note of rising costs and the challenges they created for workers.[20] Roughly twenty years later, they continued to find that the "cost of living [was] very high in Dakar."[21] The problem persisted more than two decades later, in the 1940s, with greater pressure on urban residents as the city expanded and served more regional roles.[22] Growth was rapid: Dakar's population was counted at nearly sixty thousand inhabitants in 1929,[23] and those numbers doubled by 1938.[24]

Nonetheless, the state's attitude—driven by racist premises—remained consistent over time: Africans required little and could not manage more. Entrenched in the priorities of an extractive colonial state, administrators were unwilling to consider the ways in which such an assertion was misplaced. The transactional culture of colonial Dakar constituted a rich field of interactions in which city dwellers created resources where the state would have asserted none existed, engaged in creative practices to meet obligations far more numerous than those the state counted, and made use of people and possessions in ways administrators considered irrational but locals understood as normal.

Networks of Personal Possessions

One of the clearest examples the state found of irrational economic behavior and lack of foresight was in the widespread practice of pawning material objects. Pawning personal possessions to access liquid funds was a

---

19 Population statistics for Dakar in the earlier decades of the twentieth century vary. Estimates from various sources range from nineteen thousand to twenty-five thousand. This estimate from 1915 is drawn from a confidential letter from the lieutenant-governor to the governor-general, July 18, 1915, ANS 11D1/1284.

20 In 1918, the trimester reports stated that the "rising cost of living" provoked discontent among workers on the large state projects. A strike was threatened in late 1917, and requests for a daily wage of eight francs on several worksites had already emerged by early 1918. Dakar, Trimester Reports 1918, ANS 2G18/20.

21 Inspector of Colonies, the Standard of Living of Natives in the Circumscription of Dakar, February 4, 1939, ANS 4G/107(105).

22 Letter from Sekou Keita to the attorney general, September 7, 1944, ANS 5M/270(184).

23 A 1934 report had Dakar's 1929 population at fifty-thousand Africans alone. Thus, an estimate of nearly sixty thousand is more likely by 1930—see ANS 3G2/1(1).

24 Dakar et Dépendances, Police et Sûreté, Annual Report, ANS 2G37/33.

device Dakarois, like many Africans across the colony, used commonly by the 1920s. As early as 1907, the governor-general of Senegal was already discussing the matter with Paris. The communication warned that Africans were "devoid of any notion of foresight" and too readily participated in practices leading to impoverishment.[25] In cities, pawning and credit were becoming quite commonplace, taking on new, more monetized forms than in rural areas, where farmers dealt in forecasted harvest results. Asserting that Africans disposed of "few resources," authorities were wary of pawns and loans because, they asserted, such practices robbed people of "the few objects of value" they possessed.[26] Over several decades following these early statements, pawning expanded as city dwellers sought creative ways to meet their monetary needs. Cases brought before the Tribunal de Première Instance de Dakar over the thirty-year period from 1914 to 1944 often involved pawning transactions. It was a widespread financial strategy in colonial Dakar, where money was tight.

The records of the Tribunal contradict the prevailing colonial state idea that practices such as pawning personal effects were part of a cycle of desperation or impoverishment. Contrary to officials' beliefs, pawning transactions could be configured as part of broader concrete plans. Africans pawned possessions for cash for a variety of reasons, including to generate savings. Specific case examples provide valuable evidence of transactional decisions made in a context of limited income, urban social networks, and financial strategizing. A 1918 case between Amadou Mbaye and Ousmane Ndour illustrates this well. Mbaye's complaint to the court concerned a sum he previously had left in the hands of Ndour and then sought to recover. Mbaye told court officials that the ninety francs were "savings" produced in part by pawning possessions and in part by saving wages made in Dakar.[27] Mbaye's presentation of himself was as a careful saver, who adopted a range of methods to ensure he had a cash reserve. He saved wages, pawned items, and deposited money with a third party who he believed would both protect the funds and make them available as needed. Supplementing employment earnings was common in Dakar since wages and salaries were rarely sufficient. Authorities recorded Mbaye's profession as "laborer," thus his pay was likely low. Workers like Mbaye often turned to management of material objects as resources as part of an overall financial plan to amass resources in the capital.

---

25 Secrétariat Général, 4ème Bureau, Paris, "Question des prêts sur gages et de l'assistance aux indigènes," June 2, 1907, ANS Q63.

26 Secrétariat Général, 4ème bureau, Paris, "Question des prêts sur gages et de l'assistance aux indigènes," June 2, 1907, ANS Q63.

27 Mbaye v. Ndour, February 13, 1918, ANS 5M/203(184).

In addition, a clear relationship had to exist between Mbaye and Ndour to allow the latter to function as a savings bank. The pawn was only part of the financial strategy. Once Mbaye had produced funds by pawning an object, he sought to safeguard it, trusting another individual more than himself to do so. While administrators interpreted such practices as evidence of an African absence of self-control and responsibility, Mbaye's case and those like it demonstrate that responsibility resided in relationships. The person who desired to save funds protected them from his own sphere of financial obligations by placing them with someone else. In accepting them, that individual became bound by a social contract that was perhaps more important than a financial one: operating far from any institutional rules or processes, the two parties relied on their mutual trust and social credibility to ensure the savings were kept properly.

That notion at the heart of many of the transactions that took place in the streets and homes of Dakar (rather than in its shops or banks) is reinforced in the Tribunal cases in which the willingness of people to loan possessions to others to pawn to meet immediate financial needs was clear. In a 1922 case between Diop Diame and Makha Diouf, the latter had borrowed a bracelet from the complainant with the purpose of pawning it to allow the purchase of stock for his butcher's shop. The assumption was that once Diouf had sold his butchery product, he would reclaim the bracelet and return it to Diame. When Diame encountered difficulty getting a response from Diouf, who had neither returned the bracelet nor restituted its value, he filed a grievance.[28] The same scenario occurred between Khouma M'ballo and Amadou N'diaye in 1930.[29] M'ballo came to officials after being unable to find N'diaye, a tenant to whom M'ballo had loaned jewelry to pawn when N'diaye needed money. The *M'ballo v. N'diaye* case is particularly interesting because it shows M'ballo's willingness to hand valuables over to a tenant to permit access to money in a time of need despite the unpaid housing debt to M'ballo. In the complaint to authorities, M'ballo conveys a conception of N'diaye's rental obligations and nonrental finances as discrete debts: the record listed the two debts separately and cited only the pawned object as the matter at hand. This ability to separate financial obligations, making money work to meet different urgencies and goals, was common in colonial Dakar. While court officials sought to create an overall debt case between M'ballo and N'diaye, the plaintiff had a more specific concern. M'ballo's approach is illustrative of the earmarking and creative strategies Dakarois employed.

This was rarely understood by administrators, for whom the local practice of parceling debts and channeling resources reinforced French notions of African inadequacies in financial management. Although the compounded

---

28 Diop v. Diouf, November 29, 1922, ANS 5M/208(184).
29 M'ballo v. N'diaye, June 26, 1930, ANS 5M/220(184).

debts in the *M'ballo v. N'diaye* case represented controversial transactional practices in official eyes, city dwellers understood their financial engagements as dependent on many criteria. The most important of those were urgency and social relationships. If N'diaye's need was urgent, and if an acknowledged relationship existed between M'ballo and N'diaye, the rental debt could be set aside as a solution created to assist N'diaye. Siphoning debts and lending on an individualized basis were practices anchored in new relationships of trust that were recalibrated in an urban context that had both diversity and common experience built into it. It was the combination of these two elements—diversity and common experience—that made other affinities such as place of origin recede to allow for city dwellers to transact broadly and with maximum benefit. While solidarity among immigrants from other regions of West Africa and from places further afield played a role in creating important networks in Dakar, those networks were not the sole conduits that propelled the city's transactional culture.[30] Tribunal records contain as much case evidence of transactions among people with no linkages as among parties with bonds of origin. In a context of colonial state efforts to limits people's options, urban residents multiplied their options by crafting a repertoire of practices in which all engaged with the mind to yield maximum benefit.

A 1934 case between Mr. Boucher and Ibrahima Dieng shows this well, demonstrating the practice of pawning to have been common enough that it was not limited to Dakar's African community.[31] Boucher's complaint concerned a gold chain that he had loaned to Dieng to temporarily pawn for funds Dieng needed. He indicated in his grievance that he considered the possession quite valuable.[32] Boucher gave no explanation as to the circumstances of the loan, nor did he explain his relationship to Dieng. Parting

---

30 See, for example, cases in the files ANS 5M/210(184), 5M/211(184), and 5M/218(184) for transactions among Cape Verdean Dakarois. For a clear example among Lebanese Dakarois, see El Hindaoun v. Rahmoune, December 16, 1930, ANS 5M/221(184). For a transaction between two Casançais, see Huchard v. Dalmas, May 20, 1924, ANS 5M/211(184).

31 Boucher v. Dieng, May 9, 1934, ANS 5M/232(184).

32 There is always a certain degree of risk in assuming that a French name and surname in the records confirm a person's European identity, but most typically the use of the title "Mr." before his name acts as a confirmation of that identity since the officers involved accorded the individual the term of respect they never placed before the names of Africans, Lebanese, or Cape Verdean parties. In this case, Boucher appears as "Mr. Boucher," and his first name appears only later on in the records. It is possible that Boucher was mixed race, but even if that was the case, mixed-race Dakarois to a very large extent folded into the city's European community.

with possessions of value was an act that administrators saw Africans alone as all too ready to perform, but cases such as *Boucher v. Dieng* call such assumptions into question. It was not an isolated incident. The 1940 files contain a contentious pawning case between Fatou Gueye and Dr. Sibenaler, to whom authorities referred using his title rather than his first name. Gueye explained that she had entered into a loan transaction with Sibenaler in which she pawned gold for cash. She claimed she then satisfied the terms of the loan but was unable to reclaim the gold.[33]

Such incidents demonstrate that city dwellers from different backgrounds and in varying financial conditions participated in a set of practices involving the use of objects as a means of procuring funds. Personal possessions opened up the quickest path to obtaining money to meet other obligations. The other advantage they presented was their status as objects clearly linked to individuals. By taking out a loan in the form of a personal possession of a neighbor, colleague, of family member, the person who entered into debt did so with a very strong sense of the personal nature of the loan. Rather than procuring funds devoid of meaning from a distant institution, the borrower took on an object that had value to its owner, the lender. The ramifications of defaulting on the agreement carried more than simple financial penalty as there was an added element of social shame and potential loss of respectability. City dwellers clearly understood that these types of loans could result in loss of the objects, since they regularly made cases before French officials about the expectations built into pawning transactions.

In general, grievances did not bring into question whether or not parties had the right to use items to generate loans but rather what the time delay or terms of reimbursement were. No notion that the practice was unwise, as officials held, shows itself in Tribunal records. Indeed, the 1944 case Aissatou Ndiaye brought to authorities shows the planning Dakarois attached to pawning. Earlier that year, she had pawned a jewelry box to Doudou Ndoye for twelve hundred francs, seeking funds to meet "pressing family needs."[34] Three months later, she produced the repayment and sought to reclaim the box per the agreement. The state's generalization about African lack of foresight, wasteful spending, and inability to handle funds found little resonance in urban courts.

33 Gueye v. Sibenaler, December 1939–January 1940, ANS 5M/252(184).
34 Ndiaye v. Ndoye, May 1, 1944, ANS 5M/268(184).

Credit without Collateral

Even more than pawning and using collateral for short-term cash loans, the use of credit was widespread practice in colonial Dakar. In the Tribunal files, references to credit permeate records every year from 1914 to 1944. A simple credit transaction was more accessible than a pawn agreement because there was no item to be restituted later, only outstanding debt. Credit was crucial because of the high cost of living in colonial Dakar and the consistently low wages of Africans. While this is not a full investigation of credit, it shows the ubiquity of credit as a financial device in the capital. By asking the people to survive on the bare minimum, French officials helped foster a local culture in which credit was fundamental and necessary. Dakarois employed credit in the transactions large and small, and its availability permeated nearly every type of purchase and service. As they did in pawning transactions, people engaged in credit within the boundaries of social networks, often looking to colleagues and neighbors.

Although it expanded in the 1930s, credit had existed as part of the local transactional culture well before then. Many cases from the 1910s into the 1940s reveal the importance of credit in the lives of Dakarois. It was already common enough by 1922 that shopkeeper Ibrahima Kane brought a grievance against tailor Ballo Ndiaye for selling a garment of his on credit when he was instructed not to do so.[35] Kane reported that Ndiaye had not only sold it on credit but also sold the garment for less that the instructed price. In his defense, Ndiaye explained to Kane that he had sold it for forty-five francs on credit and was awaiting payment. His explanations suggested that he expected payment to be made. The case reveals two important elements of credit. First, credit was prominent enough in Dakar's transactions that urban residents had to be vocal about avoiding it. Second, credit allowed people to create opportunities. If Ndiaye was under pressure to sell the garment and found no clients able to pay the requested price in cash, he could offer credit to acquire a client. Conversely, the client could have been able to encourage Ndiaye to accept a credit transaction—for instance, through social ties that encouraged trust.

The economic crisis of the 1930s made the need to stretch financial relationships and procure funds on the basis of credit all the more important. Credit cases proliferated in the early 1930s in the Tribunal. The increasing expense of living in Dakar, in conjunction with the new economic pressures of the era, made credit more important to supplement or even replace other resources. Court records demonstrate that Dakarois needed and used credit as the city grew and costs rose. Many cases show individual debts

---

35   Kane v. Ndiaye, July 10, 1922, ANS 5M/207(184).

compounded as people balanced needs with income and prioritized certain debts over others. In 1931, William George Diouf, a Gambian who had obtained French status, wrote a letter of complaint against another Gambian in Dakar for harassment. As authorities investigated the claim, they found that Diouf was indebted to a number of people, including the defendant.[36] When questioned, witnesses pointed to the debts—one said Diouf owed 260 francs, and another 387 francs.

Indeed, authorities often discovered deep networks of debt among litigants. Dakarois very clearly lived in a world in which expenses were greater than income. While functioning as a solution that city dwellers used at every turn, credit also held potential to aggravate situations. As city dwellers compounded different loans upon one another, they created webs of debts that became difficult to disentangle at times. Mohamed Mahmoud, a shopkeeper in the Medina district, experienced this firsthand in 1932, when unpaid debts from customers to whom he had sold on credit reached such levels that they prevented him from paying the rent for his storefront on time.[37] Credit allowed his customers to continue consuming and Mahmoud to maintain a business but at the same threatened Dakarois' financial security as much as it buttressed it.

For some, the risks were not significant enough to discourage building businesses to which credit was central. Those who provided credit turned money into business at the most local urban level, becoming creditors alongside their primary occupation, typically commerce. Creditor was commonly a shopkeeper's role because retailers were able to operate in the most local neighborhoods, a setting in which contact with one's debtors was constant, and credit was bound to people's everyday needs through common purchases. The shopkeeper and client, in constant close contact and subject to neighborhood dynamics of solidarity, were obliged each to conduct business with those social considerations in mind. The neighborhood—an urban spatial unit rather than a unit of kinship—allowed more people of diverse origins to enter into such mixed socioeconomic relationships.

While many creditors were African, other creditors—such as the Lebanese—appeared in the urban economy.[38] The Lebanese community

---

36 Diouf v. Sera, September 10, 1931, ANS 5M/222(184).

37 Mahmoud v. Faye, March 8, 1932, ANS 5M/224(184).

38 Many dossiers show this: ANS 5M/205(184) through ANS 5M/211(184); ANS 5M/211(184); ANS 5M/220(184); ANS 5M/221(184) through ANS 5M/225(184); ANS 5M/228(184); ANS 5M/231(184); ANS 5M/233(184); ANS 5M/252(184); ANS 5M/253(184); ANS 5M/261(184); ANS 5M/265(184); ANS 5M/269(184). Chapter Seven of this book explores in detail the dynamics of Lebanese insertion into Dakar's local transactional culture. Lebanese immigration was significant from the

swelled from the early 1920s into the mid-1930s as France's Syrian mandate brought new immigration to FWA and the Depression increased migration.[39] While immigration to FWA from the Levant grew rapidly across the
colony, Dakar's case was special. Most immigrants passed through Dakar,
even when destined for rural areas, and many stayed. A March 1938 report
noted "massive immigration" of Lebanese to the colony, most of whom
were in Dakar.[40] Indeed, over the thirty-year span of the records examined
here, many files contain references to Lebanese roles in trade.

An exploration of the Lebanese inclusion in Dakar's local transactional
culture is treated in Chapter Six, and the broader history of the Lebanese
in West Africa is addressed by a growing number of scholars of colonial
FWA who consider the internal networks of credit of the Lebanese and the
debates that surrounded such immigrants. Of relevance here, in an analysis
that draws on urban Tribunal records, is to note the way African Dakarois
integrated the figure of the Lebanese creditor into their shared vocabulary
of the transactional landscape in the colonial capital. The term "Syrian" was
used by Africans to refer to a merchant generally, and many litigants used
"Syrian" to denote creditor alongside merchant. Mauritanian merchants
might have been subsumed within the "Syrian" category by virtue of transla-
tion from local languages to French. Wolof-speakers used similar terms to
refer to people whose origins were north of Senegal or from the Levant, and
translators may have varied in their attention to such subtleties.[41]

1920s. Archival sources point to Lebanese commercial success in town. See also
cases noted below in this chapter, as well as administrative reports; for example:
Letter from Governor-General Carde to the minister of colonies regarding
"Immigration of Syrians in FWA," December 27, 1923, ANS 1Q322(77);
and Maurice Darchicourt, "La Question des Libanais et des Syriens," in *Les
Annales Coloniales*, March 9, 1937, ANS 1Q322(77). For the broader literature on the Lebanese in Senegal, see, for example, the following: Leichtman
"Reexamining the Transnational Migrant"; Tarraf-Najib, "Une vieille histoire
de familles"; Oliver-Saidi, *Le Liban et la Syrie au Miroir Français*.

39 ANS 1Q322 (77). This dossier contains a large and diverse collection of
documents that archivists assembled for the common theme of dealing with
foreigners. Citation of this dossier thus does not imply the use of a single doc-
ument or even set of documents. Not all documents in the dossier are named.
Where the name is obvious, it is noted. Otherwise, only the dossier is cited.
See also Arsan, *Interlopers of Empire Africa*; Laan, *Lebanese Traders in Sierra
Leone*; Leichtman, "Reexamining the Transnational Migrant"; Oliver-Saidi, *Le
Liban et la Syrie au Miroir Français*.

40 ANS 1Q322 (77).

41 The Wolof term *naar* broadly applies to Mauritanians, North Africans,
Lebanese, Syrians, Arabs, and others whom Senegalese consider part of a larger
Arabized world. While more specific terms can indicate differences between

For Africans in Dakar, the Lebanese constituted a presence external to the (fictive or real) kinship groups on which Africans commonly drew for resources and support. The immigrant presence provided Dakarois the opportunity to borrow without engaging their most intimate social circles. Lebanese shops provided an option for those seeking local access to cash or credit.[42] Patrons commonly carried balances with local stores.[43] Buying on credit was a regular practice among clients of Lebanese-owned businesses, one that was convenient to Dakarois, for whom the high cost of living prevented adequate daily liquidity.[44] Lebanese merchants also extended credit independently of purchases.[45] The interest charged on loans does not emerge from the Tribunal data, since most litigants argued over principal and time delays rather than interest. The court records also do not indicate what results ensued when a debtor could not repay loans since they do not include outcomes and thus are classified as *sans-suite*.

Just as they could borrow, African earners in Dakar could lodge funds with Lebanese merchants if they desired to shield those savings from the web of loans that commonly occurred within kinship groups. Such groups often became the ways in which funds and objects of value quickly changed hands or became depleted through mechanisms of support. Thus, Lebanese merchants served roles in the local culture of resource management that grew in Dakar over the period, serving as a niche within the broader African-driven informal credit networks in the city.

Innovating Urban Survival

The mentality of the French state about African needs, yielding deliberately low pay, limited the resources of urban people. The state went to great lengths to frame racist policies in the context of alleged African incompetence in fiscal matters. A local set of urban transactions arose out of that tension inherent to the colonial city. Dakar became a landscape of innovation

---

them, the word *naar* is the most commonly invoked. In "Syrian," *naar* also became nearly synonymous with merchant or shopkeeper.

42 See ANS 5M/232(184), 5M/210(184).

43 See ANS 5M/222(184), 5M/225(184), 5M/231(184), 5M233(184).

44 This idea became so commonplace that it made its way into local popular culture. See, for example, Sembène, *Mandabi*.

45 See, for example, Sene v. "Djamil," September 26, 1923, ANS 5M/210(184); Diop v. Salky, March 21, 1934, ANS 5M/231(184); Gueye and M'Bengue v. Badiagne, July 11, 1923, ANS 5M/209(184); Diop v. "Michel," January 4, 1924, ANS 5M/211(184); Sarr v. Rosoul, April 15, 1924, ANS 5M/211(184); Cissoko v. Jouni, July 13, 1942, ANS 5M/261(184).

Figure 4.1. Postcard image of the Palais de Justice, c. 1915. Edmond
Fortier postcard collection. Courtesy of edmondfortier.org.

Figure 4.2. Postcard image of a market in Dakar, c. 1905. Edmond
Fortier postcard collection. Courtesy of edmondfortier.org.

in transactions that permitted people not only to survive but to thrive.
Widespread use of credit, the pawning of possessions, and other creative
means of producing additional funds were so widely accepted that such practices were litigable in colonial courts. In the absence of accessible resources
available through official means, people became the most important resource
on which city dwellers could draw.

The state did not create the ways Dakarois engaged each other economically; rather, it unintentionally participated in the practices it abhorred by approaching the city with narrow notions of race and need aimed at exploitation of Africans to its own benefit. New types of community were essential in the urban environment, where the types of mechanisms of social protection and solidarity that existed in rural zones was absent. Dakarois produced trust through extended kinship links, shared profession, common origin, or neighborhood bonds. The financial and commercial networks that ran through such communities were far from the rhetoric of fiscal responsibility the colonial state employed to foster its own control.

Chapter Five

Ethnic Boundaries, Economic Niches, and Ambiguities in the Colonial City

Urban Spaces and Selves: The Cape Verdean Community of Dakar[1]

Urban life in colonial Africa involved forging selves and opportunities. Carving out economic spaces in which to operate was critical to the task. In a colonial context that foregrounded questions of race and identity, deployment of those concepts was inherent to the process of creating and maintaining economic opportunities. The jobs people occupied were significant motors of urban growth, and the holders of a vast number of such jobs were not autochthonous Dakarois. In the capital of FWA, wage earners and merchants came not only from Senegal and the larger colony but from other colonies, particularly the nearby Portuguese holdings, and from other zones of French control, such as Syria and Lebanon. Whereas those from Senegal and its region often built Dakar into a wider network of geographies of work and residence, those from Portuguese colonies and the Levant were immigrants whose intent was to stay. In many ways, the creation of permanent immigrant communities in Dakar stood in contrast to the city's tendency toward transience while contributing to the expansion of the city through the arrivals of people from elsewhere.

The transactional culture of colonial Dakar relied on factors such as proximity, origin, trust, opportunity, movement, and flexibility, and communities coalesced around those. It also was shaped by the attitudes and actions of

---

1   Contents of this chapter appeared in Petrocelli, "Painting between the Lines," and are reproduced with permission.

the colonial state. Cape Verdean success in Dakar has much to reveal about colonial urban niche economies and the dynamics of categorization that existed under colonialism. Most important is the simultaneous prominence and pliability of colonial exercises in identity definition. In his study of colonial Dar es Salaam, James Brennan has pointed to a "particular ambivalence at the heart of British interwar policy" as pertained to understanding what the colonial state perceived as native and nonnative identity categories.[2] He argues that application of categories was neither consistent nor well defined and that "the process of identity formation had multiple if unequal participants" whose motivations varied in nature.[3] The dynamic he describes was present across colonial contexts as the very act of seeking to know, define, and control identity was one that could only be fraught with assumptions and unintended consequences. Steven Fabian argues that the specificity of place is a significant factor to consider in any analysis of urban identity formation and self-perception. His study of Bagamoyo takes the relationships established with a single city as central to such processes.[4] The specific world that Dakar was—most importantly, what the state perceived it to require and what people required from it—shaped the ways in which that all took place. Immigrants from the archipelago created distinctive opportunities within the identity politics of colonial Dakar during the first half of the twentieth century and particularly in the 1930s, the pinnacle of colonialism.

In power centers such as Dakar, immigrants to town found themselves in close proximity to an administration deeply concerned with maintaining control through categorization that matched what James Scott has described as the state act of rendering populations legible so as to facilitate rule.[5] The quest for social legibility in the service of control was key to French urban policy in Dakar. By categorizing populations, administrators attempted to create discrete segments, apply rules to each, and avoid the urban disorder they feared.[6] But in Dakar, as Brennan argues was the case in Dar es Salaam, consistency in this regard was elusive. In the capital of FWA, the colonial state was just as fluid as the populations it ruled, changing over time and exercising different goals at different stages, in which broader historical shifts played a role as well. As the history of Cape Verdeans in Dakar reveals, the colonial state perceived immigrants from the nearby archipelago within a framework that integrated both racial bias and pragmatic need, weighing

---

2 Brennan, *Taifa*, 11.
3 Brennan, *Taifa*, 12–13.
4 Fabian, *Making Identity on the Swahili Coast*, 10.
5 Scott, *Seeing Like a State*.
6 Direction des Affaires Politiques et Administratives, note AP/2 "Development of large cities in AOF, Draft," June 7, 1934, ANS 21G/49.

the two in a balance that produced whatever category the state required for a specific group. The introduction of the *foreign native* category into the vocabulary of Dakar's administration occurred within that set of forces. It expressed the double insertion Cape Verdeans underwent in Dakar as they were recognized both as Africans but also as newcomers not only to the city but also to the French colonial context more generally. But officials' use of the term in placing Cape Verdeans economically revealed the underlying tension in ethno-racial and even juridical categorization, one that was obliged to negotiate the mission to dominate with the need to validate the colonial project itself.

The successful implantation of the Cape Verdean community of Dakar entailed invention, exception, and adoption all at once, both on the part of colonial authorities and Cape Verdean Dakarois. Immigrants located opportunities to mobilize boundaries in the context of the fluidity inherent to the categories French administrators applied to them. Marking off a unique identity was important in maintaining key economic niches.[7] Fredrik Barth argued that ethnic groups are not defined by broad cultural unity but rather are socially useful designations imposed from within and recognized from without.[8] As Cape Verdean immigrants inserted themselves into fields— such as the painting trade, domestic service, and barbering—they cultivated an identity that at once distinguished them from and bridged them with other city dwellers. Negotiating the colonial framework in Dakar that emphasized race and religion to exert ownership over key sectors, they located space that lay delicately in between "native" and "European."[9]

It was that gray space Cape Verdeans occupied and that permitted their creation of key niches that became strongly attached to their identity. The ability to navigate ambiguity to a successful end was perhaps in part due to experience with it. Basil Davidson drew on Cape Verdean sociologist Dulce Almada Duarte in asserting that a solid "Cape Verdeanness" emerged on the islands that was "neither European nor totally African."[10] Portuguese colonial policies starting in the 1830s solidified that space: assigned a status similar to that of the *originaires* of Senegal, Cape Verdeans were set between metropolitan whites and Africans of the continental Portuguese holdings.[11]

---

7   Guyer, *An African Niche Economy*; Guyer, *Marginal Gains*; Barth, *Ethnic Groups and Boundaries.*

8   Barth, *Ethnic Groups and Boundaries.*

9   Jane Guyer points out that economic niches in Africa are inherently productive, functioning to permit people to make a living. Guyer, *An African Niche Economy.* See also Guyer, *Marginal Gains.*

10 Davidson, "The Ancient World and Africa," 31–33.

11 Silva Andrade, *Les îles du Cap-Vert.*

Mixed heritage and a strong sense of self allowed the internal struggles with identity that existed in higher-level colonial rhetoric to work for the immigrants as they committed themselves to the protection of their niches.[12] Cape Verdeans were driven by the urgencies of emigration from a context that offered them little. So successful were they that, at the height of colonialism in 1935, a Dakar administrator asserted that to be a painter and Cape Verdean were one and the same.[13]

Dakar's Immigrant Communities in Contrast: Cape Verdeans and Lebanese

The Cape Verdean community of colonial Dakar was an immigrant community. In the historiography of this capital city, many discussions of immigration from abroad have concerned Lebanese rather than Cape Verdeans. The reasons for this complement the argument about the nature of Cape Verdean insertion in Dakar and thus it warrants a brief turn into the prominence of Lebanese immigrants in the history and the historiography of Dakar. Lebanese were very much wrapped up in the colonial trading economy. Acting as merchants, shopkeepers, and creditors, they were also active in the groundnut production zones of Senegal. From 1920, the rising position of Lebanese in the colonial trading economy and their ability to adapt to local conditions in cash crop zones frustrated French traders. Pressure rained down from French commercial interests on the state for protectionist policies, and French stakeholders waged slur campaigns in the colonial media against Lebanese during the Depression. While largely fruitless, the prominence of those dynamics has reverberated in the framing of Lebanese immigrants to Senegal.[14]

The space Cape Verdeans occupied was quite different, and this is reflected in the literature on immigration to Dakar. Although a growing literature exists on the Cape Verdean diaspora more broadly, very little work discusses the community in Senegal, where Dakar was the principal place of settlement.[15] The blue-collar economic activities of Cape Verdeans were

---

12 Guyer, *An African Niche Economy*; Guyer, *Marginal Gains*; Barth, *Ethnic Groups and Boundaries*.

13 Letter from the governor-general of FWA to the administrator of the Circumscription of Dakar, March 9, 1935, ANS K161(26).

14 O'Brien, "Lebanese Entrepreneurs in Senegal"; Bierwirth, "Initial Establishment of the Lebanese Community in Côte d'Ivoire."

15 Carreira, *People of the Cape Verde Islands*; Wils, "Emigration from Cape Verde"; Batalha, *Cape Verdean Diaspora in Portugal*; Batalha and Carling,

nonthreatening to French commercial lobbyists, sparing them the venom of the Chamber of Commerce. Just as important was the cultural and racial place Cape Verdeans held in a colony that had a history of *métissage* and local political activity dominated by mixed-race Senegalese until 1914.[16] Creole and Catholic, Cape Verdeans shared certain attributes of a certain privileged guard in Senegal, but as wage laborers in the service of Europeans, they also shared affinities with local Africans. It was in that unique spot that Cape Verdeans had a near neutrality in the colonial urban socioeconomic and political landscape that the Lebanese never enjoyed. Moreover, a more broadly Portuguese creole presence on the West African coast had deep historic roots. Over more than three centuries, Portuguese agents had contact with coastal West Africa, and a class of creole traders evolved before Europe's other powers had any significant colonial control there.[17] From the 1400s through the 1600s, fluidity existed not only in the physical movement of people between the Cape Verde archipelago and the mainland but also in ideas about race and identity.[18] Thus, unlike the sudden large wave of Lebanese immigration in the 1920s, building on foundations established forty years prior that seized the attention of French stakeholders and since fed into the historical literature on Dakar, earlier systems of movement in this region of the Atlantic made Cape Verdean arrivals to Senegal in the nineteenth and twentieth centuries anything but conspicuous. Immigrants from Cape Verde slid quietly into niches that suited the economy of the new colonial capital and negotiated the new emphasis that modern colonial politics in FWA placed on race, origin, and identity. The paucity of material on Cape Verdeans in Dakar during its formative years reflects that historical process.

Transnational Archipelago; Carter and Aulette, *Cape Verdean Women and Globalization*.

16 The authoritative work on this is Jones, *Métis of Senegal*.

17 Rodney, "Imperialist Partition of Africa"; Brooks, *Eurafricans in Western Africa*; Pérez Crosas, "Des lançados aux expatriés"; Green, *Rise of the Trans-Atlantic Slave Trade in Western Africa, 1300–1589*; Ribeiro da Silva, *Dutch and Portuguese in Western Africa*.

18 Mark, "Religion, Identity, and Slavery in the Casamance"; da Silva Horta, "Evidence for a Luso-African Identity in 'Portuguese' Accounts on 'Guinea of Cape Verde'"; Green, *Rise of the Trans-Atlantic Slave Trade in Western Africa, 1300–1589*.

Movement from Cape Verde to Dakar: 1880s–1940s

Movement away from Cape Verde in the 1800s and 1900s was the result of Portuguese colonial policies and ecological conditions on the islands. Early in the nineteenth century, Portuguese settlers migrated west via the Atlantic, especially to Brazil.[19] Left with a population both mixed and composed largely of former slaves on the islands, Portugal's labor policies sought maximum use of its subjects in Cape Verde. The state funneled people toward colonies where it required laborers for properties doled out to settlers from Portugal. Meaning to create a strong settler presence in places like Angola and Portuguese Guinea,[20] the Portuguese state instituted a system of forced migratory labor. Policies such as these prompted greater numbers of Cape Verdeans to clandestinely leave the islands.[21] The development of the new capital of FWA, Dakar, jutting out into the Atlantic toward the archipelago, drew people seeking alternatives to life under the Portuguese regime.[22]

Equally significant were ecological factors in Cape Verde. Less verdant than Portugal's more southerly possessions, the volcanic islands were historically prone to drought and famine. Nature was not the sole culprit: the importation of goats during the early Portuguese colonial period, as well as the cultivation of certain cash crops, rapidly eroded the already delicate ecological viability of the Cape Verde islands.[23] A series of serious famines plagued the islands in the late nineteenth and early twentieth centuries, draining subsistence resources and agriculture's viability as a living for many.[24] An 1830 drought brought on a famine that killed one third of the population,[25] and there were significant rates of famine-related death in 1864, 1900, and 1921.[26] Emigration patterns followed those of drought and famine. The population of Cape Verde dipped around the turn of the

---

19 Cabral, "Les migrations aux îles de Cap-Vert."
20 Confidential note no. 1222, Service of Political Affairs, September 4, 1945, ANS K108(26).
21 See the relevant sections in Carreira, *People of the Cape Verde Islands*; Batalha, *Cape Verdean Diaspora in Portugal*.
22 For more detail, see Carreira, *People of the Cape Verde Islands*; Clarence-Smith, *The Third Portuguese Empire, 1825–1975*.
23 Foy, *Cape Verde*.
24 Carreira, *People of the Cape Verde Islands*; Patterson, "Epidemics, Famines, and Population in the Cape Verde Islands"; Davidson "The Ancient World and Africa"; Silva Andrade, *Les îles du Cap-Vert*; Batalha, *Cape Verdean Diaspora in Portugal*.
25 Foy, *Cape Verde*.
26 Davidson, "The Ancient World and Africa."

century to a low of 142,000 inhabitants in 1910 before rebounding slightly over the ensuing decade.[27]

Scattered employment and census records in Senegal provide insight into the presence of Cape Verdeans before standardized administrative procedures became the norm.[28] France formally settled Dakar, and the city remained small in comparison to older Saint-Louis, but already in 1875, a Dakar census listed two "Portuguese" men out of a total 295 people counted.[29] It noted both to be literate, a possible indication that these were emigrants of Cape Verde, where the catechism was integral to most people's lives and education was available to those outside the elite classes by the mid-nineteenth century.[30] In that burgeoning population that still numbered under nine thousand inhabitants by 1890,[31] immigration was already an element of Dakar. It picked up as the city became the capital of FWA and grew in size and population. Within the first decade of Dakar's new status, nearly two hundred Cape Verdean immigrants to the city were officially counted.[32] In 1908, when Dakar's population was still under twenty thousand, two hundred Cape Verdean immigrants constituted a small but visible presence.[33] Official statistics were certainly not comprehensive. Clandestine immigration was the most common kind for Cape Verdeans coming to Dakar, and such arrivals were not documented.[34]

From 1920 to 1926, Dakar received a little more than 5 percent of the islands' emigrants, but by 1927, its popularity as a destination rose. Second only to Portugal and the Azores, it was taking in 17.5 percent of those who left the archipelago.[35] The period from 1927 to 1945 saw nearly eighteen hundred emigrants from Cape Verde record their destination as Senegal,[36] with the bulk settling in Dakar.[37] In the mid-1930s, Dakar officials noted

27 Patterson, "Epidemics, Famines, and Population in the Cape Verde Islands."
28 Commune de Gorée, Salaires municipaux, 1889–1894, ANS 3G2/93. 8. Dakar Census, 1875, 3G2/127.
29 Dakar Census, 1875, 3G2/127.
30 Foy, *Cape Verde*; Davidson, "The Ancient World and Africa"; Silva Andrade, *Les îles du Cap-Vert.*
31 Seck, *Dakar.*
32 Carreira, *People of the Cape Verde Islands.*
33 Population statistics, Gorée, 1908, ANS 3G2/135. Of 1,387 listed, 135 were noted as foreigners.
34 Interview, Jose da Silva, Sicap-Baobab, Dakar, June 2012. Similarly, see Nelson Eurico Cabral, "Les Migrations aux Iles de Cap-Vert."
35 Carreira, *People of the Cape Verde Islands.*
36 Carreira, *People of the Cape Verde Islands.*
37 Batalha, *Cape Verdean Diaspora in Portugal.*

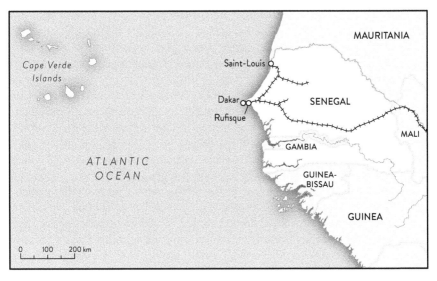

Figure 5.1. Senegal and surrounding region, with Cape Verde.

that the pace of immigration was a "constant progression."[38] Civil court records support this, with more Cape Verdeans appearing in cases from the mid-1920s to the early 1930s.[39] Movement to Dakar continued into the 1960s. The post-Second World War era brought great changes in mobility and rights in FWA, while Portugal retained oppressive colonial policies. Cape Verdean Dakarois who arrived during those years point to the importance of earlier immigrants in establishing foundations for the community.[40]

The Insertion of Cape Verdeans into the Colonial Capital

The colonial state's vision for Dakar influenced the types of opportunities available to Cape Verdean immigrants. The first was based on the growing capital's practical needs. Dakar was in need of significant expansion by the

---

38 Dakar et Dépendances, Rapport Politique, 1935, ANS 2G35/11.

39 See files ANS 5 M/210(184), 5 M/211(184), and 5 M/218(184) for the years in question.

40 Interview, Jose Da Silva, June 2012; interview, Jeanne Rodrigues, Sicap-Baobab, Dakar, June 2012; interview, Rosa Maria Delgado, Sicap-Baobab, Dakar, June 2012; interview, Camilla Guillerme, née Gomez, Sicap-Baobab, Dakar, July 2012; interview, Anna-Maria Gonzaga-Silva, Sicap-Baobab, Dakar, June 2012.

twentieth century if it was to fulfill the objectives the French state had laid out for it.[41] The physical process entailed numerous large-scale projects. Construction and public works projects brought a new demand for public works laborers, and men with experience in relevant domains were particularly desired. From the late nineteenth century into the first two decades of the twentieth century, those were sectors to which the local Lebu population did not yet flock.[42] The Lebu resisted certain types of employment in the earlier period of Dakar's expansion, seeking to maintain an economy of landowning, fishing, and small-scale farming.[43] There was little impetus for Lebu men to take jobs that offered less autonomy than that which they already enjoyed, especially before the population boom that began in the 1920s applied new economic pressure to them. The capital's autochthons were also committed to protecting their rights as *originaires* and to maintaining their roles in local urban politics. This sort of prominence, and the unique position they occupied vis-à-vis the French colonial state, caused administrators to seek workers from other regions for the manual labor needs in town.[44] Emigrants fleeing a dismal economic and political outlook in Cape Verde thus found room to work in Dakar. In 1917, for instance, officials faced a "small strike of two days" among African painters and carpenters at the Bouquereau and Leblanc companies and replaced the strikers with "Portuguese workers."[45]

It was not simply the void that created the opportunity. Possession of a preexisting skill set among some who had worked in the trades on the long-established Portuguese archipelago helped place Cape Verdeans in that labor space. Many Cape Verdean men who found work either already had training

41 Dakar's population remained under ten thousand throughout the nineteenth century, surpassing Saint-Louis's population only after the onset of major expansion projects begun in the later 1910s and early 1920s.

42 Interview with Jean-Paul Dias, Sicap-Baobab, Dakar, September 2007; interview with Antoine Dos Reis, Sacre-Coeur III, Dakar, September 2007.

43 Interview with Oumar Ba, Dakar, September 2007. Such immigrants could be from the regions of Senegal, West Africa, and further afield. Ba asserts that the early arrivals from the Futa Toro, for instance, entered easily into administration jobs because Lebu Dakarois originally did not want them. Margaret Peil makes this kind of argument about the availability of jobs to African migrants to cities in situations in which autochthons eschew certain roles. Peil, *Cities and Suburbs*, 272–74.

44 Letter from Adjoint des A.J. Aumont, Magasin du Ravitaillement, to Chef du Services des Affaires économiques, February 19, 1919, ANS K399(132).

45 Sénégal, Territoires d'administration directe: Rapport d'ensemble, 4e trimestre, 1917: Dakar, Gorée, Rufisque et Banlieue de Dakar, December 1917, ANS 2G17/26.

in trades such as masonry and painting, or were assumed to possess it.[46] They were known as masons and painters already familiar with European construction projects, and contractors sought them out. In Cape Verde, after the abolition of slavery and the institution of a formal education system geared at nonelites in the 1840s, the Portuguese colonial state established primary and, later, vocational schools.[47] In 1906, a vocational school opened that offered specialties in masonry, shoemaking, and painting, among other trades.[48] Formal training likely built on long-standing, informal experience in fields such as construction on Cape Verde, considering the number of projects that had required laborers and slaves since the sixteenth century. Prior to the rise of Dakar, Cape Verde was a major port, Atlantic fueling station, and export producer, requiring much earlier the type of manual labor that Dakar would eventually need.

Cape Verdeans exploited this reputation well in Dakar's colonial urban context. By drawing on the popular concept of preexisting experience, immigrants from the archipelago established themselves as niche workers—painters and masons from a place of origin where such trades had been long practiced and then taught. French employers recognized the ethno-economic niche as it emerged, especially since they saw the interior regions of Africa as unexposed to such "modern" skills. Labor in FWA prior to the 1930s was not a professionalized arena but rather intimately linked to taxation, or punishments assigned by the native code applied to non-*originaires*, and often was unpaid.[49] The idea that immigrant Cape Verdeans were "specialists" in the painting trade swiftly developed and was fully solidified in Dakar by the 1930s.[50]

Work and "Foreign" Identity: Cape Verdeans as Painting "Specialists"

Discussions among administrators in the 1930s revealed not only the prominence of Cape Verdeans in building and painting but also the difficulty officials

---

46   See also interview with Jose Da Silva, June 2012; interview with Bartholemy Guillerme, Sicap-Baobab, Dakar, July 2012; interview with Joe Lopes, Sicap-Baobab, Dakar, June 2012. See also Carreira, *People of the Cape Verde Islands*; Diop, "Tropical and Equatorial Africa under French, Portuguese and Spanish Domination, 1935–45"; Batalha and Carling, *Transnational Archipelago*.

47   Silva Andrade, *Les îles du Cap-Vert*.

48   Silva Andrade, *Les îles du Cap-Vert*.

49   Fall, *Le travail force en Afrique Occidentale française*.

50   Letter from the administrator of the circumscription of Dakar to the governor-general, no.148AG, 15 April 1939, ANS K142(26).

had in categorizing these Dakarois, who seemed to straddle the boundaries between native and foreigner, the latter typically implying European. One of the most revelatory exchanges took place in November 1934, and grew out of concerns over diplomatic relations with Portugal. Governor-General Brévié wrote to the administrator of the Circumscription of Dakar about a matter that had been brought to his attention by the French diplomat in Portugal. The governor of Portuguese Guinea had issued a decree stipulating that enterprises were to employ only Portuguese personnel, not foreigners.[51] The justification ostensibly was the need to address Portuguese unemployment, but FWA's governor-general saw the action as constituting a clear constraint on French regional economic interests. He responded by asking Dakar's administrator for statistics on the number and function of "Portuguese nationals" in his colonies and Dakar.[52] The information Chief Administrator Martine forwarded addressed Portuguese and other workers considered foreign in Dakar. It focused on large enterprises in public works, building, communications, shipping, and other areas integral to the colonial state and economy. Some businesses were French-owned and others foreign, and some had hundreds of foreign employees. Martine stated that a limit of 10 percent was generally fixed for the number of foreign employees an operation could have among its personnel.[53] This was the rule, "except in extraordinary circumstances, for instance, painting work."[54] He did not say specifically that these "foreign" painters were Cape Verdean.

It was Brévié who indicated in his reply to Marine that these foreign elements were Cape Verdean. He held Martine responsible for furnishing vague and inaccurate statistics on Cape Verdeans, the main object of his interest in the context of information received from the consul in Lisbon about new Portuguese policies. The governor-general was particularly dissatisfied with the statistics concerning a public works enterprise specializing in painting because they clearly underrepresented Cape Verdean employment, having noted only seven workers.

Brévié's response had much to reveal about the attitude the state meant to adopt. It clarified not only that painting was a "Portuguese" specialty but that the immigrants dominated the trade such that "all painters" were of that origin. His phrasing conveyed that this was well known to everyone in

---

51   Letter from the governor-general of FWA to the administrator of the Circumscription of Dakar, no. 175 Se/9, November 6, 1934, ANS K161(26).

52   Letter from the governor-general of FWA to the administrator of the Circumscription of Dakar, no. 175 Se/9, November 6, 1934, ANS K161(26).

53   Letter from the administrator of the Circumscription of Dakar to the governor-general of FWA, no. 47/AG, December 7, 1934, ANS K161(26).

54   Letter from the administrator of the Circumscription of Dakar to the governor-general of FWA, no. 47/AG, December 7, 1934, ANS K161(26).

Dakar and thus should have been clear in Martine's statistics. Martine then confirmed that these "Portuguese" indeed were all Cape Verdeans.

The discussion between Martine and Brévié brought to the surface the Cape Verdean immigrants' success in establishing a nearly impenetrable ethnically bounded economic niche that was integral to the constant public works going on in colonial Dakar. With Cape Verdeans clearly delineated as a distinct group with a precise occupation, newcomers from the archipelago had little problem inserting themselves into the work already associated with the identity with which they arrived. Some Cape Verdeans recount that they actually had little to no experience in areas such as painting but were quickly able to find work because other Cape Verdeans were already employed as painters; employers sought Cape Verdeans for their skills in that field.[55] Civil court records starting from roughly the 1910s and continuing into the mid-1940s confirm the association between Cape Verdean men and the painting and masonry trades.[56] "Public" knowledge about Cape Verdeans and the painting vocation, as discussed by Martine and Brévié, confirmed both the external recognition of the ethnic boundary and the productive import of the niche in colonial Dakar. Immigrants pinpointed fields on the productive side of the economy that were open in the earliest years of the city's growth, placed compatriots into them, and maintained an identity successfully attached to those niches.

While the exchange between Brévié and Martine demonstrates the pervasive presence of Cape Verdeans in the painting field, it also reveals the ambiguity surrounding these immigrant workers in terms of their status. To be a painter was to be Cape Verdean, but what did Cape Verdean mean? High-level administrators wavered between various terms, primarily "foreign," "Portuguese," and "native," in their efforts to categorize Cape Verdeans such that state policies could be applied to them. The typical categories the state employed to divide its urban population into discrete, legible units seemed to converge in this population of immigrants. It was unclear whether they were to be considered foreigners in the traditional sense, like other Europeans, which might imply a status superior to local African populations the state called natives, or if they were to be considered natives. More than a rhetorical dilemma, the issue was important if employers were to keep track of quotas for foreign workers and enact policy.

---

55   Interview with Jose Da Silva, June 2012; interview with Bartholemy Guillerme, July 2012; interview with Joe Lopes, June 2012.

56   For instance, ANS 5 M/211(184), ANS 5 M/218(184), ANS 5 M/230(184), ANS 5 M/231(184), ANS 5 M/233(184), and ANS 5 M/259(184). These dossiers contain a number of references to masons and painters of Cape Verdean origin.

When the issue originally surfaced during the economic crisis of the early 1930s, the governor-general had circulated among his lieutenant-governors and the administrator of Dakar a confidential letter instructing restriction of the number of foreigner workers to 10 percent. The definition of "foreign workers," the governor-general explained in 1932, applied to those who were "neither citizens, nor subjects, nor French protégés [populations of regions under French protection]."[57] By the end of the decade, Governor-General Cayla and his subordinates were still debating the definition, having to account for various immigrant populations such as Lebanese and Cape Verdeans, as well as those from Europe and further afield, in order to properly regulate quotas. The need for more precise definitions arose as they considered the possibility of a more generous quota of 15 percent. Such an increase would accommodate foreign workers in "certain specialties" considered particularly necessary.[58] These workers were Cape Verdean painters, as Brévié and Martine had shown.

In this next round of discussions, Cayla clearly saw Cape Verdeans as foreigners, prompting him to seek a higher quota for foreigners overall. The administrator of Dakar disagreed. There was no need for a more generous quota because the immigrants did not constitute "foreigners" in the same way non-French Europeans did. Increasing the quota would yield more competition for French nationals and *originaires*, and there was no need to permit more foreigners if the labor specialty Cayla had in mind was painting. To increase the quota for the sake of Cape Verdeans was to miss the point altogether, Dakar's head official explained, because for all intents and purposes they were natives. These immigrants differed from others, he asserted: their place of origin was African, their standard of living mirrored that of local Africans, and they worked in a niche people of French status would never occupy.

> It does not seem necessary to me, at least for the moment, to regulate native foreign labor. Laborers of this type are in essence specialized laborers and their proportion is minuscule; thus, the natives of Cape Verde who, having the identical standard of living as that of the natives of the Circumscription, cannot, in my opinion, be assimilated to Europeans and be covered by the legislation intended for foreigners.[59]

---

57   Confidential letter from the governor-general of FWA to the secretary-general of the governor- general, lieutenant-generals, and the administrator of Dakar, August 11, 1932, ANS K142(26).

58   Note from the Director of Finance to the Director of Political and Administrative Affairs, on "employment of foreigners," May 3, 1939, ANS 142(26).

59   Letter from the administrator of Dakar to the governor-general of FWA, no. 148/AG, April 15, 1939, ANS K142(26).

By differentiating between "native foreign labor" and "foreigners," he revealed a number of things. The first was that the "foreigner" category now explicitly excluded anyone of African heritage from sub-Saharan Africa. Although Dakar's top administrator pointed to standard of living as the key difference between Cape Verdeans and other foreigners, race was the key notion inherent to his assertions. The French colonial press often pointed to the ability of Lebanese immigrants to live just as Senegalese did in rural areas and even consume the local diet.[60] But Lebanese were never considered anything other than foreigners. Also clearly counted in the foreigner category in Dakar population records were Moroccans, Algerians, Vietnamese, and non-Europeans. If Cape Verdeans were confirmed as "Portuguese" or "foreigners," there could be wider implications concerning race and identity.

These comments confirmed the understanding of most administrators that labor was a native occupation. The blue-collar work Cape Verdeans performed was not the kind of work in which foreigners engaged. Lebanese were merchants, and most Europeans came to the colony for trading purposes or to work for the colonial state. Acknowledging the Cape Verdean prominence in certain laboring fields in essence bound them to those labor categories in such a way that seemed to preclude Cape Verdean economic activity in other realms. In Martine's 1934 prescriptions for retaliation against Portugal's new foreign worker policies, he pointed out that France could act against Portugal's "natives" through the simple act of requiring an immigration deposit.[61] This was enough to arrest such immigration because, although most foreigners could easily afford a deposit, poorer Cape Verdeans could not. Of course, the foreign designation could not be completely removed: by adding the term foreign to native in referring to Cape Verdeans, France potentially could use them as pawns in political maneuvering with Portugal.

This made clear how firmly Cape Verdeans had held on to their niche in the painting trade. Even while administrators struggled to pinpoint Cape Verdean legal status, which was entirely bound up in race, they recognized the key roles members of this community filled in the urban economy. Obvious in this and other correspondence on the application of policies regarding foreigners to Cape Verdeans was that race needed to conform to the economic priority at hand. In the context of such ill-defined policies, Cape Verdeans thrived by crafting a cohesive community that both defied categorization and became integral to the local economy. Cape Verdeans had established a niche-related boundary that allowed those within it to operate

---

60   "L'AOF, colonie syrienne: Comment opère un commerçant syrien," *Le Courrier Colonial*, January 14, 1938, ANS 1Q322(77).

61   Letter no. 47AG in response to Circular no. 432 Se/9, December 7, 1934, K161(26).

as a unit.[62] The outside defined those inside the boundary as it required. An example of this can be found in documentation collected in 1939 from local employers in Dakar regarding their employees. The form divided personnel into three categories—European, native, and imported. For the last, the employer was to designate the place of origin. Most employers simply left the "imported" column blank, or labeled it "nothing," writing instead that all labor was recruited on site and within the Circumscription of Dakar. One entity, the Hôtel du Palais, made particular note of Cape Verdeans, placing them in the "imported" category. One was marked as a "qualified worker" and explicitly labeled to be Cape Verdean.[63] The Hôtel du Palais was the exception. Most employers did not recognize the "imported" category. "We do not understand what 'imported' means; all of our personnel are recruited on site," the manager of Biscuterie noted.[64] It was up to the employer to categorize employees, and clearly the options the state provided could be nebulous at best.

Work and "Whiteness": Occupations outside the Trades

The reports of employers and colonial officials in Dakar eclipsed in many ways the creole background of Cape Verdean immigrants as well as the internal perspectives of the community regarding its own identity. Employment of Cape Verdeans outside fields such as painting—which was often attached to state entities and thus to official rhetoric on the immigrants and their status—helps shed light on the latter. Cape Verdeans were prominent in several services that catered to private Europeans in the city. By the same decade in which they were known as specialists of the painting trade, Cape Verdeans had acquired a nearly equal standing in domestic service for French households and in grooming for European men.[65] As in the trades, the idea of previous exposure in the Portuguese context of Cape Verde carried weight in these occupations. But domestic work and barbering carried with them deeper cultural implications: there was the expectation of training in a previous colonial context as well as of firsthand knowledge of European habits and culture. In a colonial setting in which France sought to siphon off a European urban world from the African city, French residents found the existence of a corps of semi-assimilated—even partially "white"—service staff desirable. By virtue of a historic creole background, Cape Verdeans

---

62   Barth, *Ethnic Groups and Boundaries.*
63   Foreign labor, lists submitted to the state, 193, K257(26).
64   Foreign labor, lists submitted to the state, 193, K257(26).
65   Batalha and Carling, *Transnational Archipelago.*

potentially had cultural attributes that made them appear preferable as barbers, shoemakers, housekeepers, cooks, and laundresses for the French.

The particular history of the Cape Verde islands made it possible for immigrants to propose services in which a sort of understanding of European ways on the part of the employee was implicit. The Portuguese colonies knew a deep history of *métissage*, and Cape Verde was the site of a centuries-long evolution of strong creole identity.[66] That creolization was not limited to Portugal—in fact, as Genoese and Spanish seafarers came into early contact with the islands as they sought out opportunities outside Europe.[67] Cape Verde's small size and more arid climate, compared with tropical colonies such as Guinea or Angola, allowed for a strong European presence on the ground.[68] A local creole culture evolved as a result of the impact of long-term frontline involvement in the Atlantic system. In later iterations of its colonial rule, Portugal demonstrated a commitment to assimilation among certain classes.[69] The adherence to monogamy, practice of Catholicism, preferences for Western dress and household management, and integration of European culinary elements into local cuisine constituted shared elements among Cape Verdean and French Dakarois.[70] It followed, then, that occupations related to these identity markers could become specialty niches for Cape Verdeans.

Domestic service was the most common option for Cape Verdean women in Dakar from the early moments of migration through the 1960s. Records of civil disputes contain numerous references to "Portuguese" women in such positions, and oral testimony and collective memory alike reiterate that Cape Verdean women served most commonly in French homes.[71] Cape

---

66   Meintel, *Race, Culture, and Portuguese Colonialism in Cabo Verde*; Lobban, *Cape Verde*; Fikes, "Emigration and the Spiritual Production of Difference from Cape Verde."

67   Green, *Rise of the Trans-Atlantic Slave Trade in Western Africa, 1300–1589*.

68   Green, *Rise of the Trans-Atlantic Slave Trade in Western Africa, 1300–1589*.

69   Davidson, "The Ancient World and Africa"; Mark, *"Portuguese" Style and Luso-African Identity*; Fry, "Undoing Brazil."

70   This idea also emerges clearly in the statements that appear in certain cases involving Cape Verdeans in the Tribunal de Première Instance de Dakar. In a 1932 record, one Cape Verdean complainant asked for state intervention in a family matter, citing his Catholicism as evidence of his commitment to marriage and contrasting it with what he asserted was the Muslim preference for divorce. ANS 5 M/224(184). See also Silva Andrade, *Les îles du Cap-Vert*.

71   For instance, ANS 5 M/205(184), ANS 5 M/211(184), ANS 5 M/218(184), ANS 5 M/230(184), ANS 5 M/231(184), ANS 5 M/233(184), and ANS 5 M/259(184). These dossiers contain a number of references to such jobs as laundresses and housekeepers of Cape Verdean origin.

Verdean women who recount the histories of their own experiences in Dakar and those of family members who preceded them imbue into their testimony the notion that domestic service for French households was a given fact.

Explaining why Cape Verdean women so easily found employment in private French homes, informants provide two lines of reasoning, both fully focused on identity. Cape Verdean women arrived with household habits more akin to Europeans than to Africans, and French employers sought them out for that reason. Emphasis on that point varies from one informant to another, with those drawn from more middle- and upper-class families of Cape Verde affirming that they had established a repertoire of domestic skills at home before immigrating to Dakar.[72] Even women who profess to have learned on the job assert their cultural identities predisposed them to understanding the needs of European domestic work.[73] Adeptness in handling Western clothing, which immigrant staff already wore and even made for themselves, is often cited among former domestic servants of Cape Verdean origin. Appreciation of the importance of wine at the table, and expertise in the preparation of pork, for instance, featured among the reasons Cape Verdeans were popular among French employers. Forbidden by Islamic law, consumption of alcohol and pork would not have been common to the habits of many local Africans, except those drawn from southern areas such as Casamance. Indeed, the female domestic service field was filled with women from that region of Senegal just as it employed the majority of Cape Verdean women.

The second reason emphasized in personal oral histories is similar in its emphasis on identity but is infused with a much greater colonial politic of race. Cape Verdean women argue that local African women lacked not only the proper exposure to European ways but also the propensity toward European standards of cleanliness needed to be desirable as domestics.[74] The overt references to cultural difference present in oral testimony in many ways echo the attitudes of the colonizer itself, suggesting that employment in French homes, where exposure to colonial attitudes toward local Africans likely circulated freely, might have yielded certain facets of self-perception and self-definition among Cape Verdean domestic servants. As a small immigrant community confronted with hefty competition from Senegalese, Malian, and Guinean women for domestic jobs, Cape Verdean women required a useful

---

72   Interview with Camilla Guillerme, July 2012.

73   Interview with Rose Maria Delgado, June 2012; interview with Camilla Guillerme, July 2012.

74   Many informants implicitly suggested this when speaking, as if to assume there was information known to the researcher and the informant not needing explanation. Others stated it outright in speaking about their work. Interview with Rose Maria Delgado, June 2012; interview with Camilla Guillerme, July 2012.

boundary to protect their particular niche within that field. Unlike in the painting field, in which Cape Verdean men found themselves the beneficiaries of a "native" classification that spared them the consequences of quotas on foreigners, in the domestic service field, Cape Verdean women relied on an identity that allowed for employment in "native" fields but gave them a special edge. They emphasized their mixed European heritage to oppose themselves to local Africans and create a connection that was close enough to French women to yield a privileged place in domestic service employment. Cape Verdean women make no claims to being European, as that would have erased the employment opportunity altogether and effaced the creole heritage Cape Verdeans value.[75] The ethnic boundary was positioned as a delicate but strategic liminal space for the optimal economic result.

In a similar vein, Cape Verdean women also account for hard work in their success, asserting that their local African counterparts appeared less dedicated. Their explanations, however, show that the dynamics of movement of the colonial era rather than propensity toward work played the major role in the ways household staff of different origins kept employment. Informants state that Cape Verdean servants enjoyed longer periods of employment with their households; African women were taken on and let go more frequently, Cape Verdean testimony tends to hold. Indeed, court records from 1914 to the mid-1940s attest to the significant transience that existed among African domestic staff. While the reason commonly provided by interviewees is a difference in the quality of work, the nature of the circumstances in which various workers came to colonial Dakar is the more convincing one. Operating on the basis of *refoulement* from the 1910s to the mid-1940s, the French administration consistently sought to avoid permanent installation of nonautochthonous Africans in the city. In addition, Africans had their own understandings of Dakar's utility, accessing it as they saw fit for generating income. Transience was embedded in the capital's identity, and Africans whose social and economic networks stretched into nearby regions built it into their work and residence patterns. It was less common for African workers from Dakar's hinterland to stay as long as Cape Verdean immigrants because migration between town and home was much easier for the former.

As Cape Verdean women installed themselves in domestic occupations in which they could market special knowledge and skills based on ethno-cultural criteria, their husbands and brothers entered jobs in which they could capitalize on the French colonial context. Alongside labor in construction and public works, men worked as barbers. French and African clients sought out

---

75 One informant made this view clear by asserting that local work was open to Senegalese and, thus, "if you want to work, you need to be Senegalese"; interview with Jeanne Rodrigues, June 2012.

Cape Verdean barbers, and European men assumed Cape Verdeans to possess a certain understanding of "white" hair compared to their local African counterparts.[76] The simple label "Portuguese" that the French assigned to such immigrants *sounded* European, opening up the interpretation that Cape Verdeans might be more capable of grooming French customers than local African barbers. Many Cape Verdean barbershops were in central Dakar, the zone of European residence and activity, centered in a grid of streets not far from the governor-general's palace and Dakar's main square.[77] From the 1920s through the 1940s, when the majority of customers with income for formal grooming services was European, Cape Verdeans were able to establish higher prices and create a perception of quality around their services.

These types of work all hinged on some idea of "Europeanness," an element of Cape Verdean identity that French administrators sought during the very same time period to minimize in debates about labor. There was a subtext of cultural understanding, if not affinity, running through the firm hand Cape Verdeans were able to place on barbering and domestic service. If the assumption was that ability and habit grew out of familiarity more than training, then Cape Verdeans required an ethnic identity that implied such ability and habit, allowing them to rise within the niche over Africans who could not make equal claims to qualification no matter what level of experience was involved. If adequately distanced from local Africans and just close enough to Europeans merely in terms of identity, Cape Verdeans could assure themselves a continual source of income despite their small size as a community and their immigrant status.

---

76   The most valuable comments came from an interview with Rosa Maria Delgado, June 2012, who spoke not only of her husband but also male relatives. All other formal and informal conversations with Cape Verdeans took the barbering trade as a given fact, even when interviewees had not entered the occupation. Researcher inquiries among Senegalese in Dakar's downtown city center as to where Cape Verdean pockets could be found nearly always led to a small quadrant of streets on which Senegalese said "Cape Verdean barber shops" historically had been located. Another American researcher, discussing the material, noted that in his own inquiries about where to get his own hair cut, he was directed by locals to Cape Verdean barbers because of their ability to cut "European" hair.

77   ANS 5 M/154(184) contains an entry that shows a "Cape Verdean shop" to exist on the corners of Rue Vincens and Rue Victor Hugo, the area to which I was often directed. See also Monteiro, *Manel d'Novas*.

Community in Distinctiveness

However much French perceptions of Cape Verdeans contributed to the creation and maintenance of economic opportunities, the internal workings of the immigrant community in the colonial capital were central to the endurance of the Cape Verdean presence and identity in town. Just as Lebanese immigrants employed far-reaching networks of credit and kinship ties, Cape Verdean immigrants relied on family members and employment niches to thrive in Dakar. In the same manner as they procured employment, Cape Verdeans also resided together. Households of mixed generations and extended family were common.[78] Urban court records show that complaints involving Cape Verdeans very often involved Cape Verdean neighbors.[79]

Among the mixed neighborhoods of Africans, Cape Verdeans, Lebanese, and Europeans downtown that developed even after the state's effort in 1914 to eliminate local African enclaves there, identifiable Cape Verdean enclaves existed in forms ranging from a single building to several blocks. The administration did not actively seek out the segregation of Cape Verdean immigrants as it did vis-à-vis local Africans. As downtown became increasingly expensive, and as the Medina expanded dramatically with the consistent influx of Africans to Dakar during the 1920s and 1930s, Cape Verdeans established themselves in the neighborhoods roughly between the two. The quarters just south of the broad avenue the colonial administration had designated as a *cordon sanitaire* between Dakar's center and the Medina became popular among Cape Verdean city dwellers.[80] It is key to note that the state never insisted on applying a native identity to them in matters of

---

78   ANS 5 M/230(184); ANS 5 M/219(184); ANS 5 M/264(184).

79   There are a number of cases of this nature in the 5 M collection. For clear examples, see Semedo v. Lopez, June 15, 1943, and Viegas v. Da Silva Vaz, April 22, 1943, both in ANS 5 M/265(184).

80   Rebeusse, located just south of Avenue Malick Sy and north of central Dakar and the Sandaga market, is a neighborhood known to have housed Cape Verdeans in the earlier parts of the twentieth century up to the 1960s. Later, a nearby "cité" was developed that might have been linked to Cape Verdean presence. The cité was a housing development the state planned for workers in the 1940s and realized by the late 1950s. Whether its name was derived from the heritage of Cape Verdean workers in the area or from Dakar's Cap-Vert placement is unclear. The Dakarois who submitted official requests for housing there were of all origins. See ANS 4P 2992–4P 2997, all on the "Cité Cap-Verdienne" in Dakar. References to the "Cité Cap-Verdienne" in scholarly literature on Dakar are rare and nebulous at best. It appears most commonly in Senegalese-generated work on topics addressing urban spaces and society, but even in those instances it is taken as common knowledge. On its status as an

housing regulation. Being able to keep the community essentially downtown facilitated convenient employment with well-heeled Europeans, who were concentrated in the city center.

As success solidified among immigrants, the community grew. The short distance between the archipelago and the Senegalese coast also permitted established immigrants to go back for children and other relatives, building the community steadily over time and maintaining a strong sense of connection to Cape Verde. The relatively easy maritime passage also made the trip less of a risk and investment than passage from more distant places of origin, especially as many Cape Verdean men had seafaring experience.[81] In some cases, very successful Cape Verdeans acquired vessels and ran the passage, facilitating the arrival of more immigrants to Dakar.[82] Cape Verdeans worked in wharf operations and ship supply, making it even easier to participate in the transportation of immigrants to Dakar, often clandestinely.[83] A 1935 letter from the governor-general of FWA to the administrator of Dakar asked that official to supply more information on "foreign natives" employed in such fields, and by the start of the Second World War the French state kept track of Cape Verdeans who had come to own maritime companies operating in Dakar.[84] Such internal support structures deepened the sense of solidarity among Cape Verdeans in Dakar even as they integrated into the socioeconomic and cultural spaces outlined by the city's French masters and its African majority population.

The exercise of community did not just occur in the act of migration and the acquisition of work. In the eyes of the French colonial state, as well as those of Cape Verdeans themselves, a clear element of unique identity resided in its activities outside of work. Descendants of Cape Verdean immigrants stress the attachment immigrants maintained to cultural expression and religion. In colonial Dakar, those characteristics distinguished Cape Verdeans from the largely Muslim, Wolof-speaking neighbors around them. They celebrated religious rites and festivals visibly and with enthusiasm, and drink was often part of such moments.[85] Cape Verde had a historical connection to the production of alcohol, of which the primary product was

---

old Dakar neighborhood, see, for example, Tombon-Biaye, "Les Initiatives des Jeunes dans la Lutte contre la Pauvreté Urbaine à Dakar," 30.

81 Interview with Joe Lopes, June 2012; interview with Jose Da Silva, June 2012.

82 Interview with Jose Da Silva, June 2012.

83 Interview with Jose Da Silva, June 2012.

84 Letter from the governor-general to the administrator of Dakar, March 9, 1935, ANS K161(26); list of "Foreign Businesses in Dakar," December 29, 1939, K108(26).

85 Interview with Jean-Paul Dias, September 2007; interview with Antoine Dos Reis, September 2007.

grogue, a sugar-based liquor.[86] Celebrations flowed into streets, music was abundant, and events were often communal rather than limited to single households.[87] Informants celebrate the lively and jovial reputation their grandparents and great-grandparents acquired, pointing to the loud festivals as signifiers of the preservation of their heritage in the urban environment that counted diverse expressions of religion. These public displays, for which Cape Verdeans became known, were part of the social space they created as unique among Africans and Europeans.

Colonial documentation attests to public displays of culture and community that set Cape Verdeans apart from local Africans in particular. Alcohol was an element in this. As noted above, Cape Verdean female informants place value on their comfort with alcohol since it facilitated employment in French households, where wine was counted in the state's calculation of salary allowances for white employees.[88] Police records from the 1920s into the 1940s contain very regular entries on Cape Verdeans stopped for excesses of drink, public brawls, and nighttime disturbances, typically in the form of noise or music.[89] A number of court records from the same decades also hold evidence of such tendencies.[90] The prominence of Cape Verdeans in those misdemeanors was in part due to the Muslim prohibition of alcohol. Unlike in the urban areas of central and southern Africa, alcohol was not a staple feature of African society in much of Senegal. This made for fewer instances of drinking among local Africans, although the latter were far from absent in police records for such infractions. French authorities described Cape Verdeans who were brought before police for issues ranging from brawls to running illegal bars as a nuisance.[91] In 1935, an admin-

---

86   Silva Andrade, *Les îles du Cap-Vert.* The spirit was also offered to me at inter-
     view sessions as part of the social aspect of our exchange in Cape Verdean
     homes. Food considered typical of Cape Verdean cuisine also was offered and
     discussed at interview meetings.

87   For example, cases involving Cape Verdeans in ANS 5 M/211(184), ANS 5
     M/219(184), ANS 5 M/229(184), and ANS 5 M/233(184).

88   Inspector of Colonies, Report on the Standard of Living of natives in the
     Circumscription of Dakar, February 4, 1939, and Response of the Governor-
     General to the Report of Inspector of Colonies, ANS 4G/107(105).

89   ANS 5 M/154(184); ANS 5 M/155(184); ANS 5 M/157(184). Records in
     files such as these contain many instances of public drunkenness and alterca-
     tions between Cape Verdean Dakarois.

90   ANS 5 M/210(184); ANS 5 M/219(184); ANS 5 M/233(184).

91   Numerous police and surveillance reports bear witness to this. For example,
     see deportation lists from June 3, 1941, ANS K108(26). See, for example, the
     admonishment of authorities after receiving a case involving a local quarrel in
     September 1934, ANS 5 M/233(184). See also comments about the Cape

istrator noted that Cape Verdean "behavior frequently require[d] police intervention."[92] By the later 1930s, the Security Service brought deportation requests for those who operated illegal alcohol sales.[93]

It was common for Dakar's security and political affairs officials to weave into their reports general observations on the local population, and indeed annual reports included sections on the various "populations" as they were active in town. During the Second World War, this was particularly important as wartime tensions and regime changes shaped state priorities and actions. The Vichy-controlled colonial government in Dakar during the first half of the war made surveillance a staple of its reporting system, and foreigners were under closer watch.[94] Although administration of the 1930s clearly had bent the rules concerning foreigners to maintain cheap Cape Verdean "specialized" labor by creating the concept of "foreign natives," by the middle of the war, the native emphasis had not subsumed the foreign element of that category. In its analysis of Dakar's local populations, the 1940 annual political report asserted that the "Portuguese, natives of the Cape Verde Islands and of Guinea, are only known to the police for their drunkenness, brawls, and some moral laxity."[95]

Far from a statement of fact, such a comment was nonetheless revelatory of the ways in which Cape Verdeans stood out, despite statements a few years prior that asserted how similar they were to local African populations. Cape Verdeans maintained a commitment not to a general creole heritage but to a Portuguese creole heritage. Gina Sánchez Gibau points out that "the colonial legacy of Cape Verde created a concomitant legacy of the promotion of one's Portuguese heritage over one's African heritage."[96] Dakar, and Senegal as a whole, knew a long history of *métissage* and had its own creole culture. Cape Verdeans did not assimilate to those groups; indeed, the immigrants created economic niches that were far removed from the realms of activity in which mixed-race Senegalese and many *originaires* historically had been prominent. In daily life, the standard of living Cape Verdeans shared with local Africans who might or might not have had *originaire* status did not translate into a shared culture. Transplantation of

Verdean community in Dakar et Dépendences, Annual Political Report 1940, ANS 2G40/1, and in the report five years earlier, Dakar et Dépendences, Political Report 1935, ANS 2G35/11.

92   Dakar et Dépendances, Political Report 1935, ANS 2G35/11.

93   Dakar deportation lists from June 3, 1941, ANS K108(26).

94   Renseignements politiques, Service de Sûreté, September to December 1943, ANS 17G/410.

95   Dakar et Dépendances, Annual Political Report 1940, ANS 2G40/1.

96   Gibau, "Cape Verdean Diasporic Identity Formation," 261.

cultural mechanisms of community that maintained the boundary was part of the immigration process.

Ambiguity, Stability, and the Transactional Culture of Dakar

Building on the labor roles they solidified for men and women across several sectors, Cape Verdeans continued to arrive in Dakar in the 1930s and 1940s. Their numbers rose "from 1,680 in 1939, to 1,756 in 1940," an increase "due to the regularization of certain situations as much as to the prolific qualities for which this race is well known."[97] Having carved out spaces within the fluid racial politics of Dakar, and governed by ambivalent colonial authorities who wavered in their approaches to foreigners and natives, Cape Verdeans grew from a tiny minority of specialists to an identifiable urban community. Ultimately, ambiguity had its advantages: the state's inability to firmly classify a contingent of the urban population potentially gave that group more options and yielded less pointed policies than those that could be aimed at communities whose status as foreigners or natives was undisputed. Immigrant status and the niches they occupied protected them well, making these city dwellers appear somehow preferable to others that might foster intrigue, especially since officials believed Dakar was a natural breeding ground for subversive ideas.[98] "Their loyalty is not doubted: workers with modest ambition (painters and masons, laundresses and nannies), they seem uninterested in politics, even at the local level," an administrator commented in 1940.[99]

Cape Verdeans became integral participants in Dakar's economy by occupying important labor niches valuable to the colonizer and attaching those niches to a unique identity to which only they belonged. They both exploited and overcame the label "foreigner," drawing on their particular Cape Verdean creole heritage and making themselves "specialists" in a new colonial context. Their immigrant status also afforded them a sort of stability that stood in contrast to the transience embedded in Dakar's local transactional culture.

Their experience was unique in Dakar in many ways, even if the ambivalence of the state was consistent across its efforts at categorization and control. Unlike Cape Verdeans, Lebanese Dakarois found the process of making

---

97 Dakar et Dépendances, Annual Political Report 1940, ANS 2G40/1.
98 Note de AP/2: "Détermination d'une politique de développement des grandes villes en AOF, Draft," June 9, 1934, ANS 21G/49.
99 Dakar et Dépendances, Annual Political Report 1940, ANS 2G40/1.

home in the city to be fraught with vocal critique and opposition that mobilized assertions about identity to sketch a predatory intermediary status. The gray space Cape Verdean immigrants came to occupy easily was cast by the French as innocuous, especially given the ways in which colonial officials understood themselves to require the presence of Cape Verdean wage workers in certain sectors. As Dakar expanded, utility was paramount and shaped projections of identity. As the next chapter will show, Lebanese immigrants faced a very different interpretation of that gray space, precisely because their insertion into Dakar's economic landscape was firmly by way of the transactional space that was primarily driven from below and responsive to local needs rather than through a path of wage labor controlled largely by the colonial state.

Chapter Six

The Lebanese and the Local in the Interwar Period

Foreigners, Intermediaries, Dakarois

Dakar attracted many immigrants from origins beyond sub-Saharan Africa—notably, those from Europe, North Africa, and the Levant. During the interwar period, the Lebanese became the most prominent—and most fiercely debated—immigrant, or "foreign," community in Dakar, as they established themselves in various parts of West Africa.[1] Over those decades, Lebanese Dakarois placed themselves in sectors that made them relevant to other city dwellers' needs and integral to the fabric of the city's transactional culture. The more locally entrenched the Lebanese became, the sharper became the external focus on their status as foreigners. It was the very ability of the Lebanese to harness local economic opportunities by serving the African clientele that not only made them integral to the urban sectors of retail and credit but also singled them out to the French. Their direct commerce with African communities generated hostility among French commercial stakeholders toward the Lebanese, especially during a time of global economic downturn.[2]

French business interests pointed most directly and aggressively to the role of Lebanese traders in rural areas, where the peanut trade was of great interest and importance to colonial commerce. However, the role of Lebanese merchants in Dakar was not fully understood or interpreted as

---

1   Akyeampong, "Race, Identity and Citizenship in Black Africa"; Bigo, "The Lebanese Community in the Ivory Coast"; O'Brien, "Lebanese Entrepreneurs in Senegal"; Leichtman, *Shi'i' Cosmopolitanisms in Africa*; Thioub, "Les Libano-Syriens en Afrique de l'Ouest de la fin du XIXe siècle à nos Jours"; Laan, "Migration, Mobility and Settlement of the Lebanese in West Africa."

2   Many of the works on the Lebanese in French West Africa point to the shifting attitudes toward the Lebanese, particularly the rising hostility that came about as the community became more established in commerce. Andrew Arsan, Chris Bierwirth, and Mara Leichtman, cited below, examine or refer to this in their respective works.

predatory in that way. The urban setting presented transactional options that were broad and often hidden. Like Cape Verdean Dakarois, Lebanese came to occupy a position in the colonial capital's transactional culture that was difficult for colonial administrators to classify. They operated in an economic space both French businessmen and administrators had neither truly grasped nor fully controlled, seen as neither European nor African. The state, but most frequently French commercial interests, turned to the notion of the *intermediary* to define the Lebanese. The concept of the intermediary as applied to the Lebanese in Senegal became infused with negative overtones for French stakeholders and, at times, the colonial state. The concept was a powerful one, as it appealed to the impulse to classify and know populations. In scholarship on the Lebanese in Senegal and other West African sites, the term *intermediary* has persisted as a descriptor of the community's role.[3] Yet, the notion of an intermediary role falls short in its ability to describe these dynamics as they involved Lebanese Dakarois. Far from serving as agents of the French in dealing with Africans or vice versa, the Lebanese were actors in their own right, and their interaction with other Dakarois had at its core the strategy of making the local scenario profitable and livable. Lebanese merchants, traders, and creditors were local actors embedded in equally local systems of economic interaction. At the level of the everyday transactional experience, Lebanese demonstrated the real possibilities of Dakarois to craft success in the capital city outside the parameters of French plans and paradigms.

Lebanese adeptness at inserting themselves into economic activities and networks generated French antagonism, and despite a position of relative privilege within the French colonial world after the fall of the Ottoman Empire, momentum grew among French business efforts to paint West Africa's Lebanese as predatory to Africans and damaging in relation to European commerce into the 1920s.[4] In Dakar, however, where a local transactional culture was emerging to both avoid and cope with the policies of the state, the insertion of Lebanese participants occurred beyond the economic space French interests occupied. That process entailed both reaching into African urban society and drawing on broad Lebanese social networks. Rather than placing themselves as intermediaries between one community and another, the Lebanese widened the scope of commercial activity in town. They located opportunities at the most local level, inserting themselves into the largely African transactional culture in ways French

---

3   See, for instance Bierwirth, "The Initial Establishment of the Lebanese Community in Côte d'Ivoire, ca. 1925-45"; Leichtman, "From the Cross (and Crescent) to the Cedar and Back Again"; Malki, "Competing Ontologies of Belonging."

4   Arsan, "Failing to Stem the Tide."

commerce considered outside the main poles of the urban colonial economy. Impressive Lebanese economic success in the capital, in conjunction with the decreasing profits colonial French commercial interests experienced during the Depression, infused that term with deleterious overtones.

In Dakar, Lebanese residents made space for themselves and thrived, contributing to the growing diversity of the capital in social and economic ways. If the Lebanese were intermediaries between Europeans and Africans in cultural or economic ways, this was difficult to discern in daily transactions. Everyday dispute and transaction records display a general lack of hostility among Dakarois toward the Lebanese, notable in light of the fact that court records already have a degree of antagonism built into them by virtue of the existence of a dispute. Lebanese Dakarois interfaced with each other, Africans, and Europeans along no particular pattern that would suggest such a defined role as an intermediary. The colonial city was accommodating of diversity both in the spaces the city allowed newcomers and innovators to fill and in the weakness of the colonial state's ability to prevent success among those it had not included in its plans. Examining the Lebanese in this framework of the city's dynamic transactional culture erodes the utility of the notion of the intermediary for understanding their place in colonial Dakar. It also highlights the importance of considering the most local level of the city's activity as opposed to examining only high-level rhetoric about it, since it is there that lives were carried out and long-term urban success was crafted.

Lebanese Immigration to Dakar

The Lebanese diaspora that spread out in West Africa was part of an important movement on a global scale, with enclaves in Europe, North America, South America, and Africa.[5] The end of the Ottoman Empire signaled a new era of movement. French and Lebanese sources understand the tangible beginnings of Lebanese migration toward West Africa to have begun with the French mandate in Syria following the close of World War I. September 1, 1920, saw the creation of Lebanon as a state under French oversight, and it was from Lebanon that the majority of immigrants to Senegal were drawn. France historically had a deeper degree of contact with and preference for the area's Christians, a minority population concentrated near Mount Lebanon.[6] That more heavily Christian region became the core of France's

---

5   Khater, *Inventing Home.*
6   Oliver-Saidi, *Le Liban et la Syrie au Miroir Français;* Leichtman, "Reexamining the Transnational Migrant."

creation of Lebanon in 1920.[7] While the Levantine population of Dakar came from various areas of Syria, it was from that location that a significant number originated, thus the Syrian population of Dakar from 1920 onward is more correctly termed Lebanese. Some did come from the state of Syria and were generally Muslim, as an observer in the press pointed out in the 1930s.[8] Even the Muslim population, however, was primarily Lebanese.

While some Lebanese had settled in Dakar prior to the 1920s, their numbers were relatively insignificant in comparison to those that followed France's assumption of the mandate. French authority in the Levant gave rise to new networks of mobility, primarily linking Lebanon to Marseilles, and from there to places further afield. Oral histories given by Dakarois of Lebanese origin do not discuss reasons for departure as much as explanations for landing in Senegal. Often, French West Africa was among the closer and most accessible destinations, especially as passage took place on French ships from Lebanon to Marseilles. In Marseilles, many hoped to reach the United States, but ended up on ships routed to Dakar.[9] This explanation surfaces in other studies, including a 1967 sociological examination of Lebanese in West Africa that invoked the saying, "the West Coast of Africa begins in Marseilles."[10] This was the case for various reasons, including application in Marseilles of stringent health requirements for immigration to the United

---

7   Leichtman, "Reexamining the Transnational Migrant"; Laan, *Lebanese Traders in Sierra Leone*.

8   ANS 1Q322 (77). This dossier contains a large and diverse collection of documents that archivists assembled for the common theme of dealing with foreigners. Citation of this dossier thus does not imply the use of a single document or even set of documents. Not all documents in the dossier are named. Where the name is obvious, it is noted. Otherwise, only the dossier is cited.

9   Interview with Samir Jarmache, Dakar, February 2008. Leichtman also notes this sequence of events as recounted by Lebanese in Senegal. Leichtman, *Shi'i Cosmopolitanisms*. It is worth noting here that some of the very same informants worked with me as had recently worked with Leichtman. The correspondences in the oral testimony are thus very strong. This chapter cites the interviews collected independently for this research but understands that there may be similar assertions in Leichtman's articles and her book. An effort is made to cite both. It is worth noting that when researchers request interviews with Lebanese informants, Dakarois tend to point to a core of prominent Dakarois of Lebanese origin who are accustomed to speaking about their heritage and place in local society. Leichtman also notes this in her works. Detecting this tendency, I tried to seek out less prominent Lebanese, but many preferred to refer me once more to those considered the guardians of local Lebanese history and heritage. A similar pattern emerges in requests for interviews among the Lebu.

10   Winder, "Lebanese in West Africa."

States, insufficient funds to reach the United States, or encouragement by French companies to instead seek out the opportunities of West Africa.[11]

The number of Lebanese residents in Dakar grew quite a bit over the 1920s and 1930s. Immigration to FWA from the Levant was increasing rapidly across the board, but Dakar's case was special. Most immigrants passed through Dakar to get to destinations elsewhere in the colony, but many ended up staying. Population statistics in colonial Africa are tricky to ascertain. From 1921 to 1931, the Lebanese population of Dakar increased 138 percent, as compared to the 70 percent increase outside the capital.[12] In 1921, there were 667 Lebanese in Dakar, and by 1931 the community had over 2,000 members. In 1934, when a large-scale census of the capital was performed, the state counted 2,445 Lebanese residents of Dakar.[13] The administration classified the Lebanese as white foreigners. At nearly 2,500 people, the Lebanese would have made up almost a full quarter of the so-called white population of Dakar, which was counted at 10,250. The report held the city's total population at over 76,000, the overwhelming majority of which was African.[14]

Those numbers, however, might have greatly underestimated the population statistics of the Lebanese and perhaps of the city as a whole. A 1924 communication noted that some business stakeholders estimated a Lebanese population of 2,500 in Dakar alone by that year—a good decade before nearly the exact same count came up in the census.[15] By the same vein, a confidential security report submitted in 1935 to the governor-general estimated the Lebanese population of Dakar at 3,900, noting that it had already passed 3,000 in 1931.[16] That report also showed that between 1923 and 1926, Lebanese immigration to FWA via Dakar was significant: 406 immigrants in 1923 were followed by 873 the next year.[17] The subsequent two

---

11 Winder, "Lebanese in West Africa."

12 Brissaud-Desmaillet, "L'Immigration Libano-syrienne en AOF." In the same dossier, a letter (no date) from Interim Governor-General Pierre Boisson to the Minister of Colonies notes that these statistics applied to the decade from 1921 to 1931, ANS 1Q322(77).

13 Tableau de la Population Générale de la Circonscription de Dakar, December 31, 1934, ANS 1Q322(77).

14 Tableau de la Population Générale de la Circonscription de Dakar, December 31, 1934, ANS 1Q322(77).

15 Communication no. 733, Direction des Affaires Politiques et Administratives, April 23, 1924, ANS 1Q322(77).

16 Sûreté Générale, "Note relative à la question de l'immigration syrienne" to the governor-general and cabinet director, September 13, 1935, ANS 1Q322(77).

17 Sûreté Générale, "Note relative à la question de l'immigration syrienne" to the governor-general and cabinet director, September 13, 1935, ANS 1Q322(77).

years each saw immigration exceeded by 700 in number. Those several years alone brought nearly 3,000 Lebanese through Dakar's port. Many sought lives in other towns or in rural areas, and many stayed in the city. March 1938 saw "massive immigration" of Lebanese to the colony, most of whom were in Dakar. The arrival of Lebanese immigrants "surpassed everything imaginable . . . some have called it an invasion," one administrator commented.[18] The city of Dakar had also grown dramatically, with an estimated 120,000 inhabitants by early 1938.[19]

The Anti-Lebanese Campaign of the Depression Years

The crux the rapid growth of Lebanese physical and economic presence in Dakar is that of the local. Descendants of immigrants explain the original arrival in West Africa as largely French-determined but emphasize that the subsequent success of the Lebanese lay in their ability to adapt to the local situation. They assert that their grandparents were able to create successful opportunities in town because they were flexible: they adopted certain elements of local African lifestyles and responded to the most local needs in the colonial urban economy.[20] Since French residents, commercial interests, and administrators were most concerned with the large-scale reach and impact of trade, urban development, or even broad cultural imports like language, they often overlooked the most local aspects of the city's daily workings. This was evident in all corners of urban management. The type of big-picture concern and reflection in which authorities engaged often had little to do with what was happening on the ground. Long and rehashed reflections on *refoulement* overlooked the many innovative ways Africans managed to remain in Dakar. Attempts to quell transience ignored the many different residential options Dakarois employed. Studies of salary and spending failed to take into account the deep networks city dwellers used to make money work for them. The persistent labeling of Cape Verdeans as anything other than Dakarois or Senegalese—"Portuguese" and "foreigners" among the most common—discounted the role of that long-standing community

---

18   Dakar et Dépendances, Police and Safety, Annual Report for 1937, March 1, 1938, ANS 2G37/33.

19   Dakar et Dépendances, Police and Safety, Annual Report for 1937, March 1, 1938, ANS 2G37/33.

20   Interview with Mr. Jarmache; interview with Dr. Bahroun, Plateau, Dakar, February 2008; interview with Mme. Darwiche, Hann, Dakar, February 2008. See also ANS 1Q322(77), Communication no. 733, Direction des Affaires Politiques et Administratives, April 23, 1924, for references to Lebanese adoption of an African lifestyle.

in building the city and enriching its diversity. It is no surprise, therefore, that the local was the most obscure perspective in the view of French state authorities and commercial officials. For all of Dakar's international connections, local needs and dynamics were still its driving forces, and the Lebanese were able to branch into those.

The prevailing attitudes among French authorities about who belonged in town rendered all but a select few as outsiders. "Foreigner" was broadly applied to a whole range of people in Dakar, and the Lebanese were among a larger cross section of "foreigners" that included Europeans, North Africans, Cape Verdeans, and Africans from British colonies. In fact, administrators often applied the term "colony" to each community, seeing them as discrete and disparate. A 1935 political report monitoring the activities of Dakar's Italian residents referred to the community as a "colony."[21] The Lebanese community was described similarly, as with the use of the "Libano-Syrian colony" of Dakar in a population report from the previous year.[22] The vocabulary of foreignness was applied to the Lebanese in many forms: "nationals," "foreigners," "immigrants," and "*protégés*" (people under French protection) were all used somewhat interchangeably in correspondence and reports on the local population and the place of the Lebanese therein.[23] It was difficult for administrators to come up with a consistent term to denote the growing community. Even the shift from "Syrian" to "Libano-Syrian" demonstrated the inexactness of the vocabulary they employed. What was most important to French stakeholders and officials was that the Lebanese were from elsewhere. Yet, emphasizing their foreign origins merely belied and perhaps even downplayed the depth with which the Lebanese became entrenched in the capital.

The distance between French stakeholders and the many economic corners of the colony, particularly its largest urban center, contributed to rising vocal opposition to the Lebanese that attempted to craft specific images of the community. In a context of economic crisis beginning in the later 1920s,

---

21   Dakar et Dépendances, Police and Safety, Annual Report for 1937, March 1, 1938, ANS 2G37/33.

22   Circonscription de Dakar et Dépendances, "Population—Tableau Recapitulatif de la Population Européenne," December 31, 1934, ANS 1Q322(77).

23   The examples are numerous throughout the archives. For these particular terms in documents employed here, see Letter from the president du conseil, minister of foreign affairs, to the minister of colonies, Direction des Affaires Politiques, April 23, 1932, ANS 1Q322(77); Sûreté Générale, "Note relative à la question de l'immigration syrienne" to the governor-general and cabinet director, September 13, 1935, ANS 1Q322(77); "Impressions recueillies sur le moral des populations européennes, indigènes," 1939–1940, ANS21G/150(108).

and as they failed to access the most intimate physical and economic spaces of the capital that the Lebanese were able to exploit, French—and some prominent African—voices employed the language of foreignness in their criticisms of the Lebanese. The onset of the Depression saw the birth of a massive campaign mounted by French commercial stakeholders against the Lebanese as French-owned businesses in FWA saw their profits and access to clients decline. Other studies have detailed the efforts by the Dakar Chamber of Commerce and French small businesses to cast the Lebanese as interlopers and foreigners who simultaneously took advantage of what was described as African foolishness as well as of French hospitality.[24] The mid-1930s were a time of prolific publication in local and colonial newspapers on the dangers of allowing the Lebanese not only to enter but to continue residing in FWA and its capital.[25] The language of such editorials and public letters was aimed at raising fear and resentment about the Lebanese, and it often reached vitriolic tones.

A series of articles that appeared in late 1937 and early 1938 in *Le Courrier Colonial* pursued this rhetoric in the harshest of terms. Qualifying Lebanese immigration as an "invasion," a December 24 installment asserted that "these Asians" succeeded in transforming themselves from "poor wretches" into "plush traders" after only a few years in FWA.[26] The same article referred to the newest Lebanese arrivals in Dakar as "dregs," the very lowest types of members of society.[27] The author referred to the family group as a "tribe," explaining the tendency for Lebanese men, after some time of working in the colony, to bring over wives and children.[28] The same article asserted that immigrants from the Levant lived in a "total and absolute absence of hygiene and comfort"—words that played on the French state sensitivity to public health risks that authorities saw as linked to non-European lifestyles. Publications like these often cited the willingness of immigrants to take on African habits as evidence of inferiority and inappropriate behavior in a context where France hoped to alter those very

---

24   Leichtman, "Reexamining the Transnational Migrant"; Leichtman, *Shi'i Cosmopolitanisms*; O'Brien, "Lebanese Entrepreneurs in Senegal"; Tarraf-Najib, "Une vieille histoire de familles"; Arsan, *Interlopers of Empire*.

25   See ANS 1Q322(77) for a large compilation of such newspaper articles. The state collected several dozen in its attempt to monitor and respond to the cries from the French small business lobby to expel the Lebanese.

26   "L'AOF, colonie syrienne," *Courrier Colonial*, December 24, 1937, ANS 1Q322(77).

27   "L'AOF, colonie syrienne," *Courrier Colonial*, December 24, 1937, ANS 1Q322(77).

28   "L'AOF, colonie syrienne," *Courrier Colonial*, December 24, 1937, ANS 1Q322(77).

habits. A diet of rice and onions, which were central to the local African diet, and a penchant toward learning African languages were other elements of what some public commentators termed the "Syrian" tendency to "live like the natives."[29] The analogy to Africans and use of terminology the French associated with Africans—"hygiene," "ignorance," "rice"—were tools of partisan attacks on the Lebanese presence in the colony and prominence in Dakar.[30]

The mid-1930s were not the first time such hostility surfaced, but it is the decade of its boiling over. In 1923, Governor-General Carde was already pointing to the potential problems the increase in Lebanese immigration could cause down the line. He had received complaints from the Chamber of Commerce about Lebanese encroachment on French small businesses, as well as statements from Lebanese notables in Dakar defending their activities and presence there. "It has become urgent to prevent the difficulties which will soon enough emerge," he declared to the minister of colonies in a December 27 letter detailing the local sentiment.[31] The assault he saw brewing indeed erupted a decade later, when anti-Lebanese propaganda circulated not only in Dakar but throughout FWA.[32] Even prior to that slur campaign, resentment had been steadily growing, and an administrator noted that there were some within French small business circles in Dakar that sought to blame the yellow fever epidemic of 1927–1928 on "Lebanese nationals."[33] The start of the Depression at the end of that decade opened the door to a deluge of attacks in print and official correspondence that lasted throughout the 1930s.

The government-general was not heavily swayed by the business propaganda. Even before the campaign, authorities had confronted the matter of the Lebanese status in FWA. The question of Lebanese presence in FWA and Dakar had existed since the time earliest immigration had begun, and the state saw early concerns voiced by the Chamber of Commerce as exaggerated.[34] Questions of citizenship and rights occupied the official mind more

---

29 "L'AOF, colonie syrienne: Comment opère un commerçant syrien," *Courrier Colonial*, January 14, 1938, ANS 1Q322(77).

30 "L'émigration syrienne en A.O.F.," *Dépêche Coloniale*, July 24, 1936, ANS 1Q322(77).

31 Letter from Governor-General Carde to the minister of colonies regarding "Immigration of Syrians in FWA," December 27, 1923, ANS 1Q322(77).

32 Sûreté Générale, "Note relative à la question de l'immigration Syrienne," September 13, 1935, ANS 1Q322 (77).

33 Sûreté Générale, "Note relative à la question de l'immigration Syrienne," September 13, 1935, ANS 1Q322 (77).

34 Sûreté Générale, "Note relative à la question de l'immigration Syrienne," September 13, 1935, ANS 1Q322(77); Communication no. 733, Direction

than debates about commercial practices and success. Correspondence in April and May 1932 between the minister of foreign affairs, minister of colonies, and Governor-General Jules Brévié addressed the question of legal status of immigrants from the French mandate in Lebanon and Syria to FWA.[35] The consensus was that no grounds existed for taking action to remove Lebanese in good standing from the colony. Not only was the presence of the Lebanese in FWA to be legally upheld, but Lebanese in the colony were *protégés* under the French mandate in the Levant and thus had the right to French protection, both diplomatic and administrative.[36] No difference was to be drawn in their access to such protection, nor to the right to conduct business in FWA.[37]

Lebanese Success in Dakar: Local Business

In reality, the economic activities in which the Lebanese were active posed little competition to French businesses. The Lebanese were slow to enter French-dominated commercial sectors in the colony, and commentators who defended them pointed out that the Lebanese were traditionally considered insignificant in their earnings.[38] By the time Lebanese economic activity gained momentum in the 1920s and 1930s, French commercial interests were fully involved in larger-scale operations based on the groundnut export economy, neglecting the expanding retail business in the capital to those willing to deal directly with Africans.[39] The kinds of businesses and storefronts Lebanese entrepreneurs opened in Dakar were primarily outside the orbit

---

des Affaires Politiques et Administratives, April 23, 1924, ANS 1Q322(77).

35   Correspondence between the minister of foreign affairs, minister of colonies, and governor-general of FWA, April–May, 1932, ANS 1Q322(77).

36   Letter from the minister of foreign affairs to the minister of colonies, April 23, 1932; Letter from the minister of colonies to the governor-general of FWA, Direction du Cabinet Militaire, Direction des Affaires Économiques, and Direction des Finances, May 10, 1932, ANS 1Q322(77).

37   Letter from the minister of foreign affairs to the minister of colonies, April 23, 1932; Letter from the minister of colonies to the governor-general of FWA, Direction du Cabinet Militaire, Direction des Affaires Économiques, and Direction des Finances, May 10, 1932, ANS 1Q322(77).

38   For the slow entry into higher-earning sectors, see Tarraf-Najib, "Une vieille histoire de familles," 321. For comments on the low earnings of many Lebanese merchants, see letter to the editor from Maurice Darchicourt, "La Question des Libanais et des Syriens," *Les Annales Coloniales*, March 9, 1937, ANS 1Q322(77).

39   Tarraf-Najib, "Une vieille histoire de familles," 324.

of French activity. While French commerce representatives complained of Lebanese competition, they rarely pointed out that small business in Dakar was hardly a French domain. In 1935, in a long letter to the administration about Lebanese competition, the Chamber counted four French barbers in Dakar versus thirteen "Syrian" barbers, and three French tailors versus eight Lebanese counterparts.[40] Meanwhile, of the forty-three coaches offering transport in Dakar, two belonged to "natives" and the remaining forty-one were owned by "Syrians."[41] Lebanese residents were coming to prominence in small, local retail in Dakar—they were the "masters of *petit commerce*," as one official phrased it in a 1935 analysis.[42]

The small-scale trade in which Dakar's Lebanese became "masters" was nearly entirely geared toward Africans, other Lebanese, and general non-European segments of urban society. Most Europeans in Dakar were employed by and involved with significantly larger-scale operations. A safety official pointed out in 1935, during the height of the anti-Lebanese campaign, that those large French companies did not employ Lebanese, and there were very few Lebanese commercial houses that had attained an importance such that they could pose competition to French interests.[43] The business landscape of interwar colonial Dakar was hardly dominated by Europeans. A breakdown of business licenses issued to Dakarois in 1935 showed Lebanese merchants has having received 1,481 licenses, while 1,208 were issued to French businesses. The great majority, however, were licenses obtained by Africans: 2,659.[44] Owning a business in the capital was not a European specialty. If Lebanese small business was growing, it was doing so in a context in which Africans—not Europeans—were most active. It was their insertion into the local, largely African transactional culture in the colonial capital that engendered both Lebanese success and stability there.

Lebanese merchants understood the demand for particular commodities in the urban African community. Among these were fabrics. The *procès-verbaux* contain many references to tailors and the transactions involving them, as well as to the use of credit to purchase fabric. They also contain a number of cases involving clothing orders or stolen clothing, and cases

40 Letter from the president of the Dakar Chamber of Commerce to the lieutenant-governor of Senegal, August 20, 1935, ANS 1Q322(77).

41 Letter from the president of the Dakar Chamber of Commerce to the lieutenant-governor of Senegal, August 20, 1935, ANS 1Q322(77).

42 Sûreté Générale, "Note relative à la question de l'immigration Syrienne," September 13, 1935, ANS 1Q322(77).

43 Sûreté Générale, "Note relative à la question de l'immigration Syrienne," September 13, 1935, ANS 1Q322(77).

44 Brissaud-Desmaillet, "L'Immigration Libano-syrienne en AOF," *Revue Économique Française* (1937), ANS 1Q322(77).

that entailed the purchase of fabric from Lebanese.[45] One case in 1934, for instance, was between a Lebanese shopkeeper who sold fabric and a tailor whose workshop was next door.[46] The matter was alleged theft. The store owner, having seen the tailor browse in his shop without buying, accused the latter of stealing a length of pricey fabric known as *basin*.[47] Police investigated and found no evidence that the tailor, Abdoulaye Dione, had committed any theft. Dione declared that he passed the shop of Taleb Derwiche, known locally as Ahmed, every day on his way to his workshop without a problem until that incident. The case reveals the place of fabric in local commerce, functioning as a motor of both sales and services. Fabrics were essential in the local transactional culture. They were often among the items that made up the bridewealth a husband offered a woman and her family.[48] Dakar's Lebanese businesses dealt quite a bit in fabrics, and local commercial knowledge came to understand them as major vendors of the commodity.[49]

Lebanese merchants also traded in *kola* nuts in Dakar. Like fabrics, *kola* was used in marriages and other ceremonies. Many Dakarois also chewed *kola* a daily basis, making it a staple product.[50] A number of cases brought to the Tribunal concerned or referenced *kola* commerce among Dakar's Lebanese. The purchase and sale of *kola* was also an activity in which a wide range of people participated—the *procès-verbaux* house evidence of women, Sierra Leoneans, Ivoirians, wage laborers in Dakar, Senegalese traders from the regions, and Lebanese all buying and selling *kola*.[51] It was a local business but also one that could draw on the multifaceted networks to which

---

45   See the following dossiers: ANS 5M/206(184); 5M/210(184); 5M/233(184); 5M/252(184); 5M/263(184); 5M/264(184); 5M/265(184); 5M/269(184); 5M/271(184).

46   Dione v. Derwiche, September 21, 1934, ANS 5M/233(184).

47   *Bazin* is commonly translated to "brocade" in English. It is a cotton fabric in which a pattern is woven into the fabric, producing a slightly raised texture in the pattern. *Bazin* is frequently dyed, and those from Guinea and Mali are considered particularly valuable in Dakar.

48   See, for example, Letter of complaint from Kande Kamara against a named Yalemou, August 30, 1933, ANS 5M/229(184).

49   See, for example, references in "A propos des Syriens," May 30, 1943, ANS 1Q322(77).

50   ANS 5M/229(184) contains an example of the use of *kolas* in marriage procedures.

51   Numerous examples exist in the Tribunal records of the *kola* commerce in Dakar and its variety across the three decades in question. See ANS 5M/205(184); ANS 5M/208(184); ANS 5M/211(184); ANS 5M/220(184); ANS 5M/221(184); ANS 5M/224(184); ANS 5M/225(184); ANS 5M/229(184); ANS 5M/254(184).

Dakar was connected. This was particularly important for the Lebanese *kola* trade, since Dakar's Lebanese procured *kola* from compatriots working in Côte d'Ivoire and other colonial outposts along the coast.[52] Lebanese traders drew on their networks with each other, often selecting other Lebanese as business partners, hosts, and suppliers. Connections to *kola* sources in other colonies allowed Lebanese traders to bring the product into Dakar in larger quantities and then sell to Africans who, in turn, sold *kola* in smaller quantities in the markets, streets, and courtyards of Dakar.[53] This kind of commercial orientation that focused on the African milieu and demands of the urban community set the Lebanese apart from Europeans doing business in the capital.

The provisions Lebanese merchants offered in Dakar were wide-ranging and catered to people's everyday needs. While some stores stocked fabric, clothing, footwear, glass, jewelry, and household items, other shops dealt in food stuffs and cigarettes. The art of trading and shopkeeping became the specialty of Lebanese Dakarois, so much so that the term "Syrian" was used to refer to any local Lebanese merchant or store owner. Many references in the *procès-verbaux* employed "Syrian" to denote an occupational identity as much as an ethnic one. These ethnic boundaries functioned similarly to those within the Cape Verdean community of colonial Dakar. Indeed, over the thirty-year span of the cases examined in this study, nearly each one involving Lebanese in Dakar show those city dwellers to have been owners of a store or merchants of commodities.[54] References to trading and credit round out the cases, making Lebanese relevant actors in nearly every year the Tribunal covers.

In the local transactional culture, financial means were as important as the commodities and services they bought. Lebanese traders and shop owners frequently extended credit to Dakarois and at times stored savings for them. The urban environment depended on the earning and spending of money, and administrators desired the increased usage of French money among the

---

52   See, for example, El Hindaoun v. Rahmoune, December 16, 1930, ANS 5M/221(184).

53   The records cited in footnote 51 reveal this dynamic. While the monetary value of *kola* in cases involving the Lebanese was often in the thousands, those involving Africans were more often in the hundreds and referenced the retail sale of the product in local African milieus.

54   The number of dossiers containing cases that provide evidence of this is great: ANS 5M/205(184) through ANS 5M/211(184); ANS 5M/220(184); ANS 5M/221(184) through ANS 5M/225(184); ANS 5M/228(184); ANS 5M/231(184); ANS 5M/233(184); ANS 5M/252(184); ANS 5M/253(184); ANS 5M/261(184); ANS 5M/265(184); ANS 5M/269(184).

African population.[55] Expanded use of colonial currency was accompanied by creative strategies and expansion of credit, pawning of possessions, and reserving funds for specific purposes. Lebanese shopkeepers provided an option for those seeking local access to cash.[56] A customer of a Lebanese store developed the foundations for a credit relationship with the owner by purchasing items there on a regular basis. Merchants, in turn, were willing to sell to local customers on a credit basis—the balance of a credit purchase could be paid upon the transaction of the next purchase.[57] Sometimes, balances were accrued over the course of a set period, to be paid at specific junctures. Buying on credit was a common practice in Lebanese-owned businesses, one that was convenient to Dakarois, for whom the high cost of living did not always produce correspondingly high daily liquidity. Lebanese business owners understood the necessity of offering credit and the benefit it offered them, since they could essentially establish themselves as the sole creditors to Africans. The French generally withheld services like loaning on collateral and selling on credit from Africans. They put forth that "natives, in their ignorance" and "lack of foresight" were incapable of managing debt.[58]

Lebanese merchants not only sold on credit but also extended credit independently of purchases to Africans in Dakar, especially as credit was a widespread practice in the city. Lebanese identity became associated with the local dynamics of managing money. In a 1923 dispute over a pawned necklace and sum of a hundred francs, for instance, Galo Sene told authorities that the other party, a "Syrian" named Djamil, frequently served as his creditor.[59] The business of credit between Africans and Lebanese in Dakar became widespread enough that there is evidence in the records of individuals serving as agents of such transactions. In one 1933 case, Ibrahima Diop disputed the amount Khassim Salky claimed was left of the balance Salky had lent to Diop.[60]

The Tribunal records show that African Dakarois could not only procure funds from the Lebanese but also deposit them for savings with them. In 1923, Macary Badiagne, who was brought before the Tribunal for a debt of 325 francs to two plaintiffs, said that while he did not have the money

55 Senegal, Rapport d'ensemble, Territoires d'administration directe, 1916, ANS 2G16/4.

56 See ANS 5M/232(184); 5M/210(184).

57 See ANS 5M/222(184); 5M/225(184); 5M/231(184); 5M233(184).

58 Secrétariat Général, 4ème bureau, Paris, "Question des prêts sur gages et de l'assistance aux indigènes," June 2, 1907, ANS Q63.

59 Sene v. "Djamil," September 26, 1923, ANS 5M/210(184).

60 Diop v. Salky, March 21, 1934, ANS 5M/231(184).

available immediately, he was keeping two hundred francs with a "Syrian" named Moustapha that would permit him to begin paying off the debt.[61] A case the following year also involved a deposit with a Lebanese merchant. The plaintiff, Mamadou Diop, told authorities he was unable to withdraw the two hundred francs he had deposited with a "Syrian" he referred to only as Michel.[62] Within months of that case, another dispute came before authorities in which one of the parties had put money into savings with a Lebanese store owner. Aly Mamdou and his brother Amadou Sarr claimed a Syrian[63] shopkeeper called Abdoulaye was unwilling to give back 175 francs that Aly Mamadou had deposited with him for fear the money, given to him by his brother, would be stolen.[64] The merchant, whose name was Abdel Rosoul, told authorities he took the sum as a deposit and was willing to return it but found himself unable to at the moment. His brother had taken all his merchandise and the money from the cash register, he claimed, because of a dispute in which the two men were involved.

Africans engaged Lebanese as viable options for storing funds. Of course, since these cases came before the Tribunal, they had encountered problems, showing that depositing money with the local Lebanese store owner—just as with any bank or mechanism—was not always risk-free. Since Lebanese merchants leveraged their own networks of credit and sharing, the money Africans lodged with them could move into other channels and become potentially difficult to withdraw.[65] Nevertheless, the practice was popular and continued through the 1930s and into the 1940s. A 1942 case, for instance, involved a rather significant deposit. Matene Cissoko told officials, with the support of witnesses, that he placed 790 francs in safe keeping with Aly Jouni, who claimed he had never received the deposit.[66]

Insertion into the local demand in products and credit and savings was thus crucial to Lebanese success in the urban setting, and the transactional culture in Dakar came to adopt practices that depended on members of the urban community specializing in this manner. As practices emerged and became norms, the possibilities surrounding various transactions also became

---

61   Gueye and M'Bengue v. Badiagne, July 11, 1923, ANS 5M/209(184).

62   Diop v. "Michel," January 4, 1924, ANS 5M/211(184).

63   The defendant in this case was actually Syrian, hence the absence of quotes in this instance. However, it should be noted that the usage in the original Tribunal record text could easily have been the typical usage—many customers might not have known if the merchant was Syrian or Lebanese. Generally, most were Lebanese.

64   Sarr v. Rosoul, April 15, 1924, ANS 5M/211(184).

65   See Doumbouya v. Bourdji, April, 28, 1932, ANS 5M/225(184) for an example in the 1930s.

66   Cissoko v. Jouni, July 13, 1942, ANS 5M/261(184).

shaped in certain ways. Urban clientele and those who served it engaged one another within that framework, understanding what was both possible and desirable.

Permanence through Family and Property

Lebanese Dakarois drew on themselves as their greatest resource, mobilizing endogamous credit networks that facilitated new immigration and the establishment of new shops and businesses.[67] There is evidence of such networks in the *procès-verbaux*. In one case, for instance, an African employee was able to purchase sixteen meters of fabric worth forty francs from a Lebanese shop without cash and by signing off for the purchase in the name of another Lebanese merchant.[68] In another case, from the 1920s, a dispute between brothers resulted in confiscation of one brother's merchandise by the other.[69] In a case from 1940 in which a customer claimed price gouging in a Lebanese shop, the shopkeeper asserted that the plaintiff might have been confusing him with his brother, also a store owner, who sold at lower prices.[70] Flexible capital and systems of sharing within family networks fostered prosperity, since city living was more expensive and required more robust resources.

In addition to securing capital from one another, Dakar's Lebanese settled their families in town, bolstering their local presence in the capital.[71] Since credit circulated within families and other broad kinship networks, and since families often staffed and managed the shops, this influx of women and children to Dakar was important.[72] Not only did it foster greater permanence, but it also buttressed the businesses, allowing for fuller operation and expansion. The placement of wives and children in storefronts brought unpaid labor to Lebanese urban businesses, and children raised in Dakar spoke the vernacular fluently. Evidence of this exists in some of the Tribunal

---

67 Letter number 2403 from Governor-General Carde to the minister of colonies on "Syrian Immigration to FWA," December 27, 1923, ANS 1Q322(77).
68 Ganamet v. Kange, December 12, 1923, ANS 5M/210(184).
69 Sarr v. Rasoul, April 15, 1924, ANS 5M/211(184).
70 Tourquet v. Bourghol, December 1939–January 1940, ANS 5M/252(184).
71 Tarraf-Najib, "Une vieille histoire de familles," 324.
72 The presence of family members in Lebanese business is clear throughout the archives and in interviews. Certain case years demonstrate this well: see, for example, ANS 5M/225 (184) and ANS 5M/228(184), both dossiers that treat the 1930s. Leichtman and Tarraf-Najib also reference this in their works. See specifically Tarraf-Najib, "Une vieille histoire de familles," 324.

cases. In 1930, for example, a dispute over payment for bread and butter at a Lebanese store involved a woman shopkeeper.[73] The Lebanese-born woman, Martha Milhem, appeared in the record as Mrs. Ibrahim Rahim, showing she was married. It was most likely that the shop was a family affair. Another 1930 case also involved a "Syrian" woman, this time in a dispute brought by her fiancé against her brother over marriage terms.[74] The notes recorded the occupation of the young woman, Marie Avedikiane, born in Lebanon, as "merchant." Her residence was with her sister. It was probable that Avedikiane worked with her sister, who was likely older and married, since the case referred to the young couple's room as being located in her home. Moreover, in light of Avedikiane's young age and the fact that she immigrated to Dakar, her identity in the record as a merchant was probably a reflection of her work in the shop owned by her sister's household or another family member. The case thus reinforces the ways in which kinship and work were combined within the Lebanese community of colonial Dakar. It also shows that women were key workers in such family businesses.[75] While Lebanese children rarely appear in the Tribunal records (because they were not frequently involved in complaints), there are hints of the settling of families with children in Dakar.[76]

Lebanese Dakarois facilitated the permanent status of their businesses and families by constructing buildings and residences in the city. This was often through transactions with Lebu landowners who still held large tracts of land downtown into the 1920s. The contracts were long-term leases that allowed the tenant to build at his own cost; constructions would become the property of the landowner once the lease concluded and the land reverted to its original owner.[77]

For Lebu landowners, transactions with Lebanese who were willing to build on the property were beneficial to owners. Tall edifices served to obscure from street view the older wooden dwellings the state had targeted for destruction for public health reasons. Such multilayered landscapes of taller buildings and constructions in wood and other materials became

---

73   Diallo v. Rahim, September 2, 1930, ANS 5M/220(184).

74   Fetouni v. Avedikiane family, December 15, 1930, ANS 5M/221(184).

75   See, for example, ANS 5M/223(184).

76   In one matter, a merchant claimed he no longer had a receipt to show to police in a case involving payment for laundry service because the children at home had ripped up the paper. Diallo v. Ganamet, November 7, 1922, ANS 5M/208(184).

77   This is discussed in a number of sources. Tarraf-Najib discusses it in her article to argue that the Lebanese were among the most important builders of downtown Dakar. See Tarraf-Najib, "Une vieille histoire de familles," 332–33.

common in certain areas of central Dakar.[78] A 1922 case in which a "Syrian" shopkeeper brought a complaint of theft referenced not only that his building contained both his apartment and store but that several "Wolofs"—a generic term commonly applied at the time to African or Lebu Dakarois—lived in the courtyard behind his building.[79]

The enduring presence of the Lebanese on several major arteries in central Dakar, each lined with buildings of several stories constructed by tenants from the 1920s into the 1960s, remains a highly visible sign of their place in the local economy over time. That process was well known, and it still falls victim to somewhat denigrating commentary in modern Dakar, which sees Lebanese dominance in the center of town as part of the process begun by the French by which the Lebu were displaced from their original lands downtown. This is in keeping with an undercurrent in present-day attitudes toward the Lebanese that resents their place in the urban economy, especially since the departure of the French.[80] The remnants of the rhetoric of the 1920s and 1930s should not be overlooked either—the portrait of the Lebanese painted during that era was a public one, broadcast in publications across town.[81]

The urban Lebanese were perhaps the clearest manifestation of the ways in which French commerce had misjudged both the economic context in which it operated and the capacities of the Lebanese to move beyond the intermediary paradigm originally slated for them. Building up an entire neighborhood of downtown Dakar in which Lebanese constructions, businesses, and families thrived was no intermediary project, as is commonly argued in works about the capital's physical evolution.[82] Dakar's history calls into question the notion of not only the dual city but also the tripartite city, showing that the city has an incredibly diverse population that lived in many corners of town, often alongside one another. The Lebanese were neither placed by the French in between Europeans (Plateau) and Africans

---

78   Tarraf-Najib, "Une vieille histoire de familles," 333. In casting the Lebanese as "builders" of the city, Tarraf-Najib also rejects the dual city model, arguing that the Lebanese neither occupied an intermediary role nor fell into either the white or black category.

79   ANS 5M/206 (184). See also 5M/221 (184) for references to similar building configurations.

80   See Leichtman, "Reexamining the Transnational Migrant," 139, for references to such an attitude among Senegalese.

81   O'Brien, *White Society*; see also O'Brien "Lebanese Entrepreneurs in Senegal," 103.

82   Interviewees integrate the intermediary role into their own narratives, and certain works continue to employ the notion. Interview with Jarmache; see also Marfaing and Sow, *Les Opérateurs Économiques*.

(Medina) to occupy the center of Dakar, nor did they choose their locations to strategically mediate between the two. Much like Cape Verdeans, their neighborhoods were not exclusively Lebanese. Justice records reveal diversity in Dakar's residential landscape, despite efforts on the part of the colonizer to welcome only Europeanized city dwellers.

Members of the Lebanese community harnessed local opportunities to become prominent in the urban economy, and this was done by branching into the African population, which made up the vast majority of Dakar's city dwellers. That involved being able to understand and work within the parameters of local restraints and norms while moving past the rhetoric of the French lobby and the expectations of administrators who wished to see certain types of practices evolve. Dakarois, especially Africans, worked with limited resources that they stretched and transformed to meet their needs. Lebanese transactions operated in that context. The depth and local responsiveness of Lebanese activity in interwar Dakar emerges clearly in the various Tribunal cases in which they appeared or were referenced. The most common ways Lebanese parties came to surface in such records were as shopkeepers, creditors, and employers. These were rarely discrete roles—a Lebanese shopkeeper commonly served as creditor to his African customers, employer of one or two African employees, and vendor to the neighborhood. If he constructed his building or shop on property leased from a Lebu landowner, he was also tenant of an African proprietor, or he became an urban property owner in his own right. Finally, such a figure might have also been neighbor to other Africans living in the quarter. Lebanese Dakarois were thus locally entrenched in numerous ways. The whole of the city's everyday transactions constituted a field that the state and its economic arms could not effectively control. It was a place of opportunity-making and strategy creation. Africans, Cape Verdeans, Lebanese, and Europeans navigated it as such within overlapping paradigms, each of which operated at different levels of power and access. The urban norms that drove the city were crafted from that interplay. As the 1930s gave way to a new time of global crisis that would reset those terms, Dakar's transactional culture revealed not only those changes but also the realities that had been building in the years leading to them.

Chapter Seven

War's Window

Urban Informality and Control

The Second World War as a Window

By the time of the Second World War, Dakar had become a city that coupled unique opportunities and specific barriers for those who lived there. Its fluidity, which frustrated officials, was an attribute that contributed not only to its diversity but also to the types of activities Dakarois pursued and the ways in which they did so. The war brought about two shifts in the dynamics of transactions in the colonial capital. War brought about shortages and rationing, which aggravated the "just enough" world in which Dakarois lived and catapulted the issue of daily needs to the forefront of city dwellers' minds and actions. The terms of transactions and access to resources were central to urban everyday public discourse. The grievances of the urban population regarding their daily lives also moved into a new place of prominence in the state's spectrum of concerns. Wartime generated intensified surveillance, with greater attention to the happenings of daily life. The war thus serves as a window with a special view of the city; it permits an understanding of the depth and flexibility of the transactional culture. The state became more vigilant about tracking public sentiment and activity, raising their prominence in official documentation. Those sentiments and activities put even greater pressure on Dakarois in their transactional lives. As urgency set in, a growing range of unauthorized actions emerged in the city, and preexisting illicit practices became more prominent.

As the seat of the government of colonial French West Africa, Dakar took on particular roles during World War II. It served as a strategic base and, with the regime change in France, as a Vichy stronghold outside of France.[1] Dakar became entrenched in the political and military struggles of

---

1   See, for instance: Apko-Vaché, *L'AOF et la Seconde Guerre Mondiale*; Ginio, *French Colonialism Unmasked*; Osborne, *World War II in Colonial Africa*;

the war, especially as it became a target of Allied and Free French efforts to erode Axis power in Africa.[2] Amid a global war, France also relied on its African colonies to bolster its forces, bringing about new experiences for African servicemen and shifting dynamics between soldiers and the French colonial state.[3] In Dakar, this resulted in greater military presence. Soldiers were drawn from the regions stationed in the capital, and military goods and personnel were moved through its sea and air ports of entry. International awareness of and presence in Dakar increased, particularly once American troops arrived during the later stages of the war.

In the story of the evolution of Dakarois' handling of their everyday needs—residence, earnings, consumption—the war represented as much a culmination of the preceding decades as it did a break with them. War's urgencies brought into much sharper view practices and problems that had existed and grown more robust over the 1920s and 1930s. Practices that had existed in prior decades multiplied and deepened as the war altered economic circumstances. An entrenched local transactional culture existed, and wartime dynamics became entangled in it. This resulted in new iterations of existing norms, as well as the introduction of wartime practices known in many global cities to a colonial urban setting. As it attempted to manage the capital, the state operated amid heightened anxiety and efforts at surveillance. Administrators reported more extensively on the goings-on in town, adding into the record details that had previously been hidden from official view or considered to be minor by authorities. The war also shaped the concerns that drove the administration, pushing officials to examine more closely the hidden corners of the capital's transactional culture. State documentation on illicit activity during that period is more robust than for the preceding years because of the heightened attention to anything potentially illegal during the war. In these two ways, the war acts as a window to certain elements of economic life in Dakar as it fully transitioned to a major city.

By the 1940s, an informal way of life—that is, transactions that went unregulated by the state and in which the parameters were determined by the participants—was entrenched in colonial Dakar. The state had largely

---

Crowder, *Colonial West Africa*, especially the chapter on "The Vichy Regime and Free France during the Second World War"; Cantier and Jennings, *L'Empire Colonial sous Vichy*. For the varied experiences of the war across colonial Africa, see Byfield et al., *Africa and World War II*. For the impact of military service on the process of decolonization, see Ginio, *French Army and Its African Soldiers*. For the political outlook of the period around the war, see Jennings, *Free French Africa in World War II*; Ginio, *French Colonialism Unmasked*; and Cooper, *Decolonization and African Society*.

2 Jennings, *Free French Africa in World War II*.

3 Ginio, *French Army and Its African Soldiers*; Shaka, "Vichy Dakar and the Other Story of French Colonial Stewardship in Africa."

absented itself from the city's transactional culture, leaving many issues of housing, employment terms, lending and credit, and retail commerce to Dakarois, who operated without the boundaries of particular resources and preferences. Although the administration understood the economy to be largely dominated by French commercial stakeholders in conjunction with the state, at the local level, economic activities were increasingly taken on by people of diverse backgrounds who were ready to insert themselves into opportunities the city presented. Within the context of informality arose a thriving illicit trade. Wartime in mid-century Dakar generated a robust underground market.

Evidence of Illicit Trade in the 1920s and 1930s

Evidence of illicit practices existing in the colonial capital prior to the Depression and the war runs throughout the Tribunal records. The amplitude of this gray area of the local economy was evidence that colonial authorities had not succeeded, over more than two decades of attempts, at shaping the ways city dwellers conducted their affairs. Claims of theft often led police to search stalls in the Sandaga market to determine if the goods in question were being sold there, indicating suspicion or knowledge among authorities that Dakar's main marketplace served an illicit trade. The disappearance of laundry from drying lines and clothing from personal trunks suggest the existence of channels to sell such items in the city. Cases brought against jewelers indicated that some of these craftsmen carried out a side business that fed the black market. By the 1930s, Dakarois and city authorities began speaking more openly about illicit practices, and the war ushered in new surveillance on the part of the state, bringing those practices into fuller view. The particular sources produced during the war offer a unique window into both the existence and expansion of the black market and the inability of the state to meaningfully intervene in the everyday transactions of Dakarois.

The ability to make money quickly and easily in colonial Dakar was not the invention of a wartime world. Authorities had long been fielding complaints that indicated a growing market for stolen goods in the capital. Along with debt, theft was consistently among the most common complaint brought to the Tribunal over the course of three decades, and often the investigations into theft cases revealed or suggested that stolen items were sold on the city streets and in Sandaga, its central market.[4] Sandaga did not become an offi-

---

4   The Tribunal records, for instance, record people living in the Sandaga area and calling it by that name in the 1910s; see ANS 5M/205(184). Officials did not begin serious plans to construct the market there until the 1920s. A

WAR'S WINDOW 6❧ 151

cial market housed in a structure erected by the state until the 1930s, but the area where it would be built was already known as such and served as the central marketplace in town long before the building was constructed. Its role as the place to buy and sell anything and everything emerged as soon as there was a clientele in Dakar, and Tribunal records show such action occurring as early as the 1910s. Acceleration of activity in the market, however, truly occurred in the 1920s. The reputation Sandaga acquired for being a dense maze of informal commercial activity had early roots. The transformation of Sandaga into a "flourishing marketplace that specialized in the sale of contraband goods" by the 1980s, as Catherine Boone points out in her study of merchant capital in Senegal over half a century, was not the sole result of rural-urban migration of the postcolonial period, nor uniquely related to the economic crises of the 1970s and 1980s.[5] The illicit nature of Dakar's central market had been a long-term evolution aided by an early inability of the colonial state to penetrate the informal networks that ran throughout the city.

Rarely did plaintiffs or the authorities receiving their complaints refer directly to an illegal market in the 1920s, but the records demonstrate that both city dwellers and state employees were well aware of its existence. Tribunal cases made many references to the potential for stolen items to be sold in town, especially at Sandaga. A 1923 case involved the apprehension of a man selling stolen goods in the market after a complaint regarding the missing goods was lodged with police.[6] Records from that year contained many cases in which the police were unable to locate either thieves or stolen property, indicating that merchandise moved efficiently in illicit circuits. Those who sold illegally procured items were not always anonymous perpetrators or career criminals. In fact, many cases involved individuals who held jobs in town. A 1923 record, for instance, listed numerous complaints against a jeweler whom authorities suspected of regularly melting down and reselling his clients' jewelry.[7] The following year, a case came to officials in which a roommate, employed with the Intendance Militaire and the Dakar-Saint-Louis Railroad, admitted to selling off the belongings of the other one night while the owner of the items was out.[8] The opportunity to turn a

---

1925 report noted that the project was being studied. See AOF—Résumés de Rapports d'ensemble des colonies, 1925, Circonscription de Dakar, ANS 2G25/10.

5   Boone, *Merchant Capital*, 214.
6   Unnamed plaintiff v. Diagne, September 23, 1923, ANS 5M/210(184).
7   Gueye v. Thiam, December 6, 1923, ANS 5M/210(184).
8   Huchard v. Dalmas, May 20, 1924, ANS 5M/211(184).

profit by selling stolen goods existed in Dakar in the 1920s, with no particular pattern other than the availability of buyers.

By the 1930s, this sort of unlawful activity was clearly on the rise. Cases not only addressed items that were stolen with greater frequency and amplitude but also directly referred to the presence of the items in the black market. A 1930 case in which the plaintiff told authorities about stolen laundry led inspectors to search the markets for the items.[9] The authorities who took down the details of the case commented that this was a regular occurrence. Indeed, clothing theft was common, and when police sought to retrieve stolen articles, they often headed for Sandaga. A record from 1932 is particularly revelatory of this. Alioune Diop, a clerk living downtown, brought a complaint that 750 francs worth in clothing, mostly African articles, were missing from his courtyard.[10] Diop questioned Amadou Ba, a man who had been temporarily renting in the courtyard, but Ba fled once he had been approached about the matter. Diop eventually found Ba and brought him to authorities, to whom he said he had no money and had not stolen from Diop. The police then questioned Diop's mother, Sogona Diawara, who said she had seen some of the items for sale in Sandaga. Based on that information, police swept the market and located a few of the missing articles. The record makes no indication as to how authorities dealt with the vendors of those pieces of clothing, most likely because that was a separate criminal case matter to be opened under another type of file. The fact that the police were able to return a few of the items means that inspectors were likely accustomed to searching for stolen merchandise in the market. There might have been key informants, for instance, who guided French agents when they navigated the market, which by 1932 was built and busy. In 1934, a French woman opted to perform her own search in Sandaga before lodging a complaint with authorities for housewares she claimed her houseboy had stolen and sold.[11]

Just one month prior to Diop's 1932 case, Georges Mayali complained in writing to authorities that the street vendors of Dakar should be reoriented toward the new market building.[12] He asserted that his family's stores, which had been established by his father and were registered with Dakar's Commercial Registry, were consistently encumbered by street vendors who stood in front of his doors, deterring potential clients. Mayali told officials

---

9   Theft complaint lodged by Felicia Sambo, February 11, 1930, ANS 5M/218(184).

10   Diop v. Ba, January 20, 1932, ANS 5M/224(184).

11   Jupin v. Sy, June 28, 1934, ANS 5M/233(184).

12   Complaint lodged by Georges Mayali, December 21, 1931, ANS 5M/224(184).

Figure 7.1. Sandaga market, 2004. Author's photograph.

that he had lodged verbal complaints several times before, revealing that the presence of such vendors was not a brand new one. Claims such as these indicate that the volume of informal commercial activity was becoming significant, since not only were items illegally sold at Sandaga but vendors found the streets an equally hospitable sales environment.

Shortages, Insecurity, and Distrust in a Wartime City

Although the illegal corners of Dakar's economy clearly had been established before the later 1930s, the outbreak of war brought about shifts from the prior decades. With a new wartime economy in which commodities were rationed and ration tickets became items of value, new challenges and opportunities emerged. Dakarois struggled to obtain what they needed in their daily life, and the state found itself with limited resources as well. Entrepreneurship thus took a new turn, and the illicit market expanded as it was fed ration tickets, illegal imports of rice, oil, and other foodstuffs, and military effects. While authorities attempted to monitor and crack down on such activities, other elements of wartime city dwelling worked against their efforts. Blackouts were noted to have encouraged nighttime thefts in a city where stealing was already commonplace.[13] Shortages of commodities encouraged price gouging. Military installations and the increased presence of soldiers—first French and African, then American—encouraged theft of and trade in military clothing and goods. The city struggled to disburse rations (largely reliant on food imports from the regions and metropole) and African producers found opportunities to fill local needs without going through official channels.

At the same time, the wartime regulations that the state initiated—from rations to controls on transportation—turned normal activities into unlawful ones during the late 1930s and early 1940s. Transport of goods that previously had not been controlled but became so in wartime became a law-breaking offense. Such regulations were neither clear nor known to all, especially as many people in Dakar operated on the fringes of spheres touched by the state. Thus, not every participant in illicit activity was necessarily criminal in his or her intent. In the Tribunal, Dakarois appeared or claimed to have been unaware of the new rules the state imposed. This was entirely possible, given the disconnect that existed between the colonial state and the population, although some people certainly simply disregarded new laws. Despite greater surveillance of the goings-on in town, the city's wartime circumstances engendered greater ingenuity among the population to see to their own needs, highlighting the administration's inability to keep a strong hold on the urban economy, as well as the readiness of the population to disregard the state's desires.

The war was a period in which the question of needs—crucial to managing life—was brought into greater focus for both the local population and the colonial administration. Dakar's struggles with self-sufficiency became immediately obvious during the war, especially as it came together with population increase, isolation from France, and shortage of imported supplies. After several years of war had taken a palpable toll on the city, administrators in 1943 and 1944 pointed to all of these factors, explaining what they perceived as a precarious situation. A 1943 economic report put it bluntly, stating that Dakar consumed but produced nothing.[14] Another economic report from the same year stated that since Dakar depended nearly entirely on imports from France, it was now totally cut off from the flow on which it had relied. Its other imports, meanwhile, had come from French North Africa, which was largely unable to export anything to its southern neighbors

---

13   Letter from the attorney general to the president of the court of appeals of FWA, March 24, 1944, ANS 2M51(184).

14   Dakar et Dépendances, Bureau Économique, Rapport Économique Annuel, 1943, and Rapport sur le Ravitaillement à Dakar, 1943, ANS 2G143/52.

in wartime.[15] A 1944 report restated these problems and added simply: "Dakar's is a special situation."[16] Because of this, from the earliest stages of the war, the state sought to encourage local food production. While incentives to boost small-scale agriculture around town had been in place since the mid-1930s, the administration redoubled these efforts during the war by making more land available for cultivation, passing out seeds, and offering higher prices to encourage city dwellers to farm.[17] In addition, bans on imported produce were lifted so that whatever the city could bring in to feed the population it would.[18] American imports, for instance, became important during the later years of the war, and ranged from condensed milk to generators.

Wartime rationing followed what authorities believed each urban community required or was accustomed to having. Like wages, rationing guidelines followed race-based formulas that assumed different needs for Europeans and Africans. Quantities of flour, sugar, soap, and wine were apportioned for Europeans, while rice, millet, semolina, and corn dominated the allocations for Africans. Meat, oil, fabrics, milk, and fuel were rationed as well. Certain events called for different consumption scenarios, particularly religious holidays and celebrations. In 1943, for instance, five occasions called for additional rations—the July 14 holiday, Id al-Adha (called Tabaski locally and by the administration), Id al-Fitr (known locally as Korité), Ramadan, and the arrival of the Minister of Colonies in the capital that year.[19] By the end of 1943, authorities counted 17,807 European ration recipients and 108,974 African ration recipients in Dakar. An additional 14,581 workers were "fed by their employers."[20] This total of 141,362 people sustained by either the state or employers was in relation to an urban population the administration

---

15   Dakar et Dépendances, Bureau Économique, Rapport Économique Annuel, 1943, and Rapport sur le Ravitaillement à Dakar, 1943, ANS 2G143/52.

16   Dakar et Dépendances, Annual Report for 1944, section of "Cost of Living," ANS 2G44/19.

17   Dakar et Dépendances, Bureau Économique, Rapport Économique Annuel, 1943, and Rapport sur le Ravitaillement à Dakar, 1943, ANS 2G143/52; Dakar et Dépendances, Annual Report for 1944, section of "Cost of Living," 2G44/19.

18   Dakar et Dépendances, Bureau Économique, Rapport Économique Annuel, 1943, and Rapport sur le Ravitaillement à Dakar, 1943, ANS 2G143/52.

19   Dakar et Dépendances, Bureau Économique, Rapport Économique Annuel, 1943, and Rapport sur le Ravitaillement à Dakar, 1943, ANS 2G143/52.

20   Dakar et Dépendances, Bureau Économique, Rapport Économique Annuel, 1943, and Rapport sur le Ravitaillement à Dakar, 1943, ANS 2G143/52.

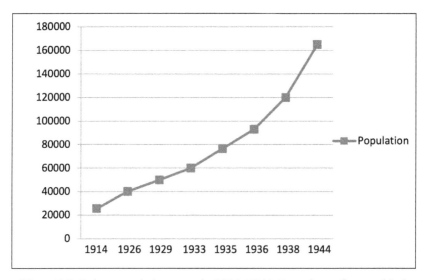

Figure 7.2. Dakar, population growth, 1914–1944. Data drawn from archival sources used in this book.

estimated at 164,614 as of January 1, 1943.[21] The measures to control distribution and consumption of foodstuffs covered the majority of the population by this later stage of the war, but 25,000 people remained outside the rationing system and thus were forced to obtain their necessities by other means.

Since Dakar's population grew over the course of the war, the number of people not officially entitled to rations expanded. During the first ten months of 1943 alone, Dakar's population grew by more than 12 percent. The size of the capital's "floating population" was never precisely understood, and the state maintained dubious statistics in its efforts to track such individuals who were clearly outside the rationing system. Rations accordingly became more severe as consumption pressure increased, and the state was obliged to further restrict the availability of certain foods as the war dragged on. Meat, for instance, was unavailable two days per week in 1943. By 1944, the number of days Dakar could neither buy nor sell meat was

---

21   Dakar et Dépendances, Bureau Économique, Rapport Économique Annuel, 1943, and Rapport sur le Ravitaillement à Dakar, 1943, ANS 2G143/52.

raised to four per week.[22] Wartime brought increased pressures and limitations such as these into all areas of the urban economy.

Grievances about the availability of necessities like fabric, flour, and milk emerged from every contingent of the population, but women became particularly important in voicing local concerns.[23] Women came to authorities most frequently with complaints about rations because the gendered division of labor in most households made them the primary managers and users of foodstuffs.[24] They also made up a sizeable proportion of the market vendors in Dakar, often voicing concern in that capacity as well.[25] Women were the first to notice and express frustration when a food product or household item was in shortage, overpriced, or of inferior quality. Authorities learned, for example, that women in the Medina were planning to send a delegation to the Governor of the Circumscription of Dakar to assert that it was "no longer possible to feed their families" and to demand the replacement of beans in the rationing plan with rice or corn.[26]

Public sentiment in Dakar at times held that the administration actively diverted or withheld resources, that better conditions existed elsewhere, and that the state did not put effort into improving matters in Dakar. Grievances sometimes carried underlying implications of neglect or even conspiracy on the part of authorities to the detriment of Dakarois who were already suffering. The claim heard around town that rice and millet were sold freely outside Dakar was an example of this: it suggested that the residents of the capital were deprived while others were able to go about business as usual. Officers collected similar claims—for instance, that the provisions stocked in Dakar were actually destined for France, or that the administration preferred to allow rice stocked in Rufisque to "spoil rather than give it to the

---

22 Dakar et Dépendances, Bureau Économique, Rapport Économique Annuel, 1943, and Rapport sur le Ravitaillement à Dakar, 1943, ANS 2G143/52.

23 Wartime brought about such issues across colonial Africa. See, for example: Rich, "Hunger and Consumer Protest in Colonial Africa during the First World War."

24 The late colonial era produced greater visibility of women's roles in this regard. See, for example, Penvenne, *Women, Migration & the Cashew Economy in Southern Mozambique.*

25 Women's prominence in markets was well established by this period throughout sub-Saharan Africa, continuing as the twentieth century progressed. See Clark, *Onions Are My Husband*; George, "Within Salvation"; Ejikeme, "From Traders to Teachers"; Allen, "Sitting on a Man"; Sheldon, *Courtyards, Markets, City Streets.*

26 Renseignements politiques, Service de Sûreté, September to December 1943, ANS 17G/410.

starved population."[27] Milk was the subject of the same type of speculation. Medications, too, were lacking, which provoked parallel reactions. A
November 1943 report raised concerns about the increasing number of
deaths in Dakar, adding that African residents "claim that the clinics and
hospitals have no more medications, and that the doctors let children die
without doing anything to save them."[28] The people of Dakar felt that they
were not merely victims of the hardships of wartime but also of neglect,
indifference, and even malice on the part of the state and its agents.

Illicitness and the Urban Wartime Economy

Against the backdrop of such sentiments, Dakarois were increasingly moti-
vated to ignore the state's rules or circumvent its channels. A number of
illicit practices arose in wartime, adding complexity and depth to the informal commerce already present in Dakar. Most common were trade in ration
tickets, sale of commodities without regard to rationing rules, and price
gouging. Tribunal records bear witness to this. Mamadou Ndiaye, a Medina
resident from the French Soudan, came to police in July 1942 to lodge a
complaint against his cousin for taking his ration cards for clothing, baby
supplies, and food to be renewed at a fee of thirty francs, and then failing
to return with them.[29] Similarly, in October of that year, Amadou Kanssain,
also a Medina resident from Soudan, lodged a complaint against Ousmane
Thiam for taking his cards to be renewed and never returning.[30] Vendors
also did business outside the legal wartime parameters. In 1942, for instance,
a perfume vendor lodged a complaint about a shopkeeper who was allegedly
selling headscarves and handkerchiefs at excessive prices and without the use
of wartime tickets or proper declaration of the merchandise to authorities.[31]

Informal economic transactions of even the smallest and most local
nature came to the attention of authorities because of the wartime context.
Authorities interrogated a Medina woman in 1941 for selling onions by the
slice in her neighborhood without proper documentation and approved
pricing.[32] The woman's business was consistent with the widespread street

---

27 Renseignements politiques, Service de Sûreté, September to December 1943,
ANS 17G/410.

28 Renseignements politiques, Service de Sûreté, September to December 1943,
ANS 17G/410.

29 Ndiaye v. Mbodj, July 7, 1942, ANS 5M/261(184).

30 Kanssain v. Thiam, October 3, 1942, ANS 5M/262(184).

31 Mbaye v. Ahmed, March 3, 1942, ANS 5M/259(184).

32 Interrogation of Magat N'diaye, September 23, 1941, ANS 5M/257(184).

vending and small-scale retail to which Dakarois had become accustomed well before the war. The microlevel at which she operated illustrates the demand that existed for even the most basic foodstuff needs during the war. The war exacerbated existing challenges in Dakar, bringing about new layers within the local economy. At the same time, the war's effects on the state's behavior—particularly intensified surveillance—brought those more intimate corners of the local transactional culture into its view. Thus, while cases in the Tribunal continued to address issues, such as the sale of stolen items and illegal practices among jewelers,[33] the justice apparatus in Dakar expanded its interventions. In the wartime context, even informal economic activities like peddling onions by the slice became issues of interest.

That interest extended into Dakar's expanding suburbs, which linked the capital to products produced in the interior. In April 1942, police in Ouakam, one of Dakar's northern neighborhoods, stopped several fishermen and women fish vendors for operating without proper documentation. Authorities informed the Lebu fishermen and vendors that they not only lacked permits to sell fish but were also without approval to transport it.[34] In August, a complaint by several Ouakam notables revealed that shopkeepers in their neighborhood were rationing corn in new, unapproved quantities. The various sellers received warnings from authorities to use the prescribed measures.[35] In May 1943, twenty-one-year-old Amadou Diallo was intercepted for transporting peanut oil without the necessary paperwork that had been instituted as part of the rationing system. When asked why he did not possess such a card, he replied that he had no idea any authorization was required to transport peanut oil and that he was taking it to his family. He added that he made no declaration with the Service des Stocks because he thought that was only required of vendors and traders rather than the general population.[36] Malick Seck asserted the same in March 1944, when he was apprehended for transporting an eighteen-liter drum of peanut oil. Seck said the oil was intended for his personal consumption and that he was unaware there were any regulations on the transportation of peanut oil.[37] The same year, authorities stopped a public transport vehicle on the outskirts of Dakar that was headed into town and found sixty kilograms of rice inside. Although they interrogated each passenger, none admitted to having any knowledge of the large sack of rice, a fact police acknowledged was to be

---

33 Diop v. Thiam, December 15, 1944, ANS 5M/271(184), for an example.
34 Police declaration of unauthorized transport, Ouakam, Dakar, April 24, 1942, ANS 5M/261(184).
35 See ANS 5M/261(184), for examples.
36 Interrogation of Amadou Diallo, May 31, 1943, ANS 5M/265(184).
37 Interrogation of Malick Seck, March 6, 1944, ANS 5M/268(184).

expected, since everyone knew there was an illicit market for such commodities.[38] The suburbs, where fish were procured, livestock were brought into town, and city dwellers and visitors alike could do business outside the central markets of town, were porous entities that made enforcement difficult. They were important nodes of the robustness that emerged in the informal spheres of the economy during the war.

In cases that range from third-party ration card renewals to the illegal transport of foodstuffs, it is certainly possible that Dakarois were unaware of the regulatory contours of wartime rationing and supply, especially given the level of disinterest the state showed in African residents in other aspects of urban life. The population of the northern fringes of Dakar, where the fishermen were apprehended, was dependent on their livelihood, and the administration had indeed encouraged local fishing and fishmongers with few formalities before the war. In the cases of Ndiaye and Kanssain, both men could have been uninformed as to the regulations for renewal when they entrusted the renewal of their rationing cards to others, even paying a fee as in Ndiaye's case. Diallo and Seck also could have lacked information on wartime rules about practices such as transporting peanut oil. Understaffed and tight on resources—even paper—during the war, the administration could have neglected to make all the technicalities of rationing and supply known to everyone in greater Dakar.

At the same time, rules were not always followed, and activities geared toward profit were pursued despite the state's efforts to the contrary. Circumvention of rules and creation of opportunities for illicit profit were corollaries of the implementation of wartime measures restricting the circulation, sale, and purchase of life's necessities. Dakar already had an underground market that evaded control because it was embedded in a world in which many legal transactions in the city were already informal. The transient nature of a port and colonial capital also made the movement of goods difficult to monitor. The war saw the black market expand, and its growth was of concern to residents and administrators alike, especially in the later phase of the war, when both the city's resources and stamina were low. Shopkeepers and traders complained that the restriction of the quantities of fabric allowed to be sold in town encouraged the growth the *marché noir*, or black market, and that customers were becoming ever more exasperated by the day, seeking what they needed "without worrying too much about the authorized prices."[39] Such a state of affairs encouraged people around Dakar

---

38 Police incident entry, interception of public transport vehicle in Thiaroye, February 27, 1944, ANS 5M/268(184).

39 Renseignements politiques, Service de Sûreté, September to December 1943, ANS 17G/410.

and even further afield to seek profit by feeding the contraband trade. Police who stopped buses and trains for inspection encountered many instances of foodstuffs being brought unlawfully into Dakar. In February 1944 alone, several cases involving rice, bread, peanut oil, and millet made it into police records; the transporters were nearly always African. Officers noted that, for the most part, production also appeared to be local and small-scale rather than commercial.[40] The black market in Dakar thus presented a real opportunity for locals, migrants, and those anchored in Senegal's various regions to profit. Authorities reported that the problem was such that people arriving in the capital from the metropole claimed Dakar's black market to be "better organized than in Marseille (which, for them, is not an understatement)."[41]

Price gouging and bribery accusations were widespread and lodged against every kind of seller. Lebanese merchants, African market women, butchers, wine sellers, and even medical providers were implicated. Authorities noted complaints in Dakar's African circles, asserting that

> nurses and municipal clinics . . . taking advantage of the scarcity of medications, ruthlessly send home the sick who don't grease their palms. These practices supposedly started a few weeks ago, purportedly made possible by the total lack of oversight. Nurses demand a minimum of twenty-five francs to provide the smallest care. Nothing is being said about the auxiliary doctors, but it is likely they are involved in similar activity.[42]

Officials were well aware of these types of issues. In the commercial and retail sphere, authorities performed regular checks to make sure that the set prices were observed—to prevent stockpiling—and oversee the proper use of rationing coupons. Between July and September 1940, police collected dozens of complaints from residents about local shops and vendors selling everything from fish to razors to pasta to cigarettes at unreasonably high prices.[43] Practices like these continued as the war dragged on. In 1944, the Service de la Répression des Fraudes et des Poids et Mesures brought 250 cases before the state.[44]

Lebanese Dakarois became particularly subjected to accusations of stockpiling, hoarding, and price gouging. These accusations came from both residents and the authorities. With the currents of vitriolic debate that had

---

40 For several examples, see dossier ANS 5M/268(184).
41 Renseignements politiques, Service de Sûreté, September to December 1943, ANS 17G/410.
42 Renseignements politiques, Service de Sûreté, September to December 1943, ANS 17G/410.
43 See cases in dossier ANS 5M/254(184).
44 Dakar et Dépendances, Annual Report for 1944, section of "Cost of Living," ANS 2G44/19.

circulated only a few years earlier during the Depression, fertile ground had been laid for a focus on Lebanese businesses during the war. By 1939, surveillance reports noted that in African milieus, people critiqued the "negative attitude" of the Lebanese, who sold household essentials, fabrics, and other imported items.[45] In January 1940, a French complainant alleged that drinking glasses were sold at fluctuating and excessive prices in Lebanese shops.[46] By 1943, complaints about sales by Lebanese became common and were lodged by both Africans and Europeans. One report noted accusations circulating in town that Lebanese merchants were taking advantage of the shortage of fabric by buying the greatest quantities possible to resell, even organizing "teams of buyers to supposedly 'wait in line all day' at the large fabric suppliers for them."[47] The idea that Lebanese shopkeepers were cheating the public was embedded in nearly every complaint collected about them. Accusations came in from Europeans about the "extraordinary and scandalous" wartime profits that, by 1943, Lebanese merchants in Dakar were making.

> Money is flowing; Libano-Syrians, shopkeepers of all sorts, who since the war's start have built up bank deposits surpassing all their hopes, act like the new rich while the majority of the population . . . can barely pay their rent at the end of the month.[48]

A lexicon heavy in references to money and profit was common even before the war, but during World War II, when resources were scarce, it became amplified and generated fiercer resentment among those who felt their own situation far from profitable.

Amid the flow of allegations in Dakar, there was a general sense that the problem of pricing and illicit trade was beyond the real control of the state. Assertions abounded in town that the Service de Ravitaillement in Sandaga could not effectively control the circulation of ration cards, and that "a real market" existed for lost cards because the administration sought no sanction against people who used them fraudulently.[49] Stolen rationing coupons continued to be used by others for months, while the families to whom they

---

45   Direction des Affaires Politiques, Impressions recueillies sur le moral des populations européennes, indigènes, 1939–1940, ANS 21G/150(108).

46   Tourquet v. Bourghol, December 1939–January 1940, ANS 5M/252(184).

47   Renseignements politiques, Service de Sûreté, September to December 1943, ANS 17G/410.

48   Renseignements politiques, Service de Sûreté, September to December 1943, ANS 17G/410.

49   Renseignements politiques, Service de Sûreté, September to December 1943, ANS 17G/410.

were allocated could be "reduced to a state of near famine."[50] The population blamed the state in its inability to manage things. A September 1943
report asserted that Dakar's African population continued "to complain
about supplies" and "claim[ed] that in the interior rice and millet are freely
sold."[51] That same month, women in Dakar protested that vegetables promised to the markets had not yet begun to be sold, and that by the time the
vegetables reached the markets, they would have already gone bad.[52]

Dakarois found particular frustration in the state's inability to abate the
skyrocketing cost of living in the city. Wartime rationing, black market activities, and general scarcity of nearly everything quickly aggravated an issue
that was already problematic for many in Dakar. Administrators admitted the
city was even more expensive than it had been in previous years. Measures
introduced in late 1939 to keep a closer watch on price gouging were put in
place, as one administrator explained, "to combat" the high cost of living.[53]

Complaints about how expensive the city had become came from every
corner of Dakar. In March 1940, objections streamed in from the capital's French residents about rising rents. One grievance declared that an
apartment that had rented for between 700 and 1,000 francs the previous
September now went for between 1,500 and 1,600 francs per month.[54]
Lebu notables asserted in 1943 that *téfankés* who waited on the outskirts of
Dakar's suburbs to buy up herds and sell the animals to city dwellers were
taking excessive commissions, with one sheep selling for 800 francs rather
than the normal 500 francs.[55] The foreign European community also felt
the pressure of rising costs. The administration noted that mail sent from
English residents in Dakar to Europe complained often about the problem.
Mail sent home by *tirailleurs* (West African artillerymen in the French colonial service) stationed in Dakar made similar statements about the expense
of life there.[56]

---

50   Renseignements politiques, Service de Sûreté, September to December 1943,
     ANS 17G/410.
51   Renseignements politiques, Service de Sûreté, September to December 1943,
     ANS 17G/410.
52   Renseignements politiques, Service de Sûreté, September to December 1943,
     ANS 17G/410.
53   Direction des Affaires Politiques, "Impressions recueillies sur le moral des
     populations européennes, indigènes," 1939–1940, ANS 21G/150(108).
54   Direction des Affaires Politiques, "Impressions recueillies sur le moral des
     populations européennes, indigènes," 1939–1940, ANS 21G/150(108).
55   Renseignements politiques, Service de Sûreté, September to December 1943,
     ANS 17G/410.
56   Direction des Affaires Politiques, Impressions recueillies sur le moral des popu-
     lations européennes, indigènes, 1939–1940, ANS 21G/150(108).

Perhaps the most vocal concerns were heard among Dakar's middle class, which administrators defined as "employees, civil servants, and lower-ranking servicemen." In short, they increasingly encountered difficulties in making ends meet.[57] A 1939 report on population "morale" cited a grievance by a lower-ranking African civil servant about "the high cost of essential foodstuffs" and described the inadequacy of "that which [was] allotted to him in relationship to the actual demands of life."[58] This particular functionary, a husband and father of "several small children," provided a schema of his monthly expenses, showing his budget to be short by a hundred francs every month, despite his monthly salary of 450 francs.[59] This case was one of the more detailed in such reports, but other civil servants also raised their concerns about the cost of living. Five months later, a February 1940 report observed: "[As] life becomes more expensive, discomfort has begun to show itself among native married, salaried employees and civil servants, who have family expenses."[60]

Such financial pressures among salaried urban Africans intensified over the course of the war. In judicial encounters, people referenced the high cost of living in Dakar. A July 1943 complaint from Amadou Niang, an employee of the Banque Commerciale Africaine, argued that Dakar was twice as expensive as Kaolack, Senegal's peanut capital.[61] By late 1943, the administration was collecting reports of complaints about salaries and the cost of living nearly every week. A report from September of that year asserted that while African civil servants had largely remained "on the margins of the atmosphere created in Dakar by certain native political leaders," they now displayed "great discontent."[62] Rumors circulated in African bureaucratic circles that the governor-general had refused salary raises to match the cost of living in Dakar. The growing sentiment of exclusion took on more global political dimensions. "These public servants," the report stated, "speak of their brothers in America who have supposedly evolved without obstacles and enjoy the same benefits as whites."[63] If the administration was surprised

---

57   Renseignements politiques, Service de Sûreté, September to December 1943, ANS 17G/410.

58   Direction des Affaires Politiques, "Impressions recueillies sur le moral des populations européennes, indigènes," 1939–1940, ANS 21G/150(108).

59   Direction des Affaires Politiques, "Impressions recueillies sur le moral des populations européennes, indigènes," 1939–1940, ANS 21G/150(108).

60   Direction des Affaires Politiques, "Impressions recueillies sur le moral des populations européennes, indigènes," 1939–1940, ANS 21G/150(108).

61   Banque Commerciale Africaine v. Niang, July 28, 1943, ANS 5M/265(184).

62   Renseignements politiques, Service de Sûreté, September to December 1943, ANS 17G/410.

63   Renseignements politiques, Service de Sûreté, September to December 1943, ANS 17G/410.

by the serious tenor of such complaints, then it had not paid heed to a grow-ing trend over the previous two decades. The problem of expensive urban life that salaried Africans—and many other Dakarois—voiced during the war was one that had materialized as early as the early 1920s. For years, Dakarois had managed shortages of affordable housing and limited access to funds to cover expenses in a city that was both increasingly costly and under the management of an administration committed to a racial hierarchy that kept Africans poor.

A Time of Waning Control

Consistent with the state's rhetoric about the capital throughout the pre-ceding decade, administrators cast problems such as shortages and rising costs of living during the war as rooted in the city's population question. Authorities saw the wartime problem of the increasing shortage of food-stuffs as directly related to the issue of the growth and nature of Dakar itself. In his 1944 report, the capital's top official discussed the matter, asserting that inadequate supplies for the city did not simply constitute a wartime problem but an urban problem. In one respect, he understood that the war brought into relief some of the capital's broader challenges. But the set of assumptions underlying such recognition were those that had been foun-dational throughout the colonial state's management of Dakar. For him, the struggles with fulfillment of basic needs in the city were not a result of the administration's own approach, which had been entrenched in racism and exclusion, but the unrelenting expansion of the city due to the constant influx of people—something the state had never favored and had struggled to control.

> This striking concentration [of population] in a . . . restricted surface area that has always had to subsist on the provision of its needs through im-ports brought about increased demand while the offerings became increas-ingly short. The reduction of foodstuffs, competing needs, and—it must be admitted—insufficiency of certain rations (sugar, oil, bread, soap) have provoked, with the appearance of a black market, a rise in prices that is dif-ficult to wrestle. Without a doubt, administrative measures . . . might have stopped this rise if Dakar had not become more and more "sprawling" in nature.[64]

Such reflections easily find their origins in the ideas that had emerged in the 1930s concerning the growth of large cities in FWA. For the colonial

---

64   Dakar et Dépendances, Annual Report for 1944, section of "Cost of Living," ANS 2G44/19.

state, the list of urban ills included overpopulation, attraction of transient elements, pressure to supply an urban population that did not produce for itself, and the tendency of the city to continue to physically expand. The city that consumed and did not produce, all the while expanding in terms of both space and population, only became a more extreme version of itself when put under the pressure of wartime shortages and a rationing regime. Dakar's chief administrator felt the onus of the problem lay on city dwellers rather than the state. He asserted that the administration might have been able to treat the issues facing the city had it not been for inexorable urban growth that produced both greater density and enlarged urban space.

The fragile veneer of urban control, already thin during the decades prior to World War II, became very obvious with the pressures the war applied to the capital. The war toppled the French state in the metropole and put new points of stress on colonies. Officials and French state employees had to make do with dramatically fewer imports from France, longer tours of duty, and vulnerability to events playing out on the world stage during the war. The decision by the government general of FWA to support the Vichy regime in mid-1940 isolated Dakar and the colonies in the federation from other French holdings in Africa that considered Free France the legitimate French authority. Only months after that declaration of Vichy alignment, Dakar endured a bombardment by the Anglo-Free France forces under the command of Charles de Gaulle. While the raid on Dakar became a brief moment of achievement for the capital's administrators, who proclaimed triumph in repelling the British attack,[65] it was a moment of trauma for the urban population. State reports and oral testimony both portray the fear among the urban population of Dakar during the three-day raid.

Oral testimonies from Dakarois paint a close picture of the event. Dakarois who lived through the raid recount having immediately sought to flee the central parts of town and found safe havens in the suburbs or less sparsely populated areas of the city.[66] As officials carried out civilian evacuations, many Dakarois fled of their own initiative without state help. Most people describe the necessity Dakarois felt to fend for themselves. One woman

---

65   Direction des Affaires Politiques, Report on the raid on Dakar, and general surveillance reports, 1940, 2D8(14). See also comments in 2G40/1 by Dakar's administrator: "The raid on the Capital of FWA would be for Dakar the chance to proudly proclaim its readiness to remain French and only French, and to bind more tightly around the head of the Federation the ties that unite the different members of the population."

66   Interview with Oumar Ba, Medina, Dakar, September 2007; interview with Lalla Ndiaye, Dakar, February 2008; interview with Ousmane Mbengue, Colobane, Dakar, September 2007.

emphasized the "running" that took place as soon as the attack began.[67] She and others recount families choosing to spend several nights in the Parc de Hann, a forestry reserve and Dakar's largest city green space, since it seemed removed from the locations targeted by the raid and provided sufficient options for remaining out of sight. One lifelong Dakarois recalls that the birth of his son occurred during the time of the raid, and notes that his wife fled to the Parc de Hann just before she gave birth.[68] These narratives of resilience and survival bear no testimony of state assistance during the raid.

State attitudes marginalizing non-Europeans were plain. Africans in and around Dakar provided support to one another during the crisis without any help from the state. A November 1940 report noted that many households in Cambérène and Yoff, both on the immediate outskirts of Dakar, received refugees from the city, generously providing for them in all respects.[69] Officials focused on only a few communities in the more central areas of Dakar, where officials concentrated their activities. Indeed, the first response of the state was a plan aimed at evacuating the central downtown area of the city, where the greatest concentration of Europeans resided. Decisions to leave town, seek refuge in the Parc de Hann, or temporarily lodge among the communities on the northern outskirts of town were strategies Dakarois devised on their own as the attack occurred. Administrators discussed local responses through the lens of African inferiority that was their default interpretive framework. The new dangers of living in an urban wartime target caused numerous Africans to leave with no intention of returning, one report claimed, while the director of political affairs declared that the "suddenness of the events left the natives in a veritable stupor."[70]

Driven by the impulse to control, the administration saw the moment of crisis as an opportunity for the state to demonstrate its ability to protect the population and attempt to generate loyalty to the colonial state. Director of Political Affairs Berthet declared that the shock of the raid permitted contact between the administration and Africans to "become more frequent than ever," noting that such contact was "marked with patience and sympathy on our part."[71] In fact, Berthet found the moment "propitious" for an "inten-

---

67 Interview with Lalla Ndiaye, Dakar, February 2008.

68 Interview with Ousmane Mbengue, Colobane, Dakar, September 2007.

69 Direction des Affaires Politiques, Report on the raid on Dakar and general surveillance reports, 1940, 2D8(14).

70 Direction des Affaires Politiques, Report on the raid on Dakar and general surveillance reports, 1940, 2D8(14); Dakar et Dépendances, Annual Political Report, 1940, 2G40/1.

71 Dakar et Dépendances, Annual Political Report, 1940, 2G40/1.

sive . . . publicity" campaign.[72] Such a rapprochement did not occur. Not only did many city dwellers see officials as unable to protect or evacuate them during the raid, but Dakarois also understood that the state was also unable to provide for the population, control prices, or manage the flow of commodities in and out of town.

The arrival of American military in Dakar in 1942 further eroded notions of French dominance. Fresh rounds of supplies came from the United States, bringing new economic influence and undermining the prewar preponderance of the French import market. Those commodities, ranging from sunglasses to cars, flowed quickly into Dakar's markets—legitimate and illicit. American military effects, for instance, fed the local black market, and American cars made their way into the theft records.[73] Since many of those cars were four-by-four vehicles and trucks, they sometimes became tools in thefts of heavier items, like construction materials, which were lacking in Dakar.[74] These construction materials also came in with the US forces.[75] Items ranging from electricity generators to condensed milk were among the supplies Americans brought into Dakar. Such imports, along with other American initiatives in the capital, constituted a visible display of the dependency on an international power other than France.

As part of the establishment of their base in Dakar, US forces also constructed an airfield, roads, radio posts, and other infrastructural elements they required in Dakar, and these remained after their departure. Informal names for streets and zones in the city developed among the urban population made reference to the American presence; the principal street in Ouakam eventually became known as Talli Américain (American Street). Indeed, with its proximity to the airfield, many residents of Ouakam found work with the Americans during that period. American influence also became obvious in Dakar's sea and air networks. The years 1943 and 1944 witnessed a dramatic increase in US maritime traffic into Dakar.[76] The installation of Pan-American in Dakar helped increase traffic through the capital, linking it via clipper service to New York, Natal, Monrovia, Lisbon, and Bermuda.[77]

---

72   Direction des Affaires Politiques, Report on the raid on Dakar and general surveillance reports, 1940, 2D8(14).

73   See cases in the following dossiers for the later 1940s: ANS 5M/269(184); ANS 5M/268(184); and ANS 5M/267(184).

74   See dossiers ANS 5M/270(184) and ANS 5M/269(184).

75   See dossiers ANS 5M/269(184); ANS 5M/268(184); and ANS 5M/267(184).

76   Dakar et Dépendances, Annual Report for 1944, section of "Cost of Living," ANS 2G44/19.

77   Dakar et Dépendances, Annual Report for 1944, section of "Cost of Living," ANS 2G44/19.

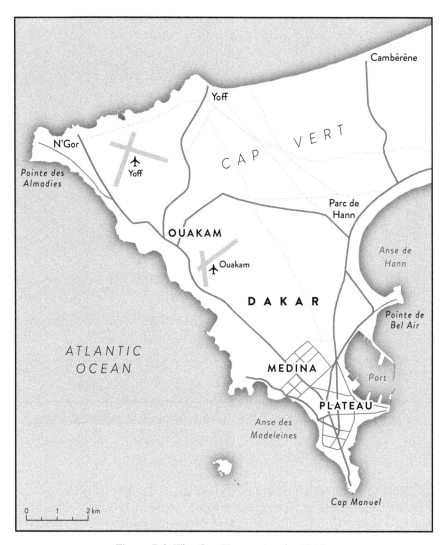

Figure 7.3. The Cap-Vert peninsula, 1940s.

If the presence of US soldiers in the capital of FWA brought new eco-nomic and physical elements that stepped beyond the French colonial paradigm, it also challenged French authority in social ways. American sol-diers who seemingly did whatever they wanted became noticeable fixtures in wartime Dakar. French colonial documents are replete with criticisms of American behavior, citing complaints from all sorts of city dwellers. Some comments indicate a general distaste among French officials for Americans,

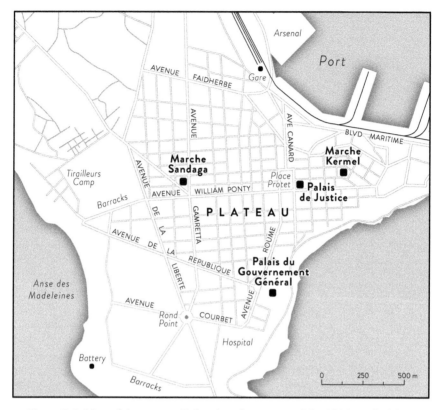

Figure 7.4. Map of downtown Dakar, based on maps of the 1920s and 1930s.

especially within Dakar's European population. French officials disliked what they interpreted as the aggressive nature of the Americans, whom they claimed sought "to penetrate the sphere of French private life" in Dakar.[78] Maurice Maillat, a former French serviceman who wrote not long after the war's conclusion about Dakar's experience of World War II, noted that even the American manner of dining at the table aggravated French residents.[79] Resentment also abounded regarding Americans' abilities to obtain blocked items, such as champagne and spirits, which French residents consistently

---

78   Renseignements politiques, Service de Sûreté, September to December 1943, ANS 17G/410.
79   Maurice Maillat, "Dakar sous la Flamme de Guerre," unpublished manuscript, ANS Library Section.

complained they were denied during the war. An anonymous letter to the police in April 1943 charged that US nationals frequented an after-hours café, well known to be a "brothel," where they consumed prohibited champagne at a thousand francs per bottle.[80]

Alongside French complaints about Americans in Dakar were reactions among non-Europeans. African grievances did not as much indict the Americans as they did the French colonial state in its ability to curb certain incidents and emerging issues. Music and dancing, which American soldiers enjoyed in various neighborhoods of the capital during the nighttime hours, were the subject of many objections. Africans living in the city proper, where such nocturnal distractions were typically organized, urged authorities to act. Residents declared "themselves and their children unable to rest at night," an official noted.[81] African Dakarois asserted that the reason such activities were allowed to continue was because they did not disturb the elite—primarily French—neighborhoods of Dakar. Authorities heard stinging criticism that the administration's top officials "couldn't care less" about these disturbances since they slept "peacefully in their villas on the Plateau," the downtown area that had many European enclaves.[82] Africans contended that if the dances took place in that area, authorities would certainly have given fewer permits for them to be held.

The notion that the administration could not control American behaviors—and that it did not care to do so even if it could—was a powerful statement about the relationship between city dwellers and the state by the 1940s. Control, the preoccupation of the colonial state, became evasive. Objections to the systems in place that had slowly been emerging became vocal and unavoidable. Practices that had lingered in the transactional culture out of sight became plainly visible. Dakar was not a French city but an African one in which diverse participants in urban life strived, acted, and exchanged. They made survival and even the possibility of success their business. The war was the final moment of Dakar's adolescence, providing a clear view of the international West African urban center—dense and vast and infused with risk and possibility—that it was becoming.

---

80 Letter of complaint against the Café du Klondyke, April 15, 1943, ANS 5M/264(184).

81 Renseignements politiques, Service de Sûreté, September to December 1943, ANS 17G/410.

82 Renseignements politiques, Service de Sûreté, September to December 1943, ANS 17G/410.

Epilogue

In 1960, Dakar became the capital of Senegal. It became an African city in the fullest sense, realizing a political status that matched its composition and urban identity. This book has shown that identity to have been forged by city dwellers as they sought to mitigate the racism embedded in colonialism to make Dakar a resource and a livable space that suited their own needs. This historical foundation, paired with Dakar's role as an economic, social, and cultural mecca in its region, poised the city for rapid growth once the changes of the mid-1940s set in. The capital grew in population, and transformative change in the city's landscape followed in the 1950s as intensive development took place in the waning years of colonialism.[1] By the time of independence in 1960, the greater agglomeration that constituted Dakar had a population of almost half a million people, a milestone it more than doubled only fifteen years later.[2]

Part of Dakar's outward-facing identity was one of transience and impermanence. The capital's involvement in local, regional, and global networks—and the movement of people inherent to them—only deepened over time. In the absence of significant natural resources on which to build a national economy, Leopold Sédar Senghor, Senegal's first president, sought to maintain the country's international standing, with Dakar at its center as an incubator of heterogenous human resources.[3] Senghor positioned Senegal to act as a global hub that was hospitable to people from all over the world. Journalists, diplomats, multinational corporation employees, researchers, nongovernmental organization workers, and others replaced French colonial administrators and their corollaries as Dakar's transient foreign community.

For many years, I was among them, inserting myself further and further over time into the transactional culture, which had become complex and expansive by Senegal's fiftieth anniversary of independence while maintaining many of the attributes established some eighty years prior. As a transient Dakarois, I found myself participating in the local transactional culture that

---

1   Diop, *Urbanisation et Gestion Du Foncier Urbain à Dakar*, 17. For the broader period of postwar developmental colonialism, Cooper's *Decolonization* is the authoritative work.

2   National Research Council, *Population Dynamics of Senegal*, 32.

3   Cooper, *Africa since 1940*, 168–70.

wove throughout the court records I read through each day. The prominence of informality, which had originated in Dakar's early years of growth, was embedded in a world that paired scarcity with prosperity and remained central to its workings. When cash machines went offline, I bought butter and eggs on credit at the local corner store. Coins handed to young men standing on the streets downtown secured me a parking space while I ran errands. My phone was refilled with credits purchased out the window of the car in traffic jams. Newcomers to Dakar passed through my apartment, finding affinity in our identities as American researchers. The bread and grilled meats I favored were the specialties of groups not native to Dakar, or even sometimes Senegal, but central to the urban food culture. The markets—produce in Thiaroye, fabrics in HLM, furniture at the Salle de Vente—represented in many ways the transactional culture, dense labyrinths that required local knowledge but drew every sort of participant.

The chapters of this book have revealed the historical roots of these dynamics, showing that local norms were neither the exclusive domain of autochthons nor of power brokers, but rather were generated from the entirety of Dakar's diverse city dwellers, each with their own conceptions of residence and priorities for urban life. As I moved through Dakar's communities in my research, my own participation in transactional spaces reflected the diversity these chapters have explored. My close confidants all considered Dakar home, despite their family origins in Futa Toro, Saloum, Casamance, or Guinea. Retirement awaited them in those places, where they also sent their children for family visits or overnight errands to deliver anything from congratulatory tidings to needed prescriptions. Dakar was formed through its accommodation and integration of diversity rooted not only in its region but in places further afield, with immigrant communities establishing themselves in the local transactional culture through economic, social, and cultural currencies. That past creation of a cosmopolitan African city reflected in my own contemporary experiences.[4] Indeed, for springtime braided bread, I sought mastic and mahlab at Lebanese shops that remained mainstays of Dakar, as did the evening parties thrown by Cape Verdeans. As I attended rooftop soirees of food, dance, and drink, I understood the ways in which the role of cultural maintenance in the making of urban niches, which this book has located as rooted in the past, has remained central to the community.

---

4   The emphasis on relocating cosmopolitanism in the African context has been present in Africanist thinking for the past decade. For an authoritative and prominent expression of Afropolitanism, see Mbembe, "Afropolitanism"; and Mbembe and Balakrishnan, "Pan-African Legacies, Afropolitan Futures."

By mining the Tribunal records, sources that present both a very pub-lic space and very private matters, the preceding chapters analyzed everyday concerns of urban life as they were expressed and lived in a very specific colonial context in which struggles, adaptations, compromises, and unin-tended consequences were present at every level, including the state level. Although my initial interest in the court records was in their capacity to reveal legal encounters and judicial process in the colonial past, the voices that emerged from the Tribunal records revealed the dynamics of city life in the making. They revealed the ways people managed to make urban life work despite state-created poverty, to define their own economic niches and exploit the holes inherent to colonial policy based on racism, to draw on one another as critical resources in a precarious landscape.

These concerns and strategies also continued in the urban dynamics of ordinary life in contemporary Dakar. At dinners in the living rooms of Senegalese friends, concerns of people who had lived nearly a century ear-lier elicited empathetic responses from knowing ears. The houseguest from out of town who never left, the friend who borrowed money to give to his mother, the wait until the first of the month to put gasoline in the car—these were the pieces of everyday life I observed, contemporary reflections of a past built upon the same foundations. Over the course of several years of work in the archives and collecting oral histories, echoes of the past were increasingly apparent in the present. A system, or set of systems, clearly at work in Dakar was the product of years of contestation and experience, and of early moments of the city as it embarked on the path to becoming a major African urban center.

The local transactional culture Dakarois established and developed was highly determinant in the type of city Dakar became. It ensured that the crucial elements to living in a big city—finding somewhere to live, negotiat-ing diversity, navigating precarity, and making ends meet—could be located without avenues created by the state and in spite of regulations meant to limit people's options. This by no means meant that barriers did not have long-term effects. As the second decade of independence set in, for instance, the majority of Dakarois did not possess the financial resources for home ownership.[5] The complex dynamic of making cities work while navigating the weight of their inequities was foundational in Dakar.

This book has harnessed the interest in modern African cities' inner work-ings to argue for the historical depth required to produce a fuller under-standing of urban processes. Dakar's marriage of bottom-up and top-down dynamics, paired with a delicate balance that enabled it to represent a brand of success in what was often an unstable region, has attracted scholars to

---

5   Bigon, *French Colonial Dakar*, 179–80.

various lines of enquiry regarding the contemporary city. The city has been identified as a unique political stage, where expression took on popular and localized forms that spoke to broad societal contemporary concerns. Youth movements, musical expression, public wall art, and grassroots initiatives that flourished in the 1980s and 1990s make up the diverse intellectual strains of Dakar studies.[6] Central to a number of works are the notions of negotiation and participation as integral parts of city life as carried out in political, economic, and sociocultural spheres.[7] That dynamic was clearly born decades prior. Although independent statehood replaced colonialism in Africa, the lingering effects of the foundations to which colonial rule was anchored have not been completely eroded. Racism, exclusion, and exploitation together constituted a specific context for the emergence of city dwelling. What emerged in Dakar, as this book has revealed, was a set of accepted strategies that entailed innovation, flexibility, and the ability to operate within parameters that were often externally drawn even if they were reshaped from within. This has remained constant in Dakar's dynamics.

Late-twentieth- and early-twenty-first-century sub-Saharan African cities are the object of much study because of their sprawl, informal economies, and grassroots solutions that both evade the state and make up for its inefficacy.[8] Much of the emphasis has been on the postcolonial and certainly the post-1970s period due to the rapid expansion in the size and population of cities. However, in African cities, the strategies people employ to live and thrive are not products of the later twentieth century. For all the transformations they have known in the postcolonial years, African cities also operate in continuity with the systems established during the colonial era. Those systems were the result of the inability and unwillingness of the colonial state to intersect with the realities of city dwellers' everyday lives. Their sights set on lofty goals, colonial officials essentially permitted Dakarois to lay the city's path underneath them. When discussions of informality are held regarding African cities such as Dakar, it is imperative to consider continuity over time. The very foundations of urban systems in cities such as Dakar, which were born in the modern era, were devised outside the purview of those possessing political and economic power. Anything that was not official was informal. My focus here has been on tracing the origins of

6   Diouf, "Fresques Murales et Ecriture de L'histoire"; Diouf, "Urban Youth and Senegalese Politics"; Fredericks, *Garbage Citizenship*; Roberts and Roberts, *A Saint in the City*; McLaughlin, "Dakar Wolof."

7   Diouf, "Urban Youth and Senegalese Politics"; Simone, *For the City Yet to Come*.

8   See, in particular, the work of AbouMaliq Simone in this area. His *For the City Yet to Come* investigates questions in a number of these areas, and his other work sustains those investigations more broadly.

the local transactional culture, which reframes informality as a historical out-growth of conditions and actions. This book has shown that transactional culture to have been viable and innovative in the same way that AbouMaliq Simone, for instance, points to the informal in contemporary African cities as constituting "a platform for the creation of a very different kind of sustain-able urban configuration."[9] A driving force in Africa today, the informal has been the historically dominant domain for the construction of urban life. Heterogenous urbanites defined it through the transactions they undertook as they engaged one another to weave the fabric of urban life.

Cities in Africa are sites of some of the most important urban processes on the planet. They are nuclei of new forms of productivity in which the world's youngest population stands to dictate the terms of a global urban future. As more visionaries strive to make their futures in and for Africa, cit-ies such as Dakar will witness transformations in the ways life is lived. This book has presented the local transactional as innovative. Even as the foun-dations laid nearly a century ago remain visible in systems today, innova-tion means that what city dwellers build atop those foundations changes in shape and substance. Dakar is a city driven by a population that diverged in its goals and activities from the visions of urbanization held by those in power. At its core, Dakar is an exercise in humanity: ambition, adaptability, and acceptance come together as its beating heart to make a city.

---

9   Simone, "Introduction: Urban Processes and Change," 4.

Bibliography

Aderinto, Saheed. *When Sex Threatened the State: Illicit Sexuality, Nationalism, and Politics in Colonial Nigeria, 1900–1958.* Champaign: University of Illinois Press, 2014.

Akyeampong, Emmanuel. "Race, Identity and Citizenship in Black Africa: The Case of the Lebanese in Ghana." *Africa: Journal of the International African Institute* 76, no. 3 (2006): 297–323.

Allen, Judith van. "'Sitting on a Man': Colonialism and the Lost Political Institutions of Igbo Women." *Canadian Journal of African Studies* 6, no. 2 (1972): 165–81.

Amselle, Jean-Loup, and Emmanuelle Sibeud, eds. *Maurice Delafosse Entre Orientalisme et Ethnographie: L'Itinéraire d'un Africaniste (1870–1926).* Paris: Maisonneuve & Larose, 1998.

Annuaire du Gouvernement Général de l'Afrique Occidentale Française, 1913–14. Paris: La Rose, 1914.

Apko-Vaché, Catherine. *L'AOF et la Seconde Guerre Mondiale: La Vie Politique (Septembre 1939–Octobre 1945).* Paris: Karthala, 1996.

Arowosegbe, Jeremiah O. "Hausa-Fulani Pastoralists and Resource Conflicts in Yorubaland." *Interventions* 21, no. 8 (2019): 1157–87.

Arsan, Andrew. "Failing to Stem the Tide: Lebanese Migration to French West Africa and the Competing Prerogatives of the Imperial State." *Comparative Studies in Society and History* 53, no. 3 (2011): 450–78.

———. *Interlopers of Empire: The Lebanese Diaspora in Colonial French West Africa.* London: Hurst, 2013.

Balandier, Georges. *Sociologie des Brazzavilles Noires.* Paris: Armand Colin, 1955.

Balandier, Georges, and Paul Mercier. *Particularisme et Évolution: Les Pêcheurs Lébu du Sénégal.* Saint-Louis: IFAN, 1952.

Baller, Susan. "Transforming Urban Landscapes: Soccer Fields as Sites of Urban Sociability in the Agglomeration of Dakar." In *Postcolonial African Cities: Imperial Legacies and Postcolonial Predicaments*, edited by Fassil Demissie, 59–72. London: Routledge, 2007.

Barbary, Olivier. "Dakar et la Sénégambie: évolution d'un espace migratoire transnational." In *Le Sénégal et Ses Voisins*, edited by Momar Coumba Diop, 142–63. Dakar: Sociétés—Espaces—Temps, 1994.

Barry, Boubacar. *Senegambia and the Atlantic Slave Trade.* Translated by Ayi Kwei Armah. Cambridge: Cambridge University Press, 1998.

Barth, Fredrik. *Ethnic Groups and Boundaries: The Social Organization of Culture Difference.* Long Grove, IL: Waveland Press, 1998.

Batalha, Luis. *The Cape Verdean Diaspora in Portugal: Colonial Subjects in a Postcolonial World.* Lanham, MD: Lexington Books, 2004.

Batalha, Luís, and Jørgen Carling, eds. *Transnational Archipelago: Perspectives on Cape Verdean Migration and Diaspora.* Amsterdam: Amsterdam University Press, 2008.

Beinart, William. *Twentieth-Century South Africa.* Oxford: Oxford University Press, 2001.

Berg, Elliot J. "Backward-Sloping Labour Supply Functions in Dual Economies: The Africa Case." *Quarterly Journal of Economics* 75, no. 3 (1961): 468–92.

Bernard-Duquenet, Nicole. *Le Sénégal et le Front Populaire.* Paris: L'Harmattan, 1985.

Betts, Raymond. "Dakar: Ville Impériale (1857–1960)." In *Colonial Cities,* edited by Robert Ross and Gerard Telkamp, 193–206. Dordrecht: Martinus Nijhoff Publishers, 1985.

Bierwirth, Chris. "The Initial Establishment of the Lebanese Community in Côte d'Ivoire, CA. 1925–45." *International Journal of African Historical Studies* 30, no. 2 (1997): 325–48.

Bigo, Didier. "The Lebanese Community in the Ivory Coast: A Non-Native Network at the Heart of Power?" In *The Lebanese in the World: A Century of Emigration,* edited by Albert Hourani and Nadim Shehadi, 509–30. London: IB Tauris, 1992.

Bigon, Liora. *French Colonial Dakar: The Morphogenesis of an African Regional Capital.* Manchester: Manchester University Press, 2016.

———. "A History of Urban Planning and Infectious Diseases: Colonial Senegal in the Early Twentieth Century." *Urban Studies Research,* Article ID 589758 (2012): 1–12.

Bigon, Liora, and Alain Sinou. "The Quest for Colonial Style in French West Africa: Prefabricating Marché Kermel and Sandaga." *Journal of Urban History* 39, no. 4 (2013): 709–25.

Bogosian, C. "Forced Labor, Resistance and Memory: The Deuxième Portion in the French Soudan, 1926–1950." PhD diss., University of Pennsylvania, 2002.

Bohannan, Paul. *Justice and Judgment among the Tiv.* Oxford: Oxford University Press, 1957.

Boone, Catherine. *Merchant Capital and the Roots of State Power in Senegal, 1930–1985.* Cambridge: Cambridge University Press, 1992.

Brantley, Cynthia. *Feeding Families: African Realities and British Ideas of Nutrition and Development in Early Colonial Africa*. Portsmouth, NH: Heinemann, 2002.

Brennan, James. *Taifa: Making Nation and Race in Urban Tanzania*. Athens: Ohio University Press, 2012.

Brooks, George E. *Eurafricans in Western Africa: Commerce, Social Status, Gender, and Religious Observance from the Sixteenth to the Eighteenth Century*. Athens: Ohio University Press, 2003.

Brunet-La Ruche, Bénédicte. "'Discipliner les villes coloniales': la police et l'ordre urbain au Dahomey pendant l'entre-deux-guerres." *Criminocorpus* (2012): article 1678.

Bryant, Kelly Duke. "Changing Childhood: 'Liberated Minors,' Guardianship, and the Colonial State in Senegal, 1895–1911." *Journal of African History* 60, no. 2 (2019): 209–28.

Bujra, Janet. *Serving Class: Masculinity and the Feminisation of Domestic Service in Tanzania*. Edinburgh: Edinburgh University Press, 2000.

Burrill, Emily. *States of Marriage: Gender, Justice, and Rights in Colonial Mali*. Athens: Ohio University Press, 2015.

Burton, Andrew. "Urchins, Loafers, and the Cult of the Cowboy: Urbanization and Delinquency in Dar es Salaam, 1919–1961." *Journal of African History* 41, no 1 (2001): 199–216.

Byfield, Judith, Carolyn Brown, Timothy Parsons, and Ahmad Alawad Sikainga, eds. *Africa and World War II*. Cambridge: Cambridge University Press, 2015.

Cabral, Nelson Eurico. "Les migrations aux îles de Cap-Vert." *Journal de la Société des Africanistes* 45, nos. 1–2 (1975): 181–86.

Callaci, Emily. *Street Archives and City Life: Popular Intellectuals in Postcolonial Tanzania*. Durham, NC: Duke University Press, 2017.

Cantier, Jacques, and Eric Jennings. *L'Empire Colonial sous Vichy*. Paris: Odile Jacob, 2004.

Cappelli, Ganriele, and Joerg Baten. "European Trade, Colonialism, and Human Capital Accumulation in Senegal, Gambia and Western Mali, 1770–1900." *Journal of Economic History* 77, no. 3 (2017): 920–51.

Carney, J. J. "Beyond Tribalism: The Hutu-Tutsi Question and Catholic Rhetoric in Colonial Rwanda." *Journal of Religion in Africa* 42, no. 2 (2012): 172–202.

Carreira, Antonio. *The People of the Cape Verde Islands: Exploitation and Emigration*. London: C. Hurst, 1982.

Carter, Katherine, and Judy Aulette. *Cape Verdean Women and Globalization: The Politics of Gender, Culture, and Resistance*. New York: Palgrave Macmillan, 2009.

Chafer, Tony, and Amanda Sackur, eds. *French Colonial Empire and the Popular Front*. New York: St. Martin's Press, 1996.

Chanock, Martin. *Law, Custom and Social Order: The Colonial Experience in Malawi and Zambia*. Cambridge: Cambridge University Press, 1985.

Christelow, Allen. *Muslim Law Courts and the French Colonial State in Algeria*. Princeton, NJ: Princeton University Press, 1985.

Clarence-Smith, William-Gervase. *The Third Portuguese Empire, 1825–1975: A Study in Economic Imperialism*. Manchester: Manchester University Press, 1985.

Clark, Gracia. *Onions Are My Husband: Survival and Accumulation by West African Market Women*. Chicago: University of Chicago Press, 1994.

Cohen, Abner. *Custom and Politics in Urban Africa: A Study of Hausa Migrants in Yoruba Towns*. Berkeley: University of California Press, 1969.

Colin, Jean-Philippe, Georges Kouamé, and Débégnoun Soro. "Outside the Autochthon-Migrant Configuration: Access to Land, Land Conflicts, and Inter-Ethnic Relationships in a Former Pioneer Area of Lower Côte d'Ivoire." *Journal of Modern African Studies* 45, no. 1 (2007): 33–59.

Cooper, Frederick. *Decolonization and African Society: The Labor Question in French and British Africa*. Cambridge: Cambridge University Press, 1996.

———. *On the African Waterfront: Urban Disorder and the Transformation of Work in Colonial Mombasa*. New Haven, CT: Yale University Press, 1987.

———, ed. *Struggle for the City: Migrant Labor, Capital, and the State in Urban Africa*. Los Angeles: Sage Publications, 1983.

———. "Urban Space, Industrial Time, and Wage Labor in Africa." In *Struggle for the City: Migrant Labor, Capital, and the State in Urban Africa*, edited by Frederick Cooper, 7–50. Los Angeles: Sage Publications, 1983.

Coquery-Vidrovitch, Catherine. "The Popular Front and the Colonial Question." In *French Colonial Empire and the Popular Front*, edited by Tony Chafer and Amanda Sackur, 157–59. New York: St. Martin's Press, 1996.

———. "Villes Coloniales et Histoire des Africains." *Vingtième Siècle: Revue d'Histoire* 20 (1988): 49–73.

Crais, Clifton. *The Politics of Evil: Magic, State Power, and the Political Imagination in South Africa*. Cambridge: Cambridge University Press, 2002.

Crowder, Michael. *Colonial West Africa: Collected Essays*. London: Frank Cass, 1978.

Curtin, Philip. *Economic Change in Precolonial Africa: Senegambia in the Era of the Slave Trade*. Madison: University of Wisconsin Press, 1975.

———. Preface to *Atlantic Port Cities: Economy, Culture and Society in the Atlantic World, 1650–1850*, edited by Franklin Wright and Peggy Liss, xi–xvi. Knoxville: University of Tennessee Press, 1991.

Da Silva Horta, José. "Evidence for a Luso-African Identity in 'Portuguese' Accounts on 'Guinea of Cape Verde' (Sixteenth–Seventeenth Centuries)." *History in Africa* 27 (2000): 99–130.

Davidson, Basil. "The Ancient World and Africa: Whose Roots?" *Journal of African Civilizations* 10 (1989): 39–52.

Deslaurier, Christine. "Des 'boys' aux 'travailleurs de maison' au Burundi; ou, le politique domestique." *Politique Africaine* 154, no. 2 (2019): 49–73.

Diop, Majhemout. "Tropical and equatorial Africa under French, Portuguese and Spanish Domination, 1935–45." In *UNESCO General History of Africa: Africa since 1935*, edited by A. Mazrui, 62–63. Berkeley: University of California Press, 1993.

Diouf, Mamadou. "Fresques Murales et Ecriture de L'histoire: le Set/Setal à Dakar." *Politique Africaine* 46 (1992): 41–54

———. "Urban Youth and Senegalese Politics: Dakar, 1988-1994." *Public Culture* 19, no. 2 (1996): 225–49.

Doho, Gilbert. *Le Code de l'indigénat; ou, Le fondement des États autocratiques en Afrique francophone*. Paris: L'Harmattan, 2017.

Duany, Jorge. "Mobile Livelihoods: The Sociocultural Practices of Circular Migrants between Puerto Rico and the United States." *International Migration Review* 36, no. 2 (2002): 355–88.

Echenberg, Myron. *Black Death, White Medicine: Bubonic Plague and the Politics of Public Health in Colonial Senegal, 1914–1945*. Portsmouth, NH: Heinemann, 2002.

Ejikeme, Anene. "From Traders to Teachers: A History of Elite Women in Onitsha, Nigeria, 1928–1940." *Journal of Asian and African Studies* 46, no. 3 (2011): 221–36.

Epstein, A. L. *The Administration of Justice and the Urban African: A Study of Urban Native Courts in Northern Rhodesia*. London: H. M. Stationary Office, 1953.

———. *Juridical Techniques and the Judicial Process: A Study in African Customary Law*. Manchester: Rhodes-Livingstone Institute, 1954.

———. *Politics in an Urban African Community*. Manchester: Manchester University Press, 1958.

Evans, Ivan. *Bureaucracy and Race: Native Administration in South Africa*. Berkeley: University of California Press, 1997.

Fabian, Steven. *Making Identity on the Swahili Coast: Urban Life, Community, and Belonging in Bagamoyo*. Cambridge: Cambridge University Press, 2019.

Fall, Babacar. *Le travail forcé en Afrique Occidentale française, 1900–1946*. Paris: Karthala, 1993.

Fallers, Lloyd. *Law without Precedent: Legal Ideas in Action in the Courts of Colonial Busoga*. Chicago: University of Chicago Press, 1969.

Faye, Cheikh Faty. *Les Enjeux Politiques à Dakar (1945–1960)*. Paris: L'Harmattan, 2000.

Faye, Ousseynou. *Dakar et ses cultures: un siècle de changements d'une ville colonial*. Paris: L'Harmattan, 2017.

Ferguson, James. *Expectations of Modernity: Myths and Meanings of Urban Life on the Zambian Copperbelt*. Berkeley: University of California Press, 1999.

Fikes, Kesha D. "Emigration and the Spiritual Production of Difference from Cape Verde." In *Cultures of the Lusophone Black Atlantic*, edited by Nancy Priscilla Naro, Roger Sansi-Roca, and David H. Treece, 159–73. New York: Palgrave Macmillan, 2007.

Fioratta, Susanne. "A World of Cheapness: Affordability, Shoddiness, and Second-Best Options in Guinea and China." *Economic Anthropology* 6, no. 1 (2019): 86–97.

Foster, Elizabeth. "Rethinking 'Republican Paternalism': William Ponty in French West Africa, 1890–1915." *Outre-Mers* 94, nos. 356–57 (2007): 211–33.

Fourchard, Laurent. "Lagos and the Invention of Juvenile Delinquency in Nigeria, 1920–60." *Journal of African History* 47, no. 1 (2006): 115–37.

Foy, Colm. *Cape Verde: Politics, Economics, Society*. London: Pinter, 1988.

Fredericks, Rosalind. *Garbage Citizenship: Vital Infrastructures of Labor in Dakar, Senegal*. Durham, NC: Duke University Press, 2018.

Freund, Bill. "Contrasts in Urban Segregation: A Tale of Two African Cities, Durban (South Africa) and Abidjan (Côte d'Ivoire)." *Journal of Southern African Studies* 27, no. 3 (2001): 527–46.

Fry, Peter. "Undoing Brazil: Hybridity versus Multiculturalism." In *Cultures of the Lusophone Black Atlantic*, edited by Nancy Priscilla Naro, Roger Sansi-Roca, and David H. Treece, 233–49. New York: Palgrave Macmillan, 2007.

Gamble, Harry. "Navigating the Fourth Republic: West African University Students between Metropolitan France and Dakar." *French Politics, Culture and Society* 39, no. 3 (2021): 73–99.

George, Abosede A. *Making Modern Girls: A History of Girlhood, Labor, and Social Development in Colonial Lagos*. Athens: Ohio University Press, 2014.

———. "Within Salvation: Girl Hawkers and the Colonial State in Development Era Lagos." *Journal of Social History* 44, no. 3 (2011): 837–59.

Geschiere, Peter. *The Perils of Belonging: Autochthony, Citizenship and Exclusion in Africa*. Chicago: University of Chicago Press, 2009.

Geschiere, Peter, and Josef Gugler. "Introduction: The Urban–Rural Connection: Changing Issues of Belonging and Identification." *Africa* 68, no. 3 (1998): 309–19.

Gibau, Gina Sanchez. "Cape Verdean Diasporic Identity Formation." In *Transnational Archipelago: Perspectives on Cape Verdean Migration and Diaspora*, edited by Luis Batalha and Jørgen Carling, 255–67. Amsterdam: University of Amsterdam Press, 2008.

Ginio, Ruth. *The French Army and Its African Soldiers*. Lincoln: University of Nebraska Press, 2017.

———. *French Colonialism Unmasked: The Vichy Years in French West Africa*. Lincoln: University of Nebraska Press, 2006.

Gluckman, Max. *Politics, Law and Ritual in Tribal Society*. Chicago: Aldine, 1968.

———. *Custom and Conflict in Africa*. Oxford: Oxford University Press, 1955.

———. "Tribalism in Modern British Central Africa." *Cahiers des Etudes Africaines* 1, no. 1 (1960): 55–70.

Gobbers, Erik. "Territorial Découpage and Issues of 'Autochthony' in Former Katanga Province, the Democratic Republic of Congo: The Role of Urban Ethnic Associations." *Ethnopolitics* 20, no. 5 (2021): 590–609.

Goerg, Odile. *Pouvoir Colonial, Municipalités et Espaces Urbains, Conakry-Freetown des Années 1800–1914*. Vols. 1 and 2. Paris: L'Harmattan, 1997.

Green, Toby. *The Rise of the Trans-Atlantic Slave Trade in Western Africa, 1300–1589*. Cambridge: Cambridge University Press, 2012.

Gueye, Ousmane. *Le Code de l'indigénat: historique en Afrique francophone 1887–1946*. Dakar: Harmattan Sénégal, 2019.

Guillot, Jean-François. *La Société française des urbanistes et l'institut d'urbanisme: deux usages du réseau pour une même cause?* Paris: Éditions du Comité des travaux historiques et scientifiques, 2017.

Guyer, Jane. *An African Niche Economy: Farming to Feed Ibadan, 1968–88*. Edinburgh: Edinburgh University Press, 2007.

———. "Households and Community in African Studies." *African Studies Review* 24, nos. 2–3 (1981): 87–137.

———. *Marginal Gains: Monetary Transactions in Atlantic Africa*. Chicago: University of Chicago Press, 2004.

———, ed. *Money Matters: Instability, Values and Social Payments in the Modern History of West African Communities*. Portsmouth, NH: Heinemann, 1995.

Guyer, Jane, and E. Stiansen, eds. *Credit, Currencies, and Culture: African Financial Institutions in Historical Perspective*. Uppsala: Nordiska Afrikainstitutet, 1999.

Hall, Bruce. *A History of Race in Muslim West Africa, 1600–1960*. New York: Cambridge University Press, 2011.

Hall, Peter. *Cities of Tomorrow: An Intellectual History of Urban Planning and Design in the Twentieth Century*. Oxford: Blackwell, 2002.

Hanson, John. *Migration, Jihad, and Muslim Authority in West Africa: The Futanke Colonies in Karta.* Bloomington: Indiana University Press, 1996.

Harris, Dustin Alan. "Constructing Dakar: Cultural Theory and Colonial Power Relations in French African Urban Development." PhD diss., Simon Fraser University, 2011.

Harrison, Christopher. *France and Islam in West Africa, 1860–1960.* Cambridge: Cambridge University Press, 2003.

Heap, Simon. "'Their Days Are Spent in Gambling and Loafing, Pimping for Prostitutes, and Picking Pockets': Male Juvenile Delinquents on Lagos Island, 1920s–1960s." *Journal of Family History* 35, no. 1 (2010): 48–70.

Hemson, David. "Dock Workers, Labour Circulation, and Class Struggles in Durban, 1940–59." *Journal of Southern African Studies* 4, no.1 (1977): 88–124.

Hindson, Doug. *Pass Controls and the Urban African Proletariat in South Africa.* Johannesburg: Ravan Press, 1987.

Hosington, William A. *The Casablanca Connection: French Colonial Policy, 1936–1943.* Chapel Hill: University of North Carolina Press, 1984.

Hunt, Nancy Rose. *A Colonial Lexicon: Of Birth Ritual, Medicalization, and Mobility in the Congo.* Durham, NC: Duke University Press, 1999.

Jackson, Julian T. *The Popular Front in France: Defending Democracy, 1934–38.* Cambridge: Cambridge University Press, 1988.

Jean-Baptiste, Rachel. *Conjugal Rights: Marriage, Sexuality, and Urban Life in Colonial Libreville, Gabon.* Athens: Ohio University Press, 2014.

Jennings, Eric. *Free French Africa in World War II.* Cambridge: Cambridge University Press, 2015.

Johnson, G. Wesley. *The Emergence of Black Politics: The Struggle for Power in the Four Communes, 1900–1920.* Stanford, CA: Stanford University Press, 1971.

Jones, Hilary. *The Métis of Senegal: Urban Life and Politics in French West Africa.* Bloomington: Indiana University Press, 2013.

———. "Women, Family and Daily Life in Senegal's Nineteenth-Century Atlantic Towns." In *African Women in the Atlantic World*, edited by Marina Candido and Adam Jones, 233–47. London: James Currey, 2019.

Keller, Kathleen. *Colonial Suspects: Suspicion, Imperial Rule, and Colonial Society in Interwar French West Africa.* Lincoln: University of Nebraska Press, 2018.

Khater, Akram. *Inventing Home: Emigration, Gender, and the Middle Class in Lebanon, 1870–1920.* Berkeley: University of California Press, 2001.

Kropiwnicki, Zosa Olenka De Sas. "The Politics of Child Prostitution in South Africa." *Journal of Contemporary African Studies* 30, no. 2 (2012): 235–65.

Laan, H. Laurens van der. *The Lebanese Traders in Sierra Leone.* The Hague: Mouton, 1975.

———. "Migration, Mobility and Settlement of the Lebanese in West Africa." In *The Lebanese in the World*, edited by Albert Hourani and Nadim Shehadi, 531–47. London: IB Tauris, 1992.

Laurent, Capitaine. *De Dakar à Zinder: Voyage en Afrique Occidentale.* New York: J. Jumel, 1911.

Law, Robin. "The 'Hamitic Hypothesis' in Indigenous West African Historical Thought." *History in Africa* 36 (2009): 293–314.

Lawrance, Benjamin, and Richard Roberts, eds., *Trafficking in Slavery's Wake: Law and the Experiences of Women and Children in Africa.* Athens: Ohio University Press: 2012.

Leichtman, Mara. "From the Cross (and Crescent) to the Cedar and Back Again: Transnational Religion and Politics among Lebanese Christians in Senegal." *Anthropological Quarterly* 86, no. 1 (2013): 35–75.

———. "Reexamining the Transnational Migrant." In *Lebanese Diaspora: History, Racism, and Belonging*, edited by Paul Tabar, 131–65. Beirut: Lebanese American University, 2005.

———. *Shi'i' Cosmopolitanisms in Africa: Lebanese Migration and Conversion in Senegal.* Bloomington: Indiana University Press, 2015.

Little, Kenneth. *West African Urbanization: A Study of Voluntary Associations in Social Change.* Cambridge: Cambridge University Press, 1965.

Lobban, Richard A. *Cape Verde: Crioulo Colony to Independent Nation.* Boulder, CO: Westview Press, 1995.

Lourenco-Lindell, Ilda. *Walking the Tight Rope: Informal Livelihoods and Social Networks in a West African City.* Stockholm: Stockholm University Press, 2002.

Lovejoy, Paul E. *Caravans of Kola: The Hausa Kola Trade, 1700–1900.* Zaria: Ahmadu Bello University Press, 1980.

———. "Islam, Slavery, and Political Transformation in West Africa: Constraints on the Trans-Atlantic Slave Trade." *Outre-mers* 89, no. 336 (2002): 247–82.

———. *Transformations in Slavery: A History of Slavery in Africa.* Cambridge: Cambridge University Press, 2011.

Lu, Hanchao. "Creating Urban Outcasts: Shantytowns in Shanghai, 1920–1950." *Journal of Urban History* 21, no. 5 (1995): 563–96.

Luke, David. "Dock Workers of the Port of Freetown: A Case Study of African Working-Class Ambivalence." *Canadian Journal of African Studies* 19, no. 3 (1985): 547–67.

Lydon, Ghislaine. *On Trans-Saharan Trails: Islamic Law, Trade Networks, and Cross-Cultural Exchange in Nineteenth-Century Western Africa.* Cambridge: Cambridge University Press, 2009.

Maiangwa, Benjamin. "'Conflicting Indigeneity' and Farmer-Herder Conflicts in Postcolonial Africa." *Peace Review* 29, no. 3 (2017): 282–88.

Malki, I. P. X. "The Competing Ontologies of Belonging: Race, Class, Citizenship, and Sierra Leone's 'Lebanese Question.'" *Dialectical anthropology* 41, no. 4 (2017): 343–66.

Mamdani, Mahmood. "The Racialization of the Hutu/Tutsi Difference under Colonialism." In *When Victims Become Killers: Colonialism, Nativism, and the Genocide in Rwanda,* 76–102. Princeton, NJ: Princeton University Press, 2020.

Manchuelle, Francois. *Willing Migrants: Soninke Labor Diasporas, 1848–1960.* Athens: Ohio University Press, 1997.

Mann, Gregory. "What Was the Indigénat? The 'Empire of Law' in French West Africa." *Journal of African History* 50, no. 3 (2009): 331–53.

Mann, Kristin. *Slavery and the Birth of an African City: Lagos, 1760–1900.* Bloomington: Indiana University Press, 2007.

Mann, Kristen, and Richard Roberts, eds. *Law in Colonial Africa.* Portsmouth, NH: Heinemann, 1991.

Marfaing, Lawrence, and Mariam Sow. *Les Opérateurs Économiques.* Paris: Karthala, 1999.

Mark, Peter. *"Portuguese" Style and Luso-African Identity: Precolonial Senegambia, Sixteenth–Nineteenth Centuries.* Bloomington: Indiana University Press, 2002.

———. "Religion, Identity, and Slavery in the Casamance." *African Studies Review* 42, no. 3 (1999): 75–80.

Martin, Phyllis. *Leisure and Society in Colonial Brazzaville.* Cambridge: Cambridge University Press, 1995.

Mayer, Philip. *Townsmen or Tribesmen: Conservatism and the Process of Urbanization in a South African City.* Cape Town: Oxford University Press, 1961.

Mbembe, Achille. "Afropolitanism." Translated by Paulo Lemos Horta. In *Cosmopolitanisms,* edited by Bruce Robbins and Paulo Lemos Horta, 102–7. New York: New York University Press, 2017.

Mbembe, Achille, and Sarah Balakrishnan. "Pan-African Legacies, Afropolitan Futures." *Transition* 120 (2016): 28–37.

M'Bokolo, Elikia. "Peste et Société Urbaine à Dakar: L'épidémie de 1914 (The Plague and Urban Society in Dakar: The 1914 Epidemic)." *Cahiers d'Études Africaines* 22, no. 85/86 (1982): 13–46.

McLaughlin, Fiona. "Dakar Wolof and the Construction of Urban Identity." *Journal of African Cultural Studies* 14, no. 2 (2001):153–72.

Meillasoux, Claude. *Urbanization of an African Community.* Seattle: University of Washington Press, 1968.

Meintel, Deirdre. *Race, Culture, and Portuguese Colonialism in Cabo Verde.* Syracuse, NY: Maxwell School of Citizenship and Public Affairs, Syracuse University, 1984.

Melly, Caroline. "Inside-Out Houses: Urban Belonging and Imagined Futures in Dakar, Senegal." *Comparative Studies in Society and History* 52, no. 1 (2010): 37–65.

Miers, Suzanne, and Richard Roberts, eds. *The End of Slavery in Africa.* Madison: University of Wisconsin Press, 1988.

Mitchell, J. Clyde. *The Kalela Dance: Aspects of Social Relationships among Urban Africans in Northern Rhodesia.* Manchester: Manchester University Press, 1956.

Monteiro, Cesar Augusto. *Manel d'Novas: Música, Vida, Caboverdianidade.* São Vicente: Gráfica do Mindelo, 2003.

Moore, Sally Falk. *Social Facts and Fabrications: "Customary" Law on Kilimanjaro, 1880–1980.* Cambridge: Cambridge University Press, 1986.

Moreau, Daniela. "Edmond Fortier (1862–1928): Photographer, Documentarian and Creator of Stereotypes in West Africa." In *Landscapes, Sources and Intellectual Projects of the West African Past*, edited by Toby Green and Benedetta Rossi, 473–89. Leiden: Brill, 2018.

Mudeka, Ireen. "Gendered Exclusion and Contestation: Malawian Women's Migration and Work in Colonial Harare, Zimbabwe, 1930s to 1963." *African Economic History* 44, no. 1 (2016): 18–43.

Nelson, David. "Defining the Urban: The Construction of French-Dominated Colonial Dakar, 1857–1940." *Historical Reflections / Réflexions Historiques* 33, no. 2 (2007): 225–55.

Njoh, Ambe. "Urban Planning as a Tool of Power and Social Control in Colonial Africa." *Planning Perspectives* 24, no. 3 (2009): 301–17.

Njwambe, Ayela, Michelle Cocks, and Susanne Vetter. "Ekhayeni: Rural-Urban Migration, Belonging and Landscapes of Home in South Africa." *Journal of Southern African Studies* 45, no. 2 (2019): 413–31.

O'Brien, Rita Cruise. "Lebanese Entrepreneurs in Senegal: Economic Integration and the Politics of Protection (Hommes d'Affaires Libanais au Sénégal: Intégration Économique et Mécanismes de Protection)." *Cahiers d'Études Africaines* 57, no. 15 (1975): 95–115.

———. *White Society in Black Africa: The French of Senegal.* Evanston, IL: Northwestern University Press, 1972.

Ochoa, Enrique. "Coercion, Reform, and the Welfare State: The Campaign against 'Begging' in Mexico City During the 1930s." *The Americas* 58, no. 1 (2001): 39–64.

Ocobock, Paul. "Earning an Age: Migration and Maturity in Colonial Kenya, 1895–1952." *African Economic History* 44, no. 1 (2016): 44–72.

Oliver-Saidi, Marie-Thérèse. *Le Liban et la Syrie au Miroir Français (1946–1991)*. Paris: L'Harmattan, 2010.

Osborne, Emily. *Our New Husbands Are Here: Household, Gender, and Politics in a West African State from the Slave Trade to Colonial Rule*. Athens: Ohio University Press, 2011.

Osborne, Richard. *World War II in Colonial Africa: The Death Knell of Colonialism*. Indianapolis, IN: Riebel-Roque, 2001.

Oyono, Ferdinand. *Une Vie de Boy*. Paris: Julliard, 1956.

Pariser, Robyn. "Masculinity and Organized Resistance in Domestic Service in Colonial Dar Es Salaam, 1919–1961." *International Labor and Working-Class History* 88 (2015): 109–29.

Parker, John. *Making the Town: Ga State and Society in Early Colonial Accra*. Portsmouth, NH: Heinemann, 2000.

Patterson, K. David. "Epidemics, Famines, and Population in the Cape Verde Islands, 1580–1900." *International Journal of African Historical Studies* 21, no. 2 (1988): 291–313.

Peil, Margaret. *Cities and Suburbs: Urban Life in West Africa*. New York: Africana, 1981.

Penvenne, Jeanne. *Women, Migration, and the Cashew Economy in Southern Mozambique: 1945–1975*. London: James Currey, 2015.

Pérez Crosas, Armonia. "Des lançados aux expatriés: 'l'Ethnie Blanche' entre les fleuves Sénégal et Casamance." *Africa Development* 34, no. 2 (2009): 129–58.

Petrocelli, Rachel M. "Painting between the Lines: The Cape Verdean Community of Colonial Dakar, 1920–1945." *Canadian Journal of African Studies* 50, no. 2 (2016): 149–68.

———. "Transactions and Informality: Financial Needs and Relationships in Colonial Dakar, 1944–1944." *Cahiers d'Études Africaines* 55, no. 2 (2015): 255–77.

Pondopoulo, Anna. "The Construction of Fulani Otherness in Faidherbe's Writings." *Cahiers d'études africaines* 36, no. 3 (1996): 421–41.

Posel, Dorrit, and Colin Marx. "Circular Migration: A View from Destination Households in Two Urban Informal Settlements in South Africa." *Journal of Development Studies* 49, no. 6 (2013): 819–31.

Premawardhana, Devaka. *Faith in Flux: Pentecostalism and Mobility in Rural Mozambique*. Philadelphia: University of Pennsylvania Press, 2018.

Prestholdt, Jeremy. "Politics of the Soil: Separatism, Autochthony, and Decolonization at the Kenyan Coast." *Journal of African History* 55, no. 2 (2014): 249–70.

Rain, David. *Eaters of the Dry Season: Circular Labor Migration in the West African Sahel*. Boulder, CO: Westview Press, 1999.

Ranger, Terence. "The Invention of Tradition in Colonial Africa." In *The Invention of Tradition*, edited by Eric Hobswam and Terence Ranger, 211–62. Cambridge: Cambridge University Press, 2014.

Ribeiro da Silva, Filipa. *Dutch and Portuguese in Western Africa*. Leiden: Brill, 2011.

Rich, Jeremy. "Hunger and Consumer Protest in Colonial Africa during the First World War: The Case of the Gabon Estuary, 1914–1920." *Food, Culture, & Society* 10, no. 2 (2007): 239–59.

———. *A Workman Is Worthy of His Meat: Food and Colonialism in the Gabon Estuary*. Lincoln: University of Nebraska Press, 2007.

Roberts, Allen, and Mary Nooter Roberts. *A Saint in the City: The Sufi Arts of Urban Senegal*. Los Angeles: University of California Press, 2003.

Roberts, Richard. *Litigants and Households: African Disputes and Colonial Courts in the French Soudan, 1895–1912*. Portsmouth, NH: Heinemann, 2005.

———. "Text and Testimony in the Tribunal De Première Instance, Dakar, during the Early Twentieth Century." *Journal of African History* 31, no. 3 (1990): 447–63.

Robinson, David. "'French Africans'—Faidherbe, Archinard, and Coppolani: The 'Creators' of Senegal, Soudan, and Mauritania." In *Democracy and Development in Mali*, edited by R. James Bingen, 23–40. Ann Arbor: Michigan State University Press, 2000.

———. *Paths of Accommodation: Muslim Societies and French Colonial Authorities in Senegal and Mauritania, 1880–1920*. Athens: Ohio University Press, 2000.

Rodney, Walter. "The Imperialist Partition of Africa." *Monthly Review* 21, no. 11 (1970): 103–14.

Roitman, Janet L. *Fiscal Disobedience: An Anthropology of Economic Regulation in Central* Africa. Princeton, NJ: Princeton University Press, 2005.

Rossi, Benedetta. "From Unfree Work to Working for Free: Labor, Aid, and Gender in the Nigerien Sahel, 1930–2000." *International Labor and Working-Class History* 92 (2017): 155–82.

Schler, Lynn. "Ambiguous Spaces: The Struggle Over African Identities and Urban Communities in Colonial Douala, 1914–45." *Journal of African History*, 44 no. 1 (2003): 51–72.

Scott, James C. *Seeing Like a State: How Certain Schemes to Improve the Human Condition Have Failed*. New Haven, CT: Yale University Press, 1998.

Seck, Assane. *Dakar: Métropole Ouest-Africaine*. Dakar: IFAN, 1970.

Sembène, Ousmane. *Mandabi (The Money Order)*. New York: New Yorker Films, 2005.

Shadle, Brett. "'Changing Traditions to Meet Currently Altering Conditions': Customary Law, African Courts, and the Rejection of Codification in Kenya, 1930–1960." *Journal of African History* 40, no. 3 (1999): 411–31.

———. *"Girl Cases": Marriage and Colonialism in Gusiiland, Kenya, 1890–1970*. Portsmouth, NH: Heinemann, 2006.

Shaka, Femi Okiremuete. "Vichy Dakar and the Other Story of French Colonial Stewardship in Africa: A Critical Reading of Ousmane Sembène and Thierno Faty Sow's 'Camp de Thiaroye.'" *Research in African Literatures* 26, no. 3 (1995): 67–77.

Shaw, Thomas. *Irony and Illusion in the Architecture of Imperial Dakar*. Lampeter: Edwin Mellen Press, 2006.

Sheldon, Kathleen. *Courtyards, Markets, City Streets: Urban Women in Africa*. New York: Routledge, 1966.

Silva Andrade, Elisa. *Les îles du Cap-Vert: de la "découverte" à l'indépendance nationale (1460–1975)*. Paris: L'Harmattan, 1996.

Simelane, Hamilton Sipho. "The State, Chiefs, and the Control of Female Migration in Colonial Swaziland, c. 1930s–1950s." *Journal of African History* 45, no. 1 (2004): 103–24.

Simone, AbouMaliq. *For the City Yet to Come: Changing African Life in Four Cities*. Durham, NC: Duke University Press, 2004.

———. "Introduction: Urban Processes and Change." In *Urban Africa: Changing Contours of Survival in the City*, edited by AbouMaliq Simone and Abdelghani Abouhani, 1–26. Dakar: Codesria, 2005.

Sinou, Alain. *Comptoirs et Villes Coloniales du Sénégal: Saint-Louis, Gorée, Dakar*. Paris: Karthala et Osrtom, 1993.

Slobodkin, Yan. "State of Violence: Administration and Reform in French West Africa." *French Historical Studies* 41, no. 1 (2018): 33–61.

Soares, Benjamin. *Islam and the Prayer Economy: History and Authority in a Malian Town*. Edinburgh: Edinburgh University Press, 2005.

Sunseri, Thaddeus. *Vilimani: Labor Migration and Rural Change in Early Post-Colonial Tanzania*. Cambridge: Cambridge University Press, 2003.

Swindell, Kenneth, and Alieu Jeng. *Migrants, Credit and Climate: The Gambian Groundnut Trade, 1834–1934*. Leiden: Brill, 2006.

Tarraf-Najib, Souha. "Une vieille histoire de familles: Les réseaux migratoires déployés entre le Liban et l'Afrique de l'Ouest, entre le Liban-Sud et la Ville de Dakar." In *Lebanese Diaspora: History, Racism, Belonging*, edited by Paul Tabar, 319–39. Beirut: Lebanese American University, 2005.

Thioub, Ibrahima. "Les Libano-Syriens en Afrique de l'Ouest de la fin du XIXe siècle à nos Jours." *Histoire de l'Afrique de l'Ouest: Etudes et Analyses* (2011). http://www.histoire-afrique.org/article159.html?artsuite=11.

Tombon-Biaye, Abdoulaye. "Les Initiatives des Jeunes dans la Lutte contre la Pauvreté Urbaine à Dakar: Le Cas des Compagnons SIGGI des Points de Dakar-Plateau, Grand-Yoff, Yeumbeul, et Diokoul." Master's thesis, Université Gaston Berger de Saint-Louis, 1999.

Tripp, Ali Mari. "Women and the Changing Urban Household Economy in Tanzania." *Journal of Modern African Studies* 27, no. 4 (1989): 601–23.

Twagira, Laura Ann. *Embodied Engineering: Gendered Labor, Food Security, and Taste in Twentieth-Century Mali*. Athens: Ohio University Press, 2021.

Underwood, David. "Alfred Agache, French Sociology, and Modern Urbanism in France and Brazil." *Journal of the Society of Architectural Historians* 50, no. 2 (1991): 130–66.

Van den Bersselaar, Dmitri. "Imagining Home: Migration and the Igbo Village in Colonial Nigeria." *Journal of African History* 46, no. 1 (2005): 51–73.

Van Onselen, Charles. *The Night Trains: Moving Mozambican Miners to and from South Africa, Circa 1902–1955*. Oxford: Oxford University Press, 2021.

———. *Studies in the Social and Economic History of the Witwatersrand, 1886–1914: 1 New Babylon; 2 New Nineveh*. Johannesburg: Ravan Press, 1982.

Van Velsen, Jaap. "Labor Migration as a Positive Factor in the Continuity of Tonga Tribal Society." *Economic Development and Cultural Change* 8, no. 3 (1960): 265–78.

Vaughan, Megan. "Food Production and Family Labour in Southern Malawi: The Shire Highlands and Upper Shire Valley in the Early Colonial Period." *Journal of African History* 23, no. 3 (1982): 351–64.

Villaneuve, R. Geoffroy. *L'Afrique; ou, Histoires, Mœurs, Usages et Coutumes des Africains: Le Sénégal*. Paris: Nepveu, 1814.

Vizcaya, Benita Sampedro. "*Houseboys*: Domestic Labour Practices in Spanish Settlers' Homes in Colonial West Africa." *Bulletin of Spanish Visual Studies* 6, no. 2 (2022): 175–96.

White, Luise. *The Comforts of Home: Prostitution in Colonial Nairobi*. Chicago: University of Chicago Press, 1990.

Whitehouse, Bruce. *Migrants and Strangers in an African City: Exile, Dignity, Belonging*. Bloomington: Indiana University Press, 2012.

Wils, Anna Babette. "Emigration from Cape Verde: Escaping the Malthusian Trap." In *Small Worlds, Global Lives: Islands and Migration*, edited by Russell King and John Connell, 77–94. London: Pinter, 1999.

Wilson, Godfrey. *An Essay on the Economics of Detribalization*. Livingstone: Rhodes-Livingstone Institute, 1942.

Winder, R. Bayley. "The Lebanese in West Africa." *Comparative Studies in History and Society* 4, no. 3 (1962): 296–333.

Wright, Gwendolyn. *The Politics of Design in French Colonial Urbanism*. Chicago: University of Chicago Press, 1991.

Zelizer, Viviana. *The Social Meaning of Money*. New York: Basic Books, 1994.

Index

www.ingramcontent.com/pod-product-compliance
Ingram Content Group UK Ltd.
Pitfield, Milton Keynes, MK11 3LW, UK
UKHW031120120325
456013UK00004B/15